Obtain the
PROMISES

by Gary Hargrave

LIVING WORD PUBLICATIONS

For your convenience, Scriptures are included as footnotes on each page; if a Scripture appears more than once in a single chapter it is footnoted at its first reference.

Living Word Publications
The Living Word
P.O. Box 958 • North Hollywood, CA 91603

Dedicated to John Robert Stevens

"And what do you have that you did not receive?"
1 Corinthians 4:7

John Stevens is the founder of The Living Word Fellowship,[1] which he began in June of 1951 when he established Grace Chapel of South Gate in California. When I think of John I am reminded of John 1:6, "There came a man, sent from God, whose name was John." This Scripture, of course, is speaking of John the Baptist. However, it memorializes the truth that God sends anointed men and women into this world at key moments in history to accomplish His purposes among men and prepare the earth for His coming Kingdom. John Robert Stevens was such a man.

Those of us who were taught and spiritually fathered by John, knew him as the expression of God's love to us. We referred to him as the apostle to the Kingdom, a fitting description for the man whose passion was to open the door for the Body of Christ to come together with one heart's cry—"Thy kingdom come. Thy will be done, on earth as it is in heaven" (Matthew 6:10). Like the Baptist, John Stevens was the voice of one crying in the spiritual wilderness of his time saying, "Make ready the way of the Lord" (John 1:23). John labored to restore true church order and worship, but he preached the Kingdom of God, and he taught us a daily walk with God through submission to the Lordship of Jesus Christ.

I am dedicating this book to John, not to build a monument to him, for he would be the first to refuse such a thing. But rather, to make his legacy available to generations that were not privileged to know him and to sit under his ministry. My hope is that this book imparts John's anointing, passion, and drive to the hearts of thousands who will out-minister him in their generations. It should also serve as a reminder to those of us who were graced to sit under this ministry of the Living Word, that we should be walking in a manner worthy of the calling which we have both heard and received (Ephesians 4:1).

[1.] www.johnrobertstevens.com

During the final stages of writing this book, my beloved wife and best friend Marilyn transitioned to be with the Lord. I therefore paused all work on the project to be by her side. Marilyn and I produced every aspect of this book together and, for that reason, it was important to me to make no major additions or revisions prior to its publication.

Acknowledgments

I would like to thank all those who supported Marilyn and myself in publishing this book. Though there are too many to name here, we would like to extend our thankfulness to every heart and hand that contributed; you are deeply important to us. It is your prayers and labors of love that have made this book possible.

In particular, I would like to acknowledge our principal editor, Steve Alder, and our faithful proofreading team: Sheryl Ferguson, Darrell Harriman, Ellen Johnston, Kelly McClane, Jeanne McDonald, and Erle Spencer. Thank you, also, to our talented art design team: Laurie Beckman, Heidi Brown, and Joleen Poole, for an outstanding cover design and layout.

Marilyn and I would like to express our sincere appreciation to Matt Walkoe and Becky Seboldt, who worked closely with us to evaluate and select the messages included in this book, and who carefully reviewed the final edits with us. And to our grandchildren, Kane, Kaylin, Leo, and Larissa, we are forever grateful to you for the love, joy, and life that you bring to us.

Finally, our special thanks to Rick and Lorena Holbrook, Steve Seboldt, and the many generations of "Word-workers" at Living Word Publications. We recognize and give thanks to the Lord for your great dedication to preserve, publish, and become the Living Word. It has been an honor to create this book with you.

"Be diligent to present yourself approved to God as a workman who does not need to be ashamed, handling accurately the word of truth" (2 Timothy 2:15).

Gary and Marilyn Hargrave

Contents

Introduction

It is important to read this introduction before reading any other part of the book, because it is essential that you understand the purpose of this book. Primarily, this book was written for God's people who are maturing; it is for all those who are pressing in to fulfill the Word regarding the sons of God coming forth (Romans 8:19). The chapters in *Obtain the Promises* reveal the spirit of the founder of The Living Word Fellowship, John Robert Stevens. This spirit was the root of who he was and of everything that he established; it was what made him the apostle to the Kingdom. You could listen to a thousand of his messages, whether on love, dedication, or faith, and still miss this foundational revelation. That is why I want to be able, through this book, to show people one thing: that the drive to obtain the promises and manifest God's Kingdom is the root of who John was. Everything else that he did grew out of that root. No matter what John said or did, this is the spiritual DNA that was imparted to our spirits when we heard him. It was that living, abiding Word of God that was implanted in our hearts (1 Peter 1:23). The Living Word, as it was spoken, imprinted on our hearts that which God had imparted to John when He first appeared to him.

It is impossible to grasp the significance of this book without understanding, at least in overview, the major changes and transitions experienced by the Church in modern history. The context of John's ministry falls chronologically in the time period of the late 1800s through the 1900s, when tremendous changes happened within Christianity. Starting in the late nineteenth century, Christianity experienced the ministry of Smith Wigglesworth, who was born in 1850, and Aimee Semple McPherson, who was born in 1890. There were also other leaders who were anointed to bring change to the Church, which had not experienced any significant change for hundreds of years. During this time period from the late 1800s on, we find God moving through outpourings and revivals, such as the outpouring at Azusa Street that began in 1906 under the ministry of William Seymour, and the Latter Rain movement which began in 1948. Many of these revivals, or movements, that happened were precursors of what would continue throughout the twentieth century.

For those who are younger in the faith, many of these more recent revivals and movements may be the only history that you know about the Church. For others, these events are very modern expressions that have come of late into the Church landscape. The changes that occurred during the 1900s were expressed by different movements and individuals who emerged during these years. For instance, Billy Graham, who was born in 1918, had a huge influence on the Evangelical movement. Part of the Evangelical movement was the formation of its own Bible translation, the New International Version, which began translation in 1965. As much as people talk about Evangelical churches and the Evangelical movement today, it was not seen as a separate movement within Christianity until 1976. Likewise, the Charismatic movement did not come into existence until the early 1960s as an outgrowth of the Pentecostal movement, which was pioneered by individuals such as McPherson, Wigglesworth, and others. The spread of the Charismatic movement into the wider Evangelical movement did not happen until the mid-1980s, which is extremely recent in our history. In 1973 Paul Crouch established the Trinity Broadcast Network (TBN). Up until that time, it was almost unheard of to have Christian television programs, yet now TBN is widely accepted as a worldwide network. Today much of what happens within Christianity is experienced, or available, through Christian television networks.

This is by no means an exhaustive history of the Church over the last 150 years, but it is important to recognize the absolute metamorphosis that the Church has gone through during this time period. It is within this historical framework that we see the ministry of John Robert Stevens and the Living Word that he spoke. Born in 1919, John Stevens began to move in the ministry at the age of fourteen. This means that John was functioning in his ministry during this same time period, along with these other individuals and movements, to bring tremendous change to what was recognized as mainstream Christianity. This was especially true during the fifties, sixties, seventies, and early eighties, when so much dynamic change was taking place in the Church. During these years, God raised up many anointed leaders in the United States and around the world to be pioneers of this new day within the Church. We can see that each individual and movement that God raised up had its own unique anointing and goals to accomplish the changes that God wanted within the Body of Christ. The specific gifts, anointing, and spiritual DNA that God imparted to and through John Stevens dealt with the coming of the Kingdom of God to the earth. He was often referred to as the apostle to the Kingdom, because that was his drive and the focus of the Word that he spoke and imparted, and it was so accurate in describing his unique ministry. John Stevens constantly challenged the believer back to the foundations which are found in the teachings of John the Baptist and of Jesus Himself: the Kingdom of God is at hand (Matthew 3:1-2; 4:17). As Jesus and John the Baptist taught, the Kingdom begins with repentance that lays the axe to the root of the tree of self and flesh (Matthew 3:10). This launches the believer into a walk with God which has this as its focus: the Kingdom of God is preached and every man must press into it (Luke 16:16). "Seek first His kingdom and His righteousness; and all these things shall be added to you" (Matthew 6:33).

In writing this book, I want to recognize John Stevens and his ministry. He is one of those who pioneered this new era of a walk with God, which has now become the mainstream Christianity embraced by most believers in the Body of Christ today. We recognize him as the source of a great river that continues to flow toward the establishment of Christ's Kingdom in the earth. I want those who are familiar with John Stevens' ministry to recognize, and have a revelation of, the true Spirit of God that was imparted to them during this time of great outpouring and change. We must continue to walk in a manner worthy of the ministry and calling that we have received through His servant (Ephesians 4:1). The spiritual DNA that Stevens imparted to those who received him created the unique expression that we are as a people today. More than this, John committed his personal deliverance to us, because he knew that without us he would not see his own deliverance. The Living Word Fellowship truly has a tremendous spiritual legacy, but we also have a job to do. This book gives us the spiritual direction we need now so that, as time goes on, we do not stray from the course that has been set before us (Hebrews 12:1).

John Stevens was worried about us drifting into denominationalism. I am not worried about that anymore, but I am worried about losing the drive that John embodied, and losing the purpose that he had in creating us as a people. My greatest hope is that as the years go by we will not lose the sharpness and clarity of our revelation of this unique anointing and impartation, but we will build upon it, obtaining the promises and ushering in the Kingdom. Bestowed upon us through the Living Word is this responsibility: without us the work will never be finished, the Word will never be fulfilled, and that which was given by revelation to John Stevens will never be completed. It is up to us to complete it (Hebrews 11:39-40).

There must be a plumb line for those who are leading us now. I know that there are many people who have recently come into our fellowship, and there are many young people who have grown up in this move of God. I am not assured that John's vision, this revelation of who we are, is as real to them as it needs to be. Instead of denominationalism, I am more concerned about us drifting into a kind of social, cultural gathering of people. It is true that God has made us a family and we love each other very much (John 13:34). We are very one with each other, and we have a lot of fun working in the Word and completing projects that the Lord has given us to do. The oneness we have is phenomenal, but we must recognize it as the vehicle God has given to us to accomplish our destiny in the earth.

Is the Living Word your focus, actually directing your life and destiny? Are you aiming by this Word, like a rifle shot, to hit the target of obtaining the promises that God has spoken? All of the provisions that we will talk about in this book are available to be experienced by the believer. This is our fight of faith: to appropriate God's promises that John Stevens made attainable by a Living Word over the years.

We have been such a people of works. When we read the story of Mary and Martha, we all love Mary because she is the one who seemed to have the faith; she sat at the feet of the Lord while Martha was busy doing all of the work that was necessary to be done (Luke 10:40-42). But the truth is that the way we live is more like Martha than Mary. Are we really accomplishing the works of God in all of the work that we are doing? Will we really accomplish the will of God if we are not taking the time to stop and wait on the Lord to obtain His promises? What shall we do to work the works of

God? Believe (John 6:28-29). That is foundational to this book and to who John Stevens was.

This book is about our fight of faith. And when you really have true faith, it is not your faith. It comes by hearing the Word of God that has been spoken to you in a Living Word (Romans 10:17). We have heard it a million times: we do not defeat satan; we appropriate Christ's victory over him. One of the great errors of our intercession, works, and walk with God is that we make it about our effort rather than the expression of faith in His perfect provision. Every Word from God is a reality that was provided by Christ's victory on the cross. But somehow, somewhere, someone has to literally appropriate the promises and bring that provision into reality as our experience in the earth today. This is the drive that is imparted as you read the chapters in *Obtain the Promises*.

CHAPTER 1

Lord, Now Is the Time

Having dedicated this book to John Stevens, I wanted to begin with a message from him. In doing this, I hope you will be able to experience firsthand the anointing and drive that was in John's heart and his demand to see the Kingdom of God manifest in our time. This message sets the tone for the whole book.

JOHN STEVENS: This message, if you read it carefully, will establish two things. The first is that Christ in His provision has defeated satan. The second is that this is the time in history for the unique manifestation of that defeat. To get this idea across, I want to bring out four points. First, I will give you some very familiar Scriptures about the complete provision of the Lord Jesus Christ for us. Second, I will show that these provisions all remain dormant until they are appropriated by faith. Third, I will dwell upon our intercession and travail for the defeat of principalities and powers, the nephilim, and satan. I will show you again that satan has been defeated by Christ, but that this remains, as with other Words from God, a provision until it is appropriated. Then once we see that the provision can be appropriated, we will go into the fourth point, which is that there is the appointed time when God moves to fulfill His promise or His provision. It was in the fullness of time that God sent His Son to be born of a woman and to be our Savior (Galatians 4:4-5). It was something that had been provided for in the heart of God from the foundation of the world, but it had to happen at a specific time (1 Peter 1:20-21). Get this, because this is the key to the entire message. This is why you are in some of the greatest travail you have ever experienced in your life. Do you wonder why you are continually in so much spiritual warfare? The warfare we are in at the present time has to be understood in light of one simple fact: this is the time when the manifestation of Christ's victory, His total defeat of satan, is to be appropriated and exercised.

It is no wonder that satan is fighting us so hard. It is no wonder that satan fights this Living Word; it is the Word for this hour. It is no wonder there is so much distraction and so much difficulty, and that satan fights the oneness so much, because this is the hour of the Kingdom. This is the hour in which the defeat of satan will be manifested. We will see fulfilled what was revealed to Paul, that it is the pleasure of God for His manifold wisdom to be manifested through the Church unto the principalities and powers (Ephesians 3:10, KJV). There has to be that time when you know that "the God of peace will soon crush Satan under your feet" (Romans 16:20). You need to get this in your mind and in your heart. You do not overcome satan yourself, but in this hour of destiny you manifest the victory of Christ over satan. We are not struggling

---

Galatians 4:4-5 But when the fulness of the time came, God sent forth His Son, born of a woman, born under the Law, ⁵ in order that He might redeem those who were under the Law, that we might receive the adoption as sons.

1 Peter 1:20-21 For He was foreknown before the foundation of the world, but has appeared in these last times for the sake of you ²¹ who through Him are believers in God, who raised Him from the dead and gave Him glory, so that your faith and hope are in God.

Ephesians 3:10, KJV To the intent that now unto the principalities and powers in heavenly places might be known by the church the manifold wisdom of God.

for victory; we are struggling with all of our hearts to walk in the faith that appropriates and manifests the victory of Christ. And to that end we travail to bring forth the Kingdom of God. We travail to see the sons of God come forth according to the Word that God has promised us.

As you read these points that I am bringing, they should do two things for you. They should make your head swim in the clouds, realizing how wonderful the provision is for you, and then they should give you a swift kick in the pants as you see how little of the provision you have really appropriated. Every truth that excites you and everything that God has done for you is wonderful, but then you face the fact that they must be accompanied by repentance. The sin of the Kingdom is that we have not claimed all that He has provided. We have not become all that He has promised and prophesied. Your problem is not that you have fallen short; it is that you have not appropriated everything that is yours. Somewhere in that process there arises an unbelief, and you become frustrated and blame everyone else. But the truth of the matter is that everyone who has a Word from God resting upon their head, and burning in their heart, has a responsibility to say, "It will never happen until I believe it!" You cannot go through the motions of prayer, intercession, and travail if you do not believe in the victories that God has for you.

Point One: Let's read about the complete provision of the Lord in the Scriptures. Fasten your seat belts, because we are about to take off. "Blessed be the God and Father of our Lord Jesus Christ, who has blessed us with every spiritual blessing in the heavenly places in Christ" (Ephesians 1:3). Now we have blasted off! We are in the heavenly places where we have **every** spiritual blessing. You will always be struggling to get someplace if you do not claim that you are blessed with every spiritual blessing in the heavenly places in Christ Jesus. When you believe that you have received it from the Lord, then you can begin to claim it. There can be instant change and fabulous blessings. Believe it! It is the Lord Jesus Christ who, "having offered one sacrifice for sins for all time, SAT DOWN AT THE RIGHT HAND OF GOD, waiting from that time onward UNTIL HIS ENEMIES BE MADE A FOOTSTOOL FOR HIS FEET. For by one offering He has perfected for all time those who are sanctified" (Hebrews 10:12-14). We also read that "he is able also to save them to the uttermost that come unto God by him, seeing he ever liveth to make intercession for them" (Hebrews 7:25, KJV).

Sometimes we get into contending with God. I think it is a good thing to remind Him of His promises. It is good to push Him a little bit. Jacob had to; he wrestled with the Lord all night. God crippled him, but Jacob was surely blessed out of it. He obtained everything that God had promised him. He was not only preserved in an hour of jeopardy, but he walked in the promises that rested upon his father, Isaac, and his grandfather, Abraham. He became a prince of God who prevailed with God and man (Genesis 32:24-29; 35:10-12). God said to him, "Do you want the blessing? Then you will have to wrestle Me for it." Sometimes it is good to wrestle with God. But in that, do not think for a moment that you are trying to persuade Him. Your struggle is for the faith to lay hold upon His willingness and His provision for you. Get that in your mind. You are not travailing to conceive; you are travailing to give birth to

---

Genesis 32:24-29 Then Jacob was left alone, and a man wrestled with him until daybreak. ²⁵ And when he saw that he had not prevailed against him, he touched the socket of his thigh; so the socket of Jacob's thigh was dislocated while he wrestled with him. ²⁶ Then he said, "Let me go, for the dawn is breaking." But he said, "I will not let you go unless you bless me." ²⁷ So he said to him, "What is your name?" And he said, "Jacob." ²⁸ And he said, "Your name shall no longer be Jacob, but Israel; for you have striven with God and with men and have prevailed." ²⁹ Then Jacob asked him and said, "Please tell me your name." But he said, "Why is it that you ask my name?" And he blessed him there.

Genesis 35:10-12 And God said to him, "Your name is Jacob; you shall no longer be called Jacob, but Israel shall be your name." Thus He called him Israel. ¹¹ God also said to him, "I am God Almighty; be fruitful and multiply; a nation and a company of nations shall come from you, and kings shall come forth from you. ¹² And the land which I gave to Abraham and Isaac, I will give it to you, and I will give the land to your descendants after you."

what the incorruptible seed, the Word of God that lives and abides forever, has put in your heart (1 Peter 1:23, KJV).

> Seeing that His divine power has granted to us everything pertaining to life and godliness, through the true knowledge of Him who called us by His own glory and excellence. For by these He has granted to us His precious and magnificent promises, in order that by them you might become partakers of the divine nature, having escaped the corruption that is in the world by lust. (2 Peter 1:3-4)

Maybe you have read this Scripture hundreds of times. Have you used it to comfort your soul, or have you used it to appropriate the divine nature? According to these verses, we can have God's very nature. How much of it have you claimed? We have everything—"all things" according to the King James Version—that pertain to life and godliness. Whether everything or all things, that is pretty big.

Point Two: God's complete provision is ours, but it has to be appropriated. I want you to see the wonders of His provision, and I want you to see the awfulness of your lack of faith. That is the thing that disturbs you when you read about the disciples. You want to kick them and say, "How dare you walk the way you walked, until the Master Himself would say, 'O you of little faith, why did you doubt?'" (Matthew 14:31). Well, how are **you** doing with your faith? It should make us repent that our faith has not been continually active and aggressive. You might be thinking, "By this time I deserve a purple heart; I have suffered so much for this Living Word." No, now is the time to cash in on every Word that God has spoken from the beginning and walk in them! The provision is there, but you have to believe it. What should really disturb you is the fact that

---

1 Peter 1:23, KJV   Being born again, not of corruptible seed, but of incorruptible, by the word of God, which liveth and abideth for ever.

Matthew 14:31   And immediately Jesus stretched out His hand and took hold of him, and said to him, "O you of little faith, why did you doubt?"

your unbelief has stopped you from the aggressiveness and the initiative of faith that lays hold upon the promises of God.

Jesus said,

> "Truly, truly, I say to you, he who believes in Me, the works that I do shall he do also; and greater works than these shall he do; because I go to the Father. And whatever you ask in My name, that will I do, that the Father may be glorified in the Son. If you ask Me anything in My name, I will do it." (John 14:12-14)

Do you believe that? Are you doing the works that He did? Are you doing greater works? We have to believe this.

> "Whenever a woman is in travail she has sorrow, because her hour has come; but when she gives birth to the child, she remembers the anguish no more, for joy that a child has been born into the world. Therefore you too now have sorrow; but I will see you again, and your heart will rejoice, and no one takes your joy away from you. And in that day you will ask Me no question. Truly, truly, I say to you, if you shall ask the Father for anything, He will give it to you in My name. Until now you have asked for nothing in My name; ask, and you will receive, that your joy may be made full." (John 16:21-24)

Ask and you will receive, that your joy may be complete. In Luke 11:9-10, the Greek verbs for "ask," "seek," and "knock" are in the active present imperative tense: ask, and keep on asking, and you will receive. Seek, and keep on seeking, and you will find. Knock, and keep on knocking, and it will be opened to you. The provisions

---

Luke 11:9-10 "And I say to you, ask, and it shall be given to you; seek, and you shall find; knock, and it shall be opened to you. [10] For everyone who asks, receives; and he who seeks, finds; and to him who knocks, it shall be opened."

of the Lord hit you hard. They shake you up. They make you want to cry. They make you want to jump up and rejoice and then fall flat on your face and repent. How can God do so much for us? And how can we give way to the indifference of unbelief and not take what God gives us? The distractions, the deception, and everything that satan throws at us are so that we will not believe God. We think that we have to get busy and do works, but what shall we do to work the works of God? Believe on Him whom He has sent (John 6:28-29). Just start believing! Start believing as you have never believed before in your life.

Point Three: Satan's defeat must be appropriated by faith. Romans 16:20 says, "Now may the God of peace crush satan under your feet shortly." God will crush satan under your feet shortly! According to Hebrews 2:14-15, Christ rendered powerless him who had the power of death, and delivered those who through fear of death were held captive all of their lives. "Submit therefore to God. Resist the devil and he will flee from you" (James 4:7). When the seventy were sent out, they rejoiced over everything they had done in His name, and Jesus told them, "Behold I give you authority over all the power of the enemy" (Luke 10:17-19). Jesus said, "In My

---

John 6:28-29 They said therefore to Him, "What shall we do, that we may work the works of God?" ²⁹ Jesus answered and said to them, "This is the work of God, that you believe in Him whom He has sent."

Romans 16:20 And the God of peace will soon crush Satan under your feet. The grace of our Lord Jesus be with you.

Hebrews 2:14-15 Since then the children share in flesh and blood, He Himself likewise also partook of the same, that through death He might render powerless him who had the power of death, that is, the devil; ¹⁵ and might deliver those who through fear of death were subject to slavery all their lives.

Luke 10:17-19 And the seventy returned with joy, saying, "Lord, even the demons are subject to us in Your name." ¹⁸ And He said to them, "I was watching Satan fall from heaven like lightning. ¹⁹ Behold, I have given you authority to tread upon serpents and scorpions, and over all the power of the enemy, and nothing shall injure you."

name they will cast out demons" (Mark 16:17). That means He did it and we execute it. We have the authority. Because He did it, in His name we can execute it. "The Son of God appeared for this purpose, that He might destroy the works of the devil" (1 John 3:8). This is the provision that Paul wrote about in Ephesians 3:8-12:

> To me, the very least of all saints, this grace was given, to preach to the Gentiles the unfathomable riches of Christ, and to bring to light what is the administration of the mystery which for ages has been hidden in God, who created all things; in order that the manifold wisdom of God might now be made known through the church to the rulers and the authorities in the heavenly places. This was in accordance with the eternal purpose which He carried out in Christ Jesus our Lord, in whom we have boldness and confident access through faith in Him.

These promises of God are very valid. While reading Ephesians, I came across one little phrase that stopped me cold: "Neither give place to the devil" (Ephesians 4:27, KJV). That bothers me. How many times have we given place to the devil? How many of us have simply been led around by the ear by satan? We have been distracted, discouraged, and depressed when really we should not be moved at all. Even as prophecies came to Paul about what he would suffer in Rome, he said, "None of these things move me. Nothing will move me from my course. I am going to finish this ministry with joy" (Acts 20:23-24, KJV). And he did. Some of the greatest epistles of joy were written by Paul in a Roman dungeon. He finished the course with joy.

Mark 16:17 "And these signs will accompany those who have believed: in My name they will cast out demons, they will speak with new tongues."

Acts 20:23-24, KJV Save that the Holy Ghost witnesseth in every city, saying that bonds and afflictions abide me. [24] But none of these things move me, neither count I my life dear unto myself, so that I might finish my course with joy, and the ministry, which I have received of the Lord Jesus, to testify the gospel of the grace of God.

Point Four: Paul's day was the beginning of the Church Age, but the Word tells us that "better is the end of a thing than the beginning thereof" (Ecclesiastes 7:8, KJV). Today we are living at the culmination of the Church Age. That is why we have to see the restoration of that which has not existed for centuries. What if we are missing the Kingdom by a hundred years? Who cares! We are not even walking in the fullness of the Church Age yet. We have to see the ministries and gifts come forth. Come on, let's move! Let's get going! Let's press in with all of our hearts. The promises of God are valid, I don't care what age you live in. By faith, in an age long before ours, Enoch was taken up so that he would not see death (Hebrews 11:5). About 5,500 years before the time people started talking about the "rapture,"[2] Enoch experienced one. We like to pigeonhole resurrection life into a certain time slot. The truth of the matter is that it has been available all the time. But in the promises of God we have a double portion when God says, "This is the time." The devils screamed and yelled, even at Jesus Christ, "Have You come here to torment us before the time?" (Matthew 8:29). But the Lord is putting His Word in our heart to say, "Oh devil, it is the time!" "Now judgment is upon this world; now the ruler of this world shall be cast out" (John 12:31). This is similar to what happened in the

---

Hebrews 11:5 By faith Enoch was taken up so that he should not see death; AND HE WAS NOT FOUND BECAUSE GOD TOOK HIM UP; for he obtained the witness that before his being taken up he was pleasing to God.

[2.] Rapture is a term in Christian eschatology which was originally used as a synonym for the first resurrection as referred to in 1 Corinthians 15:51-52. In the Scriptures, the first resurrection occurs after the tribulation period. Therefore, the original use of this term was without the belief that a group of people is caught up to heaven before the tribulation. This definition is the view that has been held historically for the longest period of time. The current, most popular use of the term "rapture," especially among fundamentalist Christians in the United States, refers to a group of people "being caught up to meet the Lord in the air" as described in 1 Thessalonians 4:16-17, and being taken to heaven. This concept was introduced by John Nelson Darby in the 1830s. It moves the first resurrection forward chronologically, referring to it as a pre-tribulation event where one group of people is caught up to heaven while another is left behind on the earth to face the tribulation.

Book of Revelation; there was no longer a place found for satan in heaven (Revelation 12:7-9). During our time, this will be duplicated. There will no longer be a place found for satan in the earth; he will be cast out. This word has to really work in our hearts, and it has to work now. We have to turn it loose.

This is the greatest rebuke to unbelief. It is the greatest stimulus of faith. It is the foundation upon which you can build. You can build your life right now at the threshold of the Kingdom of God and you can move in. It really is up to you. This is not some doctrine or theory. This word is real. It is true. We are going to make it work. Faith is an action. It is our word, and we lay hold of it, in the name of the Lord.

Revelation 12:7-9 And there was war in heaven, Michael and his angels waging war with the dragon. And the dragon and his angels waged war, [8] and they were not strong enough, and there was no longer a place found for them in heaven. [9] And the great dragon was thrown down, the serpent of old who is called the devil and Satan, who deceives the whole world; he was thrown down to the earth, and his angels were thrown down with him.

CHAPTER 2

And They Shall Flee Before You Seven Ways – Deuteronomy 28:7

How did the earth get into the condition it is in today? What is the source of all the evil and oppression in the world? It is important for us to know, and in Revelation chapter 12, we find the answer:

> And she gave birth to a son, a male child, who is to rule all the nations with a rod of iron; and her child was caught up to God and to His throne. (Revelation 12:5)

> And there was war in heaven, Michael and his angels waging war with the dragon. And the dragon and his angels waged war, and they were not strong enough, and there was no longer a place found for them in heaven. And the great dragon was thrown down, the serpent of old who is called the devil and Satan, who deceives the whole world; he was thrown down to the earth, and his angels were thrown down with him. (Revelation 12:7-9)

Jesus referred to satan as the ruler of this world (John 12:31). He had that position because he was able to usurp Adam and Eve's true

---

John 12:31 "Now judgment is upon this world; now the ruler of this world shall be cast out."

authority over the earth when they sinned. Yet satan was obviously functioning in heaven, and promoting himself and his kingdom in heaven. That ended when Jesus died on the cross, was resurrected, and ascended to the right hand of the Father. What happened to satan? He was not strong enough and there was no place found for him in heaven. He was kicked out of heaven and thrown down to the earth, where he intends to establish his kingdom. Now his focus is entirely on the earth. The whole scope of his kingdom is isolated to the natural and spiritual worlds surrounding us.

> "For this reason, rejoice, O heavens and you who dwell in them. Woe to the earth and the sea, because the devil has come down to you, having great wrath, knowing that he has only a short time." And when the dragon saw that he was thrown down to the earth, he persecuted the woman who gave birth to the male child. And the two wings of the great eagle were given to the woman, in order that she might fly into the wilderness to her place, where she was nourished for a time and times and half a time, from the presence of the serpent. And the serpent poured water like a river out of his mouth after the woman, so that he might cause her to be swept away with the flood. And the earth helped the woman, and the earth opened its mouth and drank up the river which the dragon poured out of his mouth. And the dragon was enraged with the woman, and went off to make war with the rest of her offspring, who keep the commandments of God and hold to the testimony of Jesus. (Revelation 12:12-17)

When satan finds himself on the earth, he persecutes and wars against the woman who gave birth to the male child. We know that the male child is Christ, the Messiah, who was born and caught up to the right hand of the Father. So the woman who gave birth is the Jewish nation. It is the Jews who gave birth to the Messiah, the male child who begins to move in authority and usher in the age of salvation. Because of this, when satan was cast down, he began to persecute them. He came against the Jewish people to destroy them. We have seen through the eyes of history how satan, with great rage, has come against the people of Israel. The Jewish people have been persecuted, and they have been brought almost to the point of destruction and annihilation. From the moment that satan was cast down, there has never been a time without attempts to destroy the Jewish nation and bring death to the Jewish people. But Israel will not be destroyed. In the midst of the dragon's great force to sweep her away, God brings wings of protection, and the earth itself protects the woman. Certain nations and peoples of the world have given help to the Jewish nation against this onslaught of satan to destroy her.

We also read in this passage, "And the dragon was enraged with the woman, and went off to make war with the rest of her offspring, who keep the commandments of God and hold to the testimony of Jesus" (Revelation 12:17). Not only does satan come against Israel, he comes against her children, the believers in Christ. He comes against us, the *ekklesia*.[3] Satan rages against Israel, and he rages against those who believe in Christ, against all those who serve the will of God. He is set to destroy the two branches of God's people who are really one. We know of God's great love, and an important part of that is the love that He has for His people Israel. We stand firm in God's love against satan's plan for the destruction of all of God's people.

So we have a picture of satan being cast down to the earth, and when he comes down, he comes with great wrath. This Scripture also tells us that satan is raging because he knows his time is short. It is imperative that we know this also, so that there is no passivity

---

[3.] Greek word used in New Testament texts for the coming together or assembly of believers, and translated as "church" in English.

in us that allows this time to go beyond what God has appointed. The earth is God's Kingdom, and we have to do here exactly what Jesus did in heaven. The Son, the male child, was caught up and began working in the heavenly realm to establish His Kingdom, and satan was cast out of that realm. The heavenly Kingdom that the Lord established became the gold standard for everything that is supposed to happen, and everything we are supposed to do on the earth. Therefore, in now bringing His Kingdom to the earth, we must follow the same pattern by appropriating all that Jesus is, all that He has done, and all that He has created in the Kingdom of heaven. Doing that requires that no more place be found for satan in the earth; he has to be cast out.

With this in mind, let's read Deuteronomy 28:7: "The LORD will cause your enemies who rise up against you to be defeated before you; they shall come out against you one way and shall flee before you seven ways." Ever since satan was cast down to earth, we have lived under his wrath and his pursuit of us. In his rage to destroy us, the enemy comes against us one way—as a united force—but he will be defeated and flee from us seven ways. This Scripture is our prophetic proclamation that satan's pursuit of us ends, and our pursuit of him begins. We have this confirmation from the Word that, although many times it appears as if the enemy is winning, the moment will come when the battle turns in our favor (Daniel 7:21-22). The enemy who rises up against us will be defeated before us. He will come out against us one way, but he will flee seven ways.

In the early 1970s, our founder John Stevens had a revelation from the Lord that the seven ways we pursue the enemy to his judgment are seven realms. These seven realms are very specific aspects of

---

Daniel 7:21-22 "I kept looking, and that horn was waging war with the saints and overpowering them [22] until the Ancient of Days came, and judgment was passed in favor of the saints of the Highest One, and the time arrived when the saints took possession of the kingdom."

society in our world today in which satan has established himself. It is interesting that in 1975 a revelation very similar to this came to other believers. There is still a movement in Christianity today that teaches about the seven mountains, or spheres of influence, in society. It is very close in revelation, and it came very close to the time that it was given to John Stevens. So we know that God is speaking and confirming His Word by revelation. As we bring down satan in this generation, we will not do it in a general way. We will pursue him very specifically in these realms, not with the purpose to simply make a living or pursue goals for ourselves, but with a determination to uproot satan and his angels out of every place they are entrenched.

There will be no Kingdom of God in the earth without satan being cast out; and if you are going to cast him out, you will find him in these seven realms of the world and in their functions. After he was cast out of heaven, satan fully entrenched himself in the earth. The way he did that was to take over these seven realms and fortify them. He has built them up into walled and protected cities that have become the elements that make up his kingdom in the earth. He is well-ensconced, and his perverted authority is well-protected in each of these realms. From that position of strength, he is fighting the sons of God in order to stay in control of the earth. If we understand that, then the battles we face fit perfectly into taking back these different realms of the Kingdom.

The first of these seven realms is Government, which includes politics and law. Every area of the world—every human being, every city, county, region, or country—is influenced by some form of government. And every government has some form of hierarchical structure that executes its rule over people. It is no different in the spirit realm. When God made all of creation, He formed a divine order, a hierarchical structure in which His government would function. So when satan was cast down, he took the principles of the spiritual government that God had formed and applied them to the earth. The Bible speaks of satan as the ruler, or god, of this world (John 16:11; 2 Corinthians 4:4). When satan was cast down to the earth, he established his government. Remember, it was not only satan who was cast down, but a third of the angels of heaven were cast down with him (Revelation 12:4). That is why the Scripture tells us that our battle is not against flesh and blood, but against principalities and powers (Ephesians 6:12, KJV).

This means that there is an established hierarchical structure in the satanic, demonic realm that rules this earth. This rulership of satan that the Bible speaks of is very real; it is an actual governmental structure. It exists in the realm of spirit, but as people are influenced by demonic spirits and caught up in satan's kingdom, they have established an order on the natural level that rules over every person in the earth. If we do not understand this, we will not understand the Kingdom of God, because the Kingdom of God, in its purity, is the governmental structure that God created from the beginning. He established an order to rule over creation. Mankind, represented by Adam and Eve, was part of that structure. Adam had dominion over the earth; it was his portion. It was given to him to name the animals, and he oversaw everything in the Garden of Eden. All creation that was part of this physical earth was under

---

John 16:11 "And concerning judgment, because the ruler of this world has been judged."

2 Corinthians 4:4 In whose case the god of this world has blinded the minds of the unbelieving, that they might not see the light of the gospel of the glory of Christ, who is the image of God.

Revelation 12:4 And his tail swept away a third of the stars of heaven, and threw them to the earth. And the dragon stood before the woman who was about to give birth, so that when she gave birth he might devour her child.

Ephesians 6:12, KJV For we wrestle not against flesh and blood, but against principalities, against powers, against the rulers of the darkness of this world, against spiritual wickedness in high places.

Adam's dominion (Genesis 1:28-30). In his disobedience, Adam gave up that authority; satan was then able to usurp and supplant Adam and make himself the ruler over this earth. Satan is only the ruler of the earth because he has usurped that authority. We are the ones who are to rule and reign with Jesus Christ on the earth (Revelation 5:10). Our authority and our place, established by God in the creation, have been usurped and we are taking them back.

Therefore, the issue of government becomes an important key. When you look at world governments, you see how they are the key log in the log jam that is blocking the Kingdom of God. If all you did was remove corruption from every government on the earth right now, 90 percent of the problems that we face in this world would evaporate. In many nations where poverty prevails, the country is actually rich. Most of the people who are starving are starving because their leaders are perverting the nation's finances. When other countries send food or money into those areas of need, that money tends to go into the pockets of corrupt leaders who don't care about their people. Likewise, most wars are not started by the people of a nation. Leaders seeking power, with corrupt motivations, attack other nations. We have the example of Adolf Hitler, whose motivation was a perverse drive to rule the world, which is an expression of satan himself.

Leadership and governments have to change. There is an obvious morality that simply does the right thing, which does not abuse the

---

Genesis 1:28-30 And God blessed them; and God said to them, "Be fruitful and multiply, and fill the earth, and subdue it; and rule over the fish of the sea and over the birds of the sky, and over every living thing that moves on the earth." [29] Then God said, "Behold, I have given you every plant yielding seed that is on the surface of all the earth, and every tree which has fruit yielding seed; it shall be food for you; [30] and to every beast of the earth and to every bird of the sky and to every thing that moves on the earth which has life, I have given every green plant for food"; and it was so.

Revelation 5:10 "And Thou hast made them to be a kingdom and priests to our God; and they will reign upon the earth."

finances and does not abuse the people. Of all of the things I want to see in our generation, I want to see righteousness; I want to see goodness. It starts with us as the school of prophets. That is why God continually works with us to close every open door we would have in our own spirits to the influence of satan's kingdom. It is easy to criticize leaders when you are poor and have no voice or authority to do anything about it. But what do you do when authority is put in your hands? Will you follow a pattern of perverting the righteous ways of the Lord? That is what God is changing. The Body of Christ will become the embodiment of the love and righteousness of God to one another. The key is that you love your brother as yourself (Matthew 22:36-40). When you pocket the money and pervert authority, you are directly hurting your brother. How many people have been hurt by church government or leaders who take the money and pervert authority? Before long, people are leaving churches because they are getting hurt and the whole thing seems phony. Church government is no freer from these things than the world around us.

That is why we are dropping the concept of church and striving to become the *ekklesia* of God, which is God's family coming together. The Body of Christ will not function as the Church has functioned for 2,000 years. There is something new that God is doing. We are coming into a new government where we love one another and we care one for another. As we build prophetic communities, God is teaching us and giving us opportunities. He is putting responsibilities in our hands so that we learn and are able to reject temptation in those areas. Satan has entrenched himself in this realm of government, which includes church government. So we

---

Matthew 22:36-40   "Teacher, which is the great commandment in the Law?" [37] And He said to him, "'You shall love the Lord your God with all your heart, and with all your soul, and with all your mind.' [38] This is the great and foremost commandment. [39] The second is like it, 'You shall love your neighbor as yourself.' [40] On these two commandments depend the whole Law and the Prophets."

can begin by casting him out of our churches. We cast him out by establishing a new government, a government driven by our love and our care for one another. Our prayer to God is, "Father, give us Your heart; give us Your Spirit. We cast out the false government and rulership over the Church, until it becomes the true Body of Christ in oneness and in love for every aspect of Your Body. Give us Your love that teaches us how to treat one another, not just in the house of God but in government, in leadership, and in every area of rule."

Satan has come against us but we will pursue him. We will run him out of every place that he has sought to create a fortress. Our weapons are mighty to the tearing down of fortresses (2 Corinthians 10:4). We are beginning to dismantle satan's rulership. This does not necessarily mean that we will hold positions in government. We do not have to be a senator, or a congressman, or the president, but rulers will look to us as they did to the prophet Daniel (Daniel 1:19-20). They will look to us as they did to Joseph in Egypt. Only in the throne was the authority of Pharaoh greater than that of Joseph (Genesis 41:39-40). We do not need to have a title, but we will have the authority. We will have a voice, and we will determine how things will be established.

---

2 Corinthians 10:4   For the weapons of our warfare are not of the flesh, but divinely powerful for the destruction of fortresses.

Daniel 1:19-20   And the king talked with them, and out of them all not one was found like Daniel, Hananiah, Mishael and Azariah; so they entered the king's personal service. [20] And as for every matter of wisdom and understanding about which the king consulted them, he found them ten times better than all the magicians and conjurers who were in all his realm.

Genesis 41:39-40   So Pharaoh said to Joseph, "Since God has informed you of all this, there is no one so discerning and wise as you are. [40] You shall be over my house, and according to your command all my people shall do homage; only in the throne I will be greater than you."

The second realm is the realm of Religion. Next to government, one of the greatest influences on the human race is religion. This realm includes all world religions and the areas of the occult. When you look at the broad spectrum of religion around the world, you can see how satan has made this realm another one of his fortified cities. We read that satan appears as an angel of light (2 Corinthians 11:14). He looks like the most perfect, religious person on the face of the earth. Everything in false religion looks wonderful. It appears as the true light, when in fact it is darkness. There is only one true way in God, and the perversion of religion must end. We are very anxious to bind satan and cast him out of this realm until true worship of the one true God is established. There is one Body, one Spirit, one Lord, one faith, and one baptism (Ephesians 4:4-6). We will see true worship established in the earth, but that cannot happen until we bind the perversion of religion in the Church, and throughout the world. We will not tolerate a mixture of idolatry with the worship of God. Instead, we must let God purify us. The Body of Christ is coming into oneness, and the promise in the Word is that the unity of the Spirit will lead us to the unity of the faith (Ephesians 4:3, 13). We will know true worship in every area. The Word of God will unfold with one truth, not with many opinions about its meaning. We all have the same Bible, but there is tremendous deception and confusion concerning it. That must come to an end. As we cast satan from the realm of religion, the Body of Christ will come together and we will see the Word of God come alive. We will see it live in

---

2 Corinthians 11:14 And no wonder, for even Satan disguises himself as an angel of light.

Ephesians 4:4-6 There is one body and one Spirit, just as also you were called in one hope of your calling; [5] one Lord, one faith, one baptism, [6] one God and Father of all who is over all and through all and in all.

Ephesians 4:3 Being diligent to preserve the unity of the Spirit in the bond of peace.

Ephesians 4:13 Until we all attain to the unity of the faith, and of the knowledge of the Son of God, to a mature man, to the measure of the stature which belongs to the fulness of Christ.

our hearts until, like Christ, we will become the Word made flesh (John 1:14).

The third realm is the Arts. Included in the arts are music, entertainment and media. Because they contain these areas of music and entertainment, the arts have a tremendous impact, especially in this generation, on people around the globe. We have whole generations whose morality has been framed by movies and television coming out of Hollywood. We see our thinking about family, life, and right and wrong formed by media. It is one of the greatest influences there is. We want to end that influence and bring about the influence of the pure arts from God. According to the Scriptures, the craftsmen who built the tabernacle in the wilderness were those who were chosen and anointed by God (Exodus 31:1-3). They were able to construct the ark of the covenant out of wood and overlay it with gold (Exodus 37:1-2). The realm of the arts will be one of the greatest areas in the Kingdom, expressing the true creativity of the people of God. God is creative. He cannot do anything without creating. It is the nature of God, and the arts should reflect His creativity and nature.

When you look at the magnificence of the natural world, you see that it is a beautiful work of art. The creation of this planet is one of the most beautiful works of art that you could imagine. John Stevens would often talk about the thousand faces of God that are portrayed in the Bible; for example, "God is my strong

---

John 1:14   And the Word became flesh, and dwelt among us, and we beheld His glory, glory as of the only begotten from the Father, full of grace and truth.

Exodus 31:1-3   Now the LORD spoke to Moses, saying, ² "See, I have called by name Bezalel, the son of Uri, the son of Hur, of the tribe of Judah. ³ And I have filled him with the Spirit of God in wisdom, in understanding, in knowledge, and in all kinds of craftsmanship."

Exodus 37:1-2   Now Bezalel made the ark of acacia wood; its length was two and a half cubits, and its width one and a half cubits, and its height one and a half cubits; ² and he overlaid it with pure gold inside and out, and made a gold molding for it all around.

fortress" (2 Samuel 22:33), or "The LORD is My Banner" (Exodus 17:15). If we could create artistic expressions of the thousand faces of God, people would look upon those works of art and have a meeting with God. They would see His reflection. How can we look at this created world and not see God? His nature, His very personality, is infused in everything that He touches (Romans 1:19-20). We cast satan out of the realm of the arts and bring an end to the perversion of music, of the media, of movies and video, of all the areas in which there should be the creative expression of God. Satan has usurped these areas. Many times when we look at art or listen to music, it perverts our minds; it seduces us away from the things of God. We bring an end to that in the name of the Lord. Father, instill Your creativity into Your people. We loose the creativity in the Body of Christ. We loose our children and our adults to have the keys to bring new music, new art forms, and new creativity into the earth.

The fourth realm is Finance. Under finance we find business, economics, and the world's economies. This covers what the Bible calls "mammon." Jesus said that we cannot serve God and mammon, and yet we see so many who are serving mammon (Matthew 6:24). It is one of the greatest temptations to mankind: wanting to have money, and wanting the control over money. That is not the way it was in the beginning of the Church; under the apostles, no one considered anything as his own (Acts 2:44-45). Back then, the use of finances was for the care of the Body. It was to build the places

---

Romans 1:19-20 Because that which is known about God is evident within them; for God made it evident to them. [20] For since the creation of the world His invisible attributes, His eternal power and divine nature, have been clearly seen, being understood through what has been made, so that they are without excuse.

Matthew 6:24 "No one can serve two masters; for either he will hate the one and love the other, or he will hold to one and despise the other. You cannot serve God and mammon."

Acts 2:44-45 And all those who had believed were together, and had all things in common; [45] and they began selling their property and possessions, and were sharing them with all, as anyone might have need.

of worship. In the wilderness, Moses said, "Bring me the riches that God gave you as you left Egypt." So the people brought the gold, the silver, and the fine fabrics to Moses. They brought everything that represented wealth and finances in that generation. Then what did they do with it? They built a place to worship God (Exodus 25:1-4; 36:1).

Lord, bring us back to that state of heart where our first concern regarding finances is to create a place where people can worship You. And second to that is the concern that the people themselves are cared for. In the first-century Church, not one of them had any need. Yet in this world it seems as if there is not enough wealth to go around. I do not believe that is true. The apparent lack is a manifestation of satan grabbing the finances, taking them to himself, and creating a spirit of selfishness, lust, and greed in people until they hoard all they can to themselves. Economic crashes that have affected the entire world have been born out of the corruption of people wanting money for themselves and, therefore, doing the wrong things. Today, the entire world is on the brink of financial ruin. Because of this, we are seeing riots in nations. That is evidence of satan exercising his rule and control. The truth is there is enough to take care of every man, woman, and child that God has brought forth on this earth. In the hands of the Lord's anointed ones, finances will be blessed and they will be sufficient. We prophesy the end of the satanic reign over the realm of finance. The Scripture says the gold is His and the silver is His (Haggai 2:8). All of the wealth in the

---

Exodus 25:1-4   Then the LORD spoke to Moses, saying, ² "Tell the sons of Israel to raise a contribution for Me; from every man whose heart moves him you shall raise My contribution. ³ And this is the contribution which you are to raise from them: gold, silver and bronze, ⁴ blue, purple and scarlet material, fine linen, goat hair."

Exodus 36:1   "Now Bezalel and Oholiab, and every skillful person in whom the LORD has put skill and understanding to know how to perform all the work in the construction of the sanctuary, shall perform in accordance with all that the LORD has commanded."

Haggai 2:8   "'The silver is Mine, and the gold is Mine,' declares the LORD of hosts."

entire world belongs to Him. Lord, we declare the beginning of Your repossession of the finances of the earth. Let it be by Your Word and through Your heart that wealth is distributed in the earth.

The fifth realm is Science. So many things come from science. I am very concerned about the constraint, and restraint, that satan puts on science, because in this realm are many of the answers that we need. If we made a list of all the big problems of the world, science should have the answers. But satan will not let us get to the answers. He blocks the inventions that are to come by revelation, the inventions that are really needed. We loose revelation to God's people for new inventions to answer the world's issues. We need breakthroughs in power and energy, and in the ability to see the end of waste and pollution. Satan perverts these realms, and the way he perverts science is to restrain it. Today we turn it loose. Where will the next breakthroughs in science come from? They will come from God's people. The Lord can give us the revelation, the wisdom, and the know-how. Do not wait for somebody else to do it. We have enough genius minds, engineers and scientists, just in our fellowship, to solve the problems of the world. We are the ones who are to end satan's reign. And every scientific discovery that breaks the futility of this age is a part of ending his rule.

The sixth realm is Education. Education is the next step to end satan's reign. Through education we will reverse satan's lies and the deception that has invaded every one of these other realms. We can literally teach our children **out** of futility. We know that is possible, because we have seen what education can do. The liberal, amoral education that has been so prevalent in North America has destroyed the principles of many young people. It has broken down morality and has broken down family. It has broken down truth and understanding. Education has to begin with truth. God's Word is truth (John 17:17). Jesus **is** the truth (John 14:6). Just as satan has infiltrated the other realms by controlling education, through godly education we will pursue him and cast him out of every one of these realms. We will train and educate new generations in what government really is, what religion really is, how the arts are to be done, how to manage our finances, and how to turn loose discovery and creativity in science. We will see it happen through education.

Teaching is one of the great ministries that Jesus provided for us when He ascended. He gave us apostles, prophets, evangelists, pastors, and teachers (Ephesians 4:10-11). Teaching is an anointing (1 John 2:27). It is part of the mantle that was left by Christ as He ascended to the right hand of the Father. He did not leave us as orphans (John 14:18). He left us with the anointing and the creativity that we need. And so, let's educate the next generations into the truth, releasing their anointing and creativity into every area of life. They will be turned loose into all the seven realms by the impartation of education that we release. We are not just building schools; we are imparting to and creating the next generations that God will bless with answers to liberate the world from the dying reign of satan, and to lead people into the dawning of the Lord's Kingdom.

The seventh realm is Health. It could seem as though health should be included in the realm of science, but it is too important to simply

---

John 17:17 "Sanctify them in the truth; Thy word is truth."

John 14:6 Jesus said to him, "I am the way, and the truth, and the life; no one comes to the Father, but through Me."

Ephesians 4:10-11 (He who descended is Himself also He who ascended far above all the heavens, that He might fill all things.) ¹¹ And He gave some as apostles, and some as prophets, and some as evangelists, and some as pastors and teachers.

1 John 2:27 And as for you, the anointing which you received from Him abides in you, and you have no need for anyone to teach you; but as His anointing teaches you about all things, and is true and is not a lie, and just as it has taught you, you abide in Him.

John 14:18 "I will not leave you as orphans; I will come to you."

be part of another realm. It is an area that satan has carved out with special determination. No flesh will be saved alive if satan is successful against us in this realm of health (Matthew 24:22). Our health should be a primary focus of intercession. God has spent many years raising us up, equipping us, and training us. We have gone through many things in the dealings of God. We have gone through testings and temptations. Only recently has there been enough maturity in the Body of Christ that it can start to come together like we read about in Ezekiel's vision. By the Word of the Lord, various members of Christ's Body are beginning to find a connection with one another, joint to joint and bone to bone. The sinew, the ligaments, the muscles, and the flesh are beginning to form (Ezekiel 37:7-10). God has taken great pains to bring His Body together. So satan's greatest assault is to try to kill God's sons. Our mortality is still our greatest weakness and God's biggest problem.

At the beginning of the Church, the apostles were the target of satan's destruction. It was not many years after the Church was born on the Day of Pentecost until satan was successful in destroying those who had the wisdom, the understanding, and the revelation to lead the Body of Christ. We wonder why the Church has gone through so much trouble. It is because the apostolic head was destroyed and the Body wandered blindly in darkness. But now the Church has experienced years of restoration. God is recreating globally those who can bring together and lead the Body of Christ. We cannot allow

---

Matthew 24:22 "And unless those days had been cut short, no life would have been saved; but for the sake of the elect those days shall be cut short."

Ezekiel 37:7-10 So I prophesied as I was commanded; and as I prophesied, there was a noise, and behold, a rattling; and the bones came together, bone to its bone. [8] And I looked, and behold, sinews were on them, and flesh grew, and skin covered them; but there was no breath in them. [9] Then He said to me, "Prophesy to the breath, prophesy, son of man, and say to the breath, 'Thus says the Lord GOD, "Come from the four winds, O breath, and breathe on these slain, that they come to life."'" [10] So I prophesied as He commanded me, and the breath came into them, and they came to life, and stood on their feet, an exceedingly great army.

our own mortality to cut this off prematurely. We must bring an end to the access that satan has to destroy us, to destroy mankind, and to destroy the world. Health is too important to simply be an area under science. It is more than medicine. There are ways of health; there are revelations that God is beginning to show us about how to maintain our health. We believe in resurrection life, but on the road to resurrection life, we believe in divine health. We believe in God's intervention for our physical bodies. More than just healings like we have known, we need divine health and strength.

This is something that God's people had in the days of Moses. Moses had it. Joshua had it. Caleb had it. Their strength was never abated (Deuteronomy 34:7; Joshua 14:11). They lived in health. They lived in strength. We do not have that kind of health anymore. It has been too long since the world has seen true health, divine anointing and glory resting on human vessels until their strength does not dissipate. Throughout the wilderness wanderings, Israel had none of the diseases that were on the surrounding people (Exodus 15:26). Yet today, in the Body of Christ, we accept disease. We think it is a way of life. Our minds have been perverted by the deception of satan to believe in being sick, to believe in losing our health and our strength. We end that perverted thinking! That is not the way men like Joshua and Caleb lived. Their strength did not abate. There was such a force of life and health on Israel in that day that even their

---

Deuteronomy 34:7 Although Moses was one hundred and twenty years old when he died, his eye was not dim, nor his vigor abated.

Joshua 14:11 "I am still as strong today as I was in the day Moses sent me; as my strength was then, so my strength is now, for war and for going out and coming in."

Exodus 15:26 And He said, "If you will give earnest heed to the voice of the Lord your God, and do what is right in His sight, and give ear to His commandments, and keep all His statutes, I will put none of the diseases on you which I have put on the Egyptians; for I, the Lord, am your healer."

clothes and shoes did not wear out (Deuteronomy 29:5). Futility was suspended.

Satan is the force of futility, and it is futility that drains away our life and energy. We should be done with it. We should contend before the Father and pray, "Give us life! Give us strength!" If we have been buried with Christ in baptism, then we should be raised with Him into His life, His resurrection (Romans 6:4-5). Lord, we loose that life to course through our veins, to course through our physical bodies. Give us strength, Lord. Let there be life for Your people. We will not have a Church that is sick and weak. We will be filled with Your Spirit, with life, and with faith. If we are going to cast satan out of these other six realms, we need Your strength, Lord. You have not raised us up that we should die in sickness.

Who is going to put an end to satan? You will! There had better be an intensity in your spirit, because it is the time. From this day forward, we are no longer being pursued by satan. He is defeated and we pursue him seven ways. Not one area of his rule will continue or stand. He is cast out of Government, out of Religion, out of the Arts, out of Finance, out of Science, out of Education, and out of Health. We are free! We pursue satan and we see him being cast out of this earth, just as he was cast out of heaven. We will not rest until it is done. Now when we prophesy as the school of prophets, it is not generalized: "We bind you, satan." No, we pursue him. We very specifically end his involvement and rulership in every one of these realms. We declare the vision that John Stevens had will be fulfilled today by a people who have believed the Living Word that he spoke.

Deuteronomy 29:5 "And I have led you forty years in the wilderness; your clothes have not worn out on you, and your sandal has not worn out on your foot."

Romans 6:4-5 Therefore we have been buried with Him through baptism into death, in order that as Christ was raised from the dead through the glory of the Father, so we too might walk in newness of life. [5] For if we have become united with Him in the likeness of His death, certainly we shall be also in the likeness of His resurrection.

It will manifest today in specific judgments against satan in every realm, in the name of the Lord.

CHAPTER 3

What Stops Us Now?

Those who know me know that I am determined to see something happen in this generation. I am very concerned that we do not stop our intensity and our drive of appropriation. What future generations will have is their concern; I am concerned about God moving in this generation. As a people, we have something very important in the Living Word that was spoken to us by John Robert Stevens. In that Word there are many prophecies and many promises that are a covenant between us as a people and God. I believe there are many other groups in the Body of Christ who have this same reality—not just generalized promises, but very specific promises that should be obtained, that should be walked in. We ourselves need to know very specifically what we should have. There must be access to these prophecies, so that our future generations will know and understand the covenant that was made with them by God through His Word. In this message, I want to help you understand, through the Scriptures, what a covenant actually means and the process that takes place by virtue of that covenant.

The reason the Bible was divided into the Old Testament and the New Testament is because the word "testament" is another word for covenant. Therefore, the Bible is about the old covenant and the new covenant that God made with man. The New Testament writers made reference to this concept (2 Corinthians 3:14; 1 Corinthians 11:25). A study of the Bible reveals that it is really a series of covenants that God made with mankind. To understand the significance of this, we have to first understand what a covenant is. A covenant is an agreement made between two parties, in which each party promises to abide by the terms of the agreement. For example, the first covenant in the Bible is the covenant God made with Adam and Eve. In this agreement, He told them to rule over the earth. In turn, He would provide the plants and trees for food, on the condition that they did not eat from the tree of the knowledge of good and evil (Genesis 1:27-29; 2:16-17). We know that they broke that covenant; and because they did not adhere to the agreement, there were consequences. What God did then for Adam and Eve was to make a new covenant with them (Genesis 3:16-19).

---

2 Corinthians 3:14 But their minds were hardened; for until this very day at the reading of the old covenant the same veil remains unlifted, because it is removed in Christ.

1 Corinthians 11:25 In the same way He took the cup also, after supper, saying, "This cup is the new covenant in My blood; do this, as often as you drink it, in remembrance of Me."

Genesis 1:27-29 And God created man in His own image, in the image of God He created him; male and female He created them. [28] And God blessed them; and God said to them, "Be fruitful and multiply, and fill the earth, and subdue it; and rule over the fish of the sea and over the birds of the sky, and over every living thing that moves on the earth." [29] Then God said, "Behold, I have given you every plant yielding seed that is on the surface of all the earth, and every tree which has fruit yielding seed; it shall be food for you."

Genesis 2:16-17 And the LORD God commanded the man, saying, "From any tree of the garden you may eat freely; [17] but from the tree of the knowledge of good and evil you shall not eat, for in the day that you eat from it you shall surely die."

Genesis 3:16-19 To the woman He said, "I will greatly multiply your pain in childbirth, in pain you shall bring forth children; yet your desire shall be for your husband, and he shall rule over you." [17] Then to Adam He said, "Because you have listened to the voice of your wife, and have eaten from the tree about which I commanded you, saying, 'You shall not eat from it'; cursed is the ground because of you; in toil you shall eat of it all the days of your life. [18] Both thorns and thistles it shall grow for you; and you shall eat the plants of the field; [19] by the sweat of your face you shall eat bread, till you return to the ground, because from it you were taken; for you are dust, and to dust you shall return."

What we really find in what we call the Old Testament, or old covenant, are many covenants, and those covenants were usually made with blood. These were very serious agreements. In the Scriptures where we read that God made a covenant with someone, the Hebrew word *karat* is used, meaning He "cut" a covenant. One of the reasons for this is that these covenants were instituted with blood; and that blood, of course, represents Christ. Do you believe that Christ was in the Garden of Eden, and that He was covering the sin of Adam and Eve (1 Peter 1:18-20)? The covenant that was made between God and Adam and Eve was made with blood. You may think, "I don't see that in the Bible. Where was the sacrifice of the animal?" We know that animals were sacrificed, because God clothed them with animal skins. From the very beginning, blood was spilled to create the covenant. For Adam and Eve, that symbol of Christ in the spilling of His blood was something they wore, and it is what covered their nakedness. God cut a covenant with them; it was made with blood.

That was the beginning of the covenants that came down through the Scriptures, all the way until the time of Christ. The Bible is full of covenants. God made a covenant with Abraham, promising him a child, and telling him that his descendants would possess the land where he was dwelling. In Genesis chapter 15 this covenant was sealed with the blood of sacrificed animals. Then He made the covenant of circumcision with Abraham, promising him that he would be the father of many nations. These covenants had specific requirements for Abraham and his descendants to walk in. If any male descendant was not circumcised, that person would have broken the covenant and would be cut off from his

---

1 Peter 1:18-20 Knowing that you were not redeemed with perishable things like silver or gold from your futile way of life inherited from your forefathers, [19] but with precious blood, as of a lamb unblemished and spotless, the blood of Christ. [20] For He was foreknown before the foundation of the world, but has appeared in these last times for the sake of you.

people (Genesis 17:10, 14). Abraham tried to fulfill God's promise of a son through Sarah's maid, Hagar, but God told him that the covenant would only be fulfilled through Sarah in the birth of his son, Isaac (Genesis 17:15-16, 18-19).

God also made a covenant with Israel to be His people at Mount Sinai; this covenant too was sealed with blood (Exodus 19:5-6; 24:7-8). God told them to observe the laws He gave them, or they would be removed from the land that He had promised (Deuteronomy 4:23, 26-27). We know that they broke that covenant,

---

Genesis 17:10 "This is My covenant, which you shall keep, between Me and you and your descendants after you: every male among you shall be circumcised."

Genesis 17:14 "But an uncircumcised male who is not circumcised in the flesh of his foreskin, that person shall be cut off from his people; he has broken My covenant."

Genesis 17:15-16 Then God said to Abraham, "As for Sarai your wife, you shall not call her name Sarai, but Sarah shall be her name. ¹⁶ And I will bless her, and indeed I will give you a son by her. Then I will bless her, and she shall be a mother of nations; kings of peoples shall come from her."

Genesis 17:18-19 And Abraham said to God, "Oh that Ishmael might live before Thee!" ¹⁹ But God said, "No, but Sarah your wife shall bear you a son, and you shall call his name Isaac; and I will establish My covenant with him for an everlasting covenant for his descendants after him."

Exodus 19:5-6 " 'Now then, if you will indeed obey My voice and keep My covenant, then you shall be My own possession among all the peoples, for all the earth is Mine; ⁶ and you shall be to Me a kingdom of priests and a holy nation.' These are the words that you shall speak to the sons of Israel."

Exodus 24:7-8 Then he took the book of the covenant and read it in the hearing of the people; and they said, "All that the Lord has spoken we will do, and we will be obedient!" ⁸ So Moses took the blood and sprinkled it on the people, and said, "Behold the blood of the covenant, which the Lord has made with you in accordance with all these words."

Deuteronomy 4:23 "So watch yourselves, lest you forget the covenant of the Lord your God, which He made with you, and make for yourselves a graven image in the form of anything against which the Lord your God has commanded you."

Deuteronomy 4:26-27 "I call heaven and earth to witness against you today, that you shall surely perish quickly from the land where you are going over the Jordan to possess it. You shall not live long on it, but shall be utterly destroyed. ²⁷ And the Lord will scatter you among the peoples, and you shall be left few in number among the nations, where the Lord shall drive you."

and God did to them exactly as He had said. They were driven from the land and scattered among the nations. Still He promised them a new covenant, and this covenant is recorded in Jeremiah chapter 31:

> "Behold, days are coming," declares the LORD, "when I will make a new covenant with the house of Israel and with the house of Judah, not like the covenant which I made with their fathers in the day I took them by the hand to bring them out of the land of Egypt, My covenant which they broke, although I was a husband to them," declares the LORD. "But this is the covenant which I will make with the house of Israel after those days," declares the LORD, "I will put My law within them, and on their heart I will write it; and I will be their God, and they shall be My people. And they shall not teach again, each man his neighbor and each man his brother, saying, 'Know the LORD,' for they shall all know Me, from the least of them to the greatest of them," declares the LORD, "for I will forgive their iniquity, and their sin I will remember no more." (Jeremiah 31:31-34)

Our concept of the New Testament is based on this promise of a new covenant. What we forget is that it was only new to the Jews. As Gentiles, we exclaim, "We have a new covenant!" No, the Gentiles had no covenant at all. It is only new to us in the sense that we never had a covenant before. But for the Jews, it was truly a new covenant because they had an old one. This new covenant was to be made with Israel and with Judah; but when God made this covenant with them, He also, by the blood of Jesus Christ, included the Gentiles. God made a new covenant with the Jewish nation, and in Christ He made a covenant with us as Gentiles.

Today, Christians understand the New Testament as being about salvation in Jesus Christ. We emphasize being "saved." When you come to Christ, your sins are forgiven, and you have a salvation experience. In reality, it is about the covenant that God made with us, and the blood of Christ was the sealing of that covenant. Salvation is an aspect of that covenant; it is a paragraph in the agreement. In this covenant God says, "If you confess your sin, I will forgive your sin by the blood of Christ" (1 John 1:9). That is definitely part of the covenant. But because we focus on that part, we tend to forget what the whole covenant says. What is really in the new covenant, this contract that we have with God? We know that God is serious about this contract, because He signed it with the blood of Christ. And when you receive Christ, you are agreeing to the contract. You have entered into a covenant with God, just as Adam and Eve did, as Abraham did, as Israel did. You cannot simply take one part of the covenant and say, "Now I'm done. I have received salvation." That covenant is a relationship between you and God. It is a daily walk with the Lord, and it is important to understand what our commitment is in this new covenant. Let's look at Hebrews the 11th chapter to see how people of faith walked with God in their covenant:

> By faith Enoch was taken up so that he should not see death; AND HE WAS NOT FOUND BECAUSE GOD TOOK HIM UP; for he obtained the witness that before his being taken up he was pleasing to God. And without faith it is impossible to please Him, for he who comes to God must believe that He is, and that He is a rewarder of those who seek Him. [Now we will look at some of these covenants that we were talking about.] By faith Noah, being warned by God about things not yet seen, in reverence prepared an ark for the salvation of his household, by which he condemned the world, and became an heir of the righteousness which is according to faith. By faith Abraham, when he was called, obeyed by going out to a place which he was to receive for

---

1 John 1:9 If we confess our sins, He is faithful and righteous to forgive us our sins and to cleanse us from all unrighteousness.

an inheritance; and he went out, not knowing where he was going. By faith he lived as an alien in the land of promise, as in a foreign land, dwelling in tents with Isaac and Jacob, fellow heirs of the same promise. (Hebrews 11:5-9)

And all these, having gained approval through their faith, did not receive what was promised. (Hebrews 11:39)

We see illustrated here the process of walking with God according to a covenant. This entire chapter is about covenants that existed between God and specific individuals. When you read the rest of the chapter, it tells how Abraham offered up Isaac by faith, and describes acts of faith by Jacob, Moses, Gideon, Samson, David, and many others. All of these people had specific covenants with God, and by faith they brought down armies, did acts of righteousness, and performed tremendous miracles all within the context of their covenant. Then we read that all of these people, who gained approval through their faith, did not receive what was promised. They were committed to performing their part of the agreement, but the fulfillment of their promises had to wait for Christ to come. In other words, if the covenant that we call the Old Testament was the agreement, then the fulfillment of that agreement was dependent upon Christ.

That is staggering. We read about all of the things these people did, all of the wonderful works, all of the authority and power that they moved in, and yet in the end they did not receive what was promised. Today, as Christians, we talk about the fact that we have a new covenant, but we are satisfied to experience it as they experienced the old covenants. In our conditioning, we are used to having a covenant that does not seem to work. We see generation after generation of believers dying in faith, never receiving the promises (Hebrews 11:13). You cannot say that they did not have faith. They did many wonderful things, real acts of faith, real works of God, but they also died never receiving what was promised. So, in a sense, we see the Church living in an old covenant way. Yet having the new covenant, we are supposed to live possessing the promises. There has been a great deal of criticism of the Old Testament, saying, "That was the old covenant. That never worked. But now we have Christ." Okay, I agree; we have Christ. Then, let's see it work! Are we waiting for another blood sacrifice? Do we need another covenant because we cannot keep this covenant?

Every covenant between God and man ended up being broken, because man could never do his part; so God was free to break the covenant. We can look at the Scripture in Jeremiah chapter 31 and say, "Was God a liar? He made a promise previously, but it seems as if He is breaking that promise by making a new covenant." God's response to that would be, "No, they broke the covenant. They never did what they agreed to do." This is the nature of a contract, or an agreement: "We will both keep this covenant. I agree to do certain things, and you agree to do certain things. As long as you keep doing what you promised, I will keep doing what I promised." When you break the covenant, then God is no longer responsible to you. I don't care what He promised you. I don't care what He said He would give you. If you break the covenant, then He does not have to fulfill His part. However, according to Hebrews chapter 8, we are able to keep this new covenant:

> But now He has obtained a more excellent ministry, by as much as He is also the mediator of a better covenant, which has been enacted on better promises. For if that first covenant had been faultless, there would have been

---

Hebrews 11:13 All these died in faith, without receiving the promises, but having seen them and having welcomed them from a distance, and having confessed that they were strangers and exiles on the earth.

no occasion sought for a second. For finding fault with them, He says,

"Behold, days are coming, says the Lord,
When I will effect a new covenant
With the house of Israel and with the house
    of Judah;
Not like the covenant which I made with
    their fathers
On the day when I took them by the hand
To lead them out of the land of Egypt;
For they did not continue in My covenant,
And I did not care for them, says the Lord.
For this is the covenant that I will make
    with the house of Israel
After those days, says the Lord:
I will put My laws into their minds,
And I will write them upon their hearts.
And I will be their God,
And they shall be My people." (Hebrews 8:6-10)

People have broken every covenant they have had with God. No one was able to perform their part of the agreement. That is why Christ is so important, because walking in this new covenant is not dependent on us being perfect; it is dependent on Him having been perfect. Therefore, it is not by works (Ephesians 2:8-9). In this new covenant, there is not something we have to do like the Israelites had to do in their covenant with God at Sinai. They had to hold to the agreement in minute detail in order for God to keep His side of the agreement. And they never were able to do it. So Christ came as the performer of our part of the agreement. This new covenant is not between you and Jesus; it is between you and God. Jesus is the

---

Ephesians 2:8-9   For by grace you have been saved through faith; and that not of yourselves, it is the gift of God; ⁹ not as a result of works, that no one should boast.

mediator of the new covenant (Hebrews 9:15). He is the One who makes the covenant possible. He negotiates the covenant for both sides. That is why God said, "This covenant is not like the covenant which I made with their fathers, My covenant which they broke."

What then is supposed to happen in this covenant? As you read Jeremiah chapter 31 and Hebrews chapter 8, ask, "What is God's part of the agreement? What is He supposed to do for me?" In this covenant, He is to write His Law on your heart. He is to make you capable of walking in the covenant. What is your part? Your part is to know Him. "For they shall all know Me, from the least of them to the greatest of them" (Jeremiah 31:34). You are to know God personally. God's promise is "I will be their God, and they shall be My people" (Jeremiah 31:33). That is the relationship we are looking for. I know there are many other promises, but I am going to concentrate on this one right here. The fact that I am bringing this message is proof that we are not walking in the covenant. Why am I teaching you? Because something is missing. The promise is that "they shall not teach again, each man his neighbor and each man his brother, saying, 'Know the LORD'" (Jeremiah 31:34).

The new covenant is emphasized again in the New Testament, because this covenant applies to us as Christians as well as to Israel and Judah. If any covenant that God made with man had worked, there would have been no need for a new covenant. The point is that everyone, not just Israel and Judah, has broken their covenant with God, and He has found fault with them. Now will He find fault with us? What happened to all those people with whom God made covenants? According to Hebrews 11, they walked by faith, they performed acts of righteousness, they made many things happen,

---

Hebrews 9:15 And for this reason He is the mediator of a new covenant, in order that since a death has taken place for the redemption of the transgressions that were committed under the first covenant, those who have been called may receive the promise of the eternal inheritance.

but they never received the promise. I keep waiting for Christianity to wake up and say, "For 2,000 years we have walked just like the people walked in the Old Testament. We have done many things, but we still don't have what is promised in this new covenant." It has been a reality in Christianity that many people have done mighty works, but they have not received the promise. The Word is to be written on our hearts. It is to be written in our minds. Something is supposed to happen where the problem of the human nature is taken away.

Honestly ask yourself, "Do I have that experience?" Do you wake up with the Word written on your heart, empowered to do the will of God? Or do you wake up still striving with the flesh? We continually fight the downward pull of our old nature, but we are supposed to be a new creation in Christ (2 Corinthians 5:17). It is time to obtain the promise, not just have some works of faith. We are not waiting for Christ; He has already come. So we have to ask ourselves, "What stops us now?" Abraham had to wait for Christ to come. Noah had to wait. Isaiah had to wait. Jeremiah had to wait. What are we waiting for? What is the Body of Christ waiting for today? Do we just want to do a few good works? I love that we have healings and wonderful works of faith. I love seeing miracles. I am not taking away from that. But the promise of the new covenant is resurrection life. I do not want people to talk about all the mighty words I brought or the mighty works that I did. If I die in the faith, it means I did not receive what was promised.

You have a covenant with God in Christ. Do you know what promises you have? What do they say? What are you supposed to do? What is God supposed to do? Do you even know? We have so much in the new covenant, but there are other promises as well. There are prophecies that have come to us as The Living Word Fellowship.

---

2 Corinthians 5:17 Therefore if any man is in Christ, he is a new creature; the old things passed away; behold, new things have come.

We have covenants that God has made with us by prophecy and by a Word. What are those promises? Do you know? Do your children know them? Do you contend daily for what you have been promised? Or do you only want to do good works? We have to honestly ask ourselves, "Will we be a generation that is satisfied with doing good works but ends up dying without receiving the promises?" We will either be happy starting new projects, having fellowship, enjoying our oneness, and doing many good things, or we will be those who receive the promise of God writing His Word on our hearts.

"And all these, having gained approval through their faith, did not receive what was promised" (Hebrews 11:39). I do not want this to continue being said about the Body of Christ. This was written for us so that we might understand what not to do. It is not enough to gain approval by our faith. We have to obtain the promise, because "God has provided something better for us." We are not at the same impasse that they were. We have Christ. What are they waiting for? What perfects them? Apart from us they will not be made perfect (Hebrews 11:40). Our obtaining the promises is what releases them into their perfection. They are not waiting for us to be good Christians and perform acts of faith. It is more than being saved. Christ has taken away our sins; they are forgiven. But then we cannot say, "That's it. I'm satisfied. If I just hold on to that belief, then I can die in the faith." Dying in the faith does not receive the promise. What are we waiting for? What stops us? Is it something in our own minds that cannot grasp what God has provided for us, what this covenant is all about? Is it our passivity? Is it the outward battle of the satanic world blinding our eyes to the potential that exists in the Body of Christ? It is all of that and more. Whatever it is, we have to throw it off.

Hebrews 11:40 Because God had provided something better for us, so that apart from us they should not be made perfect.

God promised to write His Word upon our minds and upon our hearts. He promised that we would know Him. It is time for us to have understanding. It is time for us to be driven by an internal force of the Word of God that has been written within us. If we start there, then every other promise will become clear. We refuse to stop at a certain place in our walk with God. We refuse to stop with just acts of faith. Do you remember the parable that Christ told of those who will come to Him and say, "Lord, Lord, have we not done many mighty works in Your name?" And He says, "Depart from Me; I never knew you" (Matthew 7:22-23). The promise of the new covenant in Jeremiah chapter 31 is that "they shall all know Me." The fact that we do not know Him as we should means that we have not obtained the promise. I do not want to appear before the Lord and say, "Didn't I do many mighty works? Didn't I speak many Words from God? Didn't I bless a lot of people? Didn't I administrate a lot of churches?" I do not want to face Him that way. I want to know Him before I stand before Him.

As a school of prophets we are going to cry out to the Lord to end this cycle of having a walk of faith but never obtaining the promises. Do you think we can do it? Do you think it will take a long time? Look how many years went by in the Old Testament, and Christians have been going at it for another 2,000 years. I know it seems too big, and we don't even know where to start, but we can reach into it in our worship and let the Lord transform our minds. For the Bible says, "While beholding Him, we will be changed" (2 Corinthians 3:18). We read in Romans chapter 12, "I urge you therefore, brethren, by

---

Matthew 7:22-23 "Many will say to Me on that day, 'Lord, Lord, did we not prophesy in Your name, and in Your name cast out demons, and in Your name perform many miracles?' 23 And then I will declare to them, 'I never knew you; DEPART FROM ME, YOU WHO PRACTICE LAWLESSNESS.'"

2 Corinthians 3:18 But we all, with unveiled face beholding as in a mirror the glory of the Lord, are being transformed into the same image from glory to glory, just as from the Lord, the Spirit.

the mercies of God, to present your bodies a living and holy sacrifice, acceptable to God, which is your spiritual service of worship" (Romans 12:1). That is a beautiful description of worship. It comes from everything within us. It is giving our physical bodies unto the Lord in a determination not to be conformed to this world, but to be transformed by the renewing of your mind (Romans 12:2). Worship is an expression of our appropriation. It is an expression of our drive and determination that brings the transformation of our minds.

We no longer have to have a resistance within our being. We no longer have to walk like our fathers walked, in an unending cycle of not obtaining the promises. There is nothing more that has to happen in a sacrifice that will enable us to appropriate and experience the promises. Christ, in His perfection, has already given us the ability to put on His righteousness, to fulfill the covenant. We can obtain the promises. Let us walk with that awareness, and set something new in motion. There is nothing that can stop us!

Romans 12:2   And do not be conformed to this world, but be transformed by the renewing of your mind, that you may prove what the will of God is, that which is good and acceptable and perfect.

CHAPTER 4

The Living Word:
The Fight of Faith

I want to read out of a message titled "You're Free! Fight!" from the book *Violent Proclamation* by John Robert Stevens. I want us to take a practical step into what this message is talking about and really receive something from the Lord. We want to have new eyes and ears created in us, filled with the capacity to grasp the new level that God is bringing forth in His Kingdom. These are things that belong to this new day, but have been confusing to us in the old age. I believe that our hearts can be enlightened so that many of these things will simply clear up for us (Ephesians 1:18).

> There is one problem that exists in every believer's mind: How can we reconcile the fact that God has provided so much for us when we see that we are not walking in as much of His provision as we should. This applies not only to the words of responsibility, but also to the privileges and promises and blessings that are ours. We are somewhat

---

Ephesians 1:18 I pray that the eyes of your heart may be enlightened, so that you may know what is the hope of His calling, what are the riches of the glory of His inheritance in the saints.

reluctant to admit how far short we fall in coming into the full appropriation.

There is a scriptural principle involved in this. If we would rewrite the twenty-third Psalm the way it actually operates in the average person's life, we would not say, "My cup runneth over"; instead, we would have to say, "My cup is half-empty." People are not living on the overflow. Their lives do not reflect the idea that God is doing exceeding abundantly above all that they ask or think. Even when they ask largely, they are usually grateful to receive only ten percent of what they asked. We need to recognize the fact that God is not tithing the blessings to us; He wants to give us the entire blessing, plus a little more. We cannot talk "cream" and live "skim milk." If we are going to talk about the riches of the Lord, then let us walk in them. If God meant for us to have an abundance of blessing, then we want to have it all. We are continually making an effort to come up, up, up to all that God has provided. We must be determined to walk in whatever He says is ours. How do we arrive at that place? By truly believing.

People place themselves in a position of unbelief when they feel that they have to fight the devil and overcome him. You are not the Son of God, born of a virgin, and if you were to go out in the wilderness to battle the devil, he would surely stomp you to death. That battle was fought once; you do not need to fight it again. You do not have to find a cross and die on it. All you need to do is believe in Jesus Christ and in what He has done for you. He made a perfect, full provision for your need. And by the precious blood of Jesus Christ you are saved; you are delivered. Hebrews 10:14 tells us that by one sacrifice

---

Hebrews 10:14 For by one offering He has perfected for all time those who are sanctified.

He has forever perfected those who are sanctified. That sacrifice is provided forever, and if you are not walking in the provision, then you will have to fight for it. You do not fight the devil as if he is the undefeated foe who still has to be defeated. Your fight is a fight of faith, whereby you accept satan as a defeated foe. It is one thing to accept Jesus Christ as Lord of lords and King of kings, but it is quite another thing to accept the devil as a defeated foe.

We are not ignorant of satan's wiles and schemes, the various devices he uses in trying to overcome us. How do we prevail over those schemes? Not by fighting him as though he were an undefeated foe, but by believing. The fight is a fight of faith.[4]

The way we related to the Living Word in our intercession for John Stevens was very much like an old covenant for us. This message, spoken by John during that time, lays out very simply the foundation of the new covenant and the new day that we are in. We are in a fight of faith. You could say, "I thought we were fighting satan in our intercession for John." No, we were giving birth to the Living Word in that old covenant. Now we have entered into a time when this is very simply a fight of faith. What is going on with you, in you, and around you is a fight of faith. This is where we have to be careful not to bring with us the baggage of an old age, because much of what we have done contains the seeds of unbelief. In this new covenant we are not backing up to try something again. We are doing something that we have never done before. Why didn't we do it before? I cannot answer that, but I do know one thing—we have entered into the fight of faith over the Living Word. How do we arrive at the place where we possess all that the Lord says is ours? By truly believing. Does that mean that we have not truly believed

---

4. John Robert Stevens, "You're Free! Fight!," in *Violent Proclamation* (North Hollywood: The Living Word, 1977), 50-51.

the Living Word? If we are honest, I think we have to admit that we have not. In some ways, I do not know that we had time to. We were fighting for our lives, and fighting to bring forth this Living Word. It was literally a life-or-death struggle, and it was won or lost by virtue of our intercession. Of course, it would have helped if our intercession had been more from a position of believing. But now it truly can be, if we go back and listen to and read this Living Word, and discover that it is a Word that we have never really heard before.

I believe that we tried to hear the Living Word, but we were focused on accomplishing something. We were in the thick of the battle over whether the Living Word would even be birthed. It would have helped us a great deal if we had really heard the Living Word at that time, but I'm not sure it wasn't the very battle itself that prevented us from hearing it. There is no worse time to figure out the cross experience than when you are in it. Christ Himself said on the cross, "Father, why have You forsaken Me?" (Matthew 27:46). I don't know if we have the faculties to perceive these things yet. I don't know if the ears to hear and the eyes to see have really been created. We were not fully hearing the Living Word, because that was not what we were doing. The fight was the fight to birth the Word. We did not have time to talk about our college education, our pensions—all the things that would happen after the Living Word was birthed. We only had time to birth it. We were in the battle that was set to prevent us from birthing it. Something has to happen now to magnify the Living Word in our eyes so that we literally go back to that Word as though we have never seen it, heard it, read it, or even been involved with it before.

We have never absorbed the Living Word with the purpose of fulfilling and walking in that Word the way we are going to now. I am sure that you have listened to messages by John Stevens and said,

Matthew 27:46 And about the ninth hour Jesus cried out with a loud voice, saying, "Eli, Eli, lama sabachthani?" that is, "My God, My God, why hast Thou forsaken Me?"

"That Word changed my life! It turned everything around for me." Isn't it amazing how you can listen to a Word that is many years old, and it is still so real for you today? That is because the Living Word is a Word for today. It is not just something that we have had around for a long time, which we all know and love and are familiar with. In reality, it is something that we have never really encountered. There is an old segment in John's Living Word library consisting of about 2,000 messages. At one point we recognized that more than 1,500 of those messages had never been released and did not exist in any church library—something that we have been working to correct. Yet we feel we know the Living Word. New generations have grown up in our midst who have never really known it. There is also a sense among some people that it is not really important, that there is not much in these Words for them. But I am here to tell you that this Word is living and powerful and sharper than any two-edged sword (Hebrews 4:12)! There is something in this Word for you to live and walk in, because as you hear it and read it, you are united with it by faith (Hebrews 4:2). We are going to walk as a people who believe the Living Word.

Everything in the world will attempt to block you from getting this, because this is literally where we stand or fall as we walk into a new day appropriating this Living Word. The way we get into that new day is to lay hold of the Living Word and believe it. We will live in a fight of faith, because God is making us a people of faith. God will make you a spiritual son who believes until your faith cannot be moved. He is at work in you to will and do of His good

---

Hebrews 4:12 For the word of God is living and active and sharper than any two-edged sword, and piercing as far as the division of soul and spirit, of both joints and marrow, and able to judge the thoughts and intentions of the heart.

Hebrews 4:2 For indeed we have had good news preached to us, just as they also; but the word they heard did not profit them, because it was not united by faith in those who heard.

pleasure (Philippians 2:13). He will work in you to believe; then He will test your faith and continue to work in you to believe. We are entering into a time when the only thing that is really happening is a fight of faith. Nothing we are doing has any real significance other than that. When we believe the Word more than we believe what we see and feel, then we will have the victory. How do you win the fight of faith? By believing. "For by one offering He has perfected for all time those who are sanctified" (Hebrews 10:14). That sacrifice is provided forever, and if you are not walking in that provision, then you will have to appropriate it. Our pattern has been that whenever something does not work, we turn and start fighting for it, rather than believing. We have been conditioned by the spiritual battle to fight the enemy, and we constantly position ourselves in that fight. But we are not in a fight with an enemy; we are in a fight of faith. The enemy, the impasse, or the battle is never the issue. It is always secondary. The elimination of the enemy or the impasse is a by-product of having won the fight of faith.

In the message "You're Free! Fight!" John Stevens goes on to say,

> "Beloved, while I was making every effort to write you about our common salvation, I felt the necessity to write to you appealing that you contend earnestly for the faith which was once for all delivered to the saints" (Jude 3). Notice: you are to contend earnestly for that faith. The faith does not come because it is taught to you. Jesus said, "All things are possible to him who believes" (Mark 9:23). You could memorize this promise and assent to it, knowing that it is the truth; but that is not the same as truly believing that all things are possible to you.[5]

Philippians 2:13 For it is God who is at work in you, both to will and to work for His good pleasure.

[5.] Stevens, "You're Free! Fight!," 51.

Faith does not come because it is taught to you. Faith comes by hearing, and that by the Word of God (Romans 10:17). Faith comes because you hear the Word and contend earnestly for it. This takes us out of giving mental assent to believing something, and shows us the way to have the reality of the Living Word implanted within our hearts. John Stevens can no longer be our apostle in an old covenant where we just mentally assent to the Word that he spoke. We can't just sit around and say, "Oh John, that was such an awesome Living Word!" We have to enter into a new covenant where we believe the Living Word with him. John continues,

> You must have the faith for all things to be possible. When the New Testament speaks about fighting, it is not referring to fighting flesh and blood, nor is it talking about fighting satan as an undefeated foe. We wrestle against principalities and powers (Ephesians 6:12). We wrestle against them; therefore, in one sense it is true that we fight against satan and his hordes, but in another sense it is not true because our main battle is begun and resolved within ourselves. It is a fight of faith.
>
> Paul wrote in 1 Timothy 1:18: "This command I entrust to you, Timothy, my son, in accordance with the prophecies previously made concerning you, that by them you may fight the good fight." Does this mean that you are going to fight over your prophecies? Yes, that is exactly what Paul meant. When a prophecy or a revelation comes over you, you must fight a good fight as you contend to believe, without any wavering, those Words that God has spoken.[6]

Romans 10:17 So faith comes from hearing, and hearing by the word of Christ.

Ephesians 6:12 For our struggle is not against flesh and blood, but against the rulers, against the powers, against the world forces of this darkness, against the spiritual forces of wickedness in the heavenly places.

[6] Stevens, "You're Free! Fight!," 51-52.

"Our main battle is begun and resolved within ourselves. It is a fight of faith." I don't know about you, but I am ready to resolve that battle. There is nothing in the Living Word more difficult to believe than what it says about you personally. The reason it took so much intercession to walk with John Stevens is because we were right up against this fight of faith. John would come to us and say, "You have to pray for me," because he had to believe. He was fighting a fight of faith. How do you move as the apostle to the Kingdom? How do you speak the Living Word that will end one age and usher in a new one? John had to fight that fight of faith. Can we drink the same cup (Matthew 20:22)? It is time that we do. It is time to enter into the same kind of faith about ourselves, fighting the fight to believe the Word over us, to believe who the Living Word says we are. This Living Word is not generic. Read the prophecies that have come. They are speaking to each one of us personally. They are talking about what we are to do as a body together, and they are talking about what we are to be individually as part of that body. This is why Paul said to fight over the prophecies. It is by those Words that we wage this warfare. Let's read some more from John:

> Many of the practical truths that we have learned simply unfolded for us line upon line and precept upon precept (Isaiah 28:13). But now that we understand more about them, we realize that there can be no passivity in our walk with God. When God gives you a Word, and it is transcribed, it is not to be filed in a drawer where you look at it once every six months or so and forget about it the rest of the time. That is not the way to make that Word effective in your life. It is by those prophecies that you are to war a

---

Matthew 20:22 But Jesus answered and said, "You do not know what you are asking for. Are you able to drink the cup that I am about to drink?" They said to Him, "We are able."

Isaiah 28:13 So the word of the LORD to them will be, "Order on order, order on order, line on line, line on line, a little here, a little there," that they may go and stumble backward, be broken, snared, and taken captive.

good warfare. You must have faith in them, even though your feelings and many factors in your circumstances may tell you that those prophecies are not valid. Even when everything that happens seems to contradict them, you still believe; then they will come to pass. Fulfillment is a fight of faith.[7]

If you are honest with yourself, you will realize that you stopped before you got to that point of believing. That is why it is important that we understand what we did, and our effectiveness in it. We interceded, and we saw the birthing of a Living Word. We watched John Stevens overcome satan. How did he do it? By faith. Where did he get the faith? We helped him get that faith because we prayed for him. What was the faith for? It was faith in the Word that was over him. Now we are entering into the same battle; we are confronted with the same fight of faith. We all want to see the fulfillment of this Living Word, but fulfillment only comes in the fight of faith. What is it that we are fighting? What is the dispute about? Is it the impasses? No, impasses have their place. When we are finished, we will rejoice and worship God for our impasses. We should be so thankful for the hindrances, the obstacles, the battles, and everything that stands against us having fulfillment. We are going to love everything that is now fighting to delay us and seeking to kill us. What the Scriptures teach will make sense to us: love your enemy (Luke 6:27). Why should you love everything that hates you and is set against you? Because it refines your faith.

> Beloved, do not be surprised at the fiery ordeal among you, which comes upon you for your testing, as though some strange thing were happening to you; but to the degree that you share the sufferings of Christ, keep on rejoicing;

Luke 6:27 "But I say to you who hear, love your enemies, do good to those who hate you."

[7.] Stevens, "You're Free! Fight!," 52.

so that also at the revelation of His glory, you may rejoice with exultation. (1 Peter 4:12-13)

Get out of your thinking the idea that you are in a battle. Your hindrances and the attacks against you are not battles. They are the Lord allowing the testing and proving of your faith (1 Peter 1:7). We think, "I read the Word; of course I believe it." But the Lord says, "You believe it? Okay, let's see." Then He lets something come against you, and you fall flat on your face. Why? You say, "The enemy defeated me." That's nonsense! It is impossible for the enemy to defeat you, because he is already defeated. Then what happened? You wavered. You did not believe. Your faith is everything. There is no fight going on; there is either believing or not believing. This is a fight of faith, but you are not fighting something that is outside of you. The fight of faith takes place within you. What is happening on the outside is essentially meaningless; it is secondary. You say, "Then what are all these circumstances that I am thrown into?" They are the proving of your faith.

When we were doing construction work at Shiloh, before the engineers would let us pour concrete, they would take a sample of the concrete and put it under a stress test. They wanted to see if it could really hold the weight that it had to hold. If it failed, we had to deal with it somehow before we could move forward. We had to reinforce it, or even tear out a section and start over, to make sure that the concrete would not fail. Do you get the picture? Of course you have faith. But will it hold? We may look really good in what we are doing, but can we bear the weight of the Kingdom? Is our faith something that God can put His weight on, or will it collapse?

---

1 Peter 1:7 That the proof of your faith, being more precious than gold which is perishable, even though tested by fire, may be found to result in praise and glory and honor at the revelation of Jesus Christ.

We must build ourselves up on our most holy faith (Jude 20). Then what happens? It seems as if God Himself keeps knocking us over; then we develop a bad spirit toward the Lord. How many times have we stood in a service and said, like Peter, "Lord, I believe this Word. I will never waver. I will never back off" (Matthew 26:33)? Then how long was it before the rooster crowed (Matthew 26:74-75)? When that happens, are you angry? Do you get a wrong spirit? Is it God's fault? Is it a problem with the Word, or with John Stevens, or maybe with your brother or sister? What really happened to you? We are talking about the fight of faith, so I cannot tell you that nothing will ever happen to you. Everything will happen to you. After you set your heart to believe a Word, just give it five minutes and things will start happening to you. You can say, "This is part of the same old battle we had with John." No it is not, because this time you are the issue; this time you must walk in the Word about you. This time you are not going to collapse. This time you will understand in your heart and mind what is taking place. Do we have faith? Yes, and that faith is being proven. It is being tested, because it needs to bear the weight of the Kingdom. It has to be load-bearing so that God can put His weight down upon it. God is simply being a good engineer. When we come running up to Him and say, "We're ready now. We believe. We've got it this time," He is making sure that we really are ready. He puts a little weight down on our faith to see whether it will hold up or collapse.

That is it. It is so simple. We are going to love the persecution; we are going to love our enemies; we are going to love the impasses. Think

---

Jude 20 But you, beloved, building yourselves up on your most holy faith; praying in the Holy Spirit.

Matthew 26:33 But Peter answered and said to Him, "Even though all may fall away because of You, I will never fall away."

Matthew 26:74-75 Then he began to curse and swear, "I do not know the man!" And immediately a cock crowed. [75] And Peter remembered the word which Jesus had said, "Before a cock crows, you will deny Me three times." And he went out and wept bitterly.

about it. How can an impasse possibly stand against the Word of the Lord? If you have a revelation of the Living Word of God, you know that nothing can stop it. That is the truth of the Word. But it has to be your truth. In the spirit realm, it is never what you see; it is only what you accept. The entirety of the spirit realm works upon the principle of believing. The odds never matter. Only what you accept matters. When you accept that whatever is raging against you is the reality rather than the Word—whether it is a circumstance, something in your physical body, or another person—then your faith collapses. You did not lose the victory. You simply let go of the Word. You were convinced of something different. That, in its simplicity, is called unbelief. Actually, we should not call it unbelief, because it really is believing in something more than you believe in the Word. We tend to go into condemnation, struggling to get rid of our unbelief. You do not need to try to get rid of your unbelief; you just need to believe the Word. You need to believe it so much that the next time you are confronted with something that is contrary to the Word, you believe the Word instead of believing in what is coming against you.

My impasses and personal problems are only valid when I believe in them. They are not valid otherwise. My personal problems may in fact strengthen me to walk in the Word. Have you ever read about Winston Churchill? Here was a man who was driven. Even President Roosevelt would fall asleep in meetings with Churchill, because he could not keep up the same pace. Nobody could; he was so driven. Yet Churchill had a problem with depression, and when he was alone at night by himself, he could become suicidal. So he always worked late and kept going. He made sure that when he sat down, he was focused; and when he was thinking, he was thinking about the solutions that he needed to find. He never let his mind wander from the issues that were important to him and his goals, because as soon as his mind wandered, it could literally be life-threatening to him. Now, tell me, was that a problem, or was it the salvation of

Europe? What is your problem? How big is it? Is it bigger than the Word? The Word is living and powerful and sharper than any two-edged sword; it cannot be stopped (Hebrews 4:12). The Word of God is the greatest force that exists in the universe. The Word is God (John 1:1). Heaven and earth could pass away, but the Word would not be touched; it will never pass away (Matthew 24:35).

I do not know if we have ever let the Word of God have free course. It would be interesting to see what would happen if the Word truly had free course. What could it do if we really turned it loose? The reality is that we are never neutral. We are always believing in something. Let's not kid ourselves by saying, "No, we're neutral. We just let the Word flow. We step back and let God move." No we do not. In every situation that we are faced with, we always believe something. The question is, what are we believing?

Let's continue our reading from "You're Free! Fight!":

> Paul wrote to Timothy: "Fight the good fight of faith; take hold of the eternal life to which you were called, and you made the good confession in the presence of many witnesses" (1 Timothy 6:12). Fight the good fight of faith. When all is said and done, your fight is that of being a believer. Because the unredeemed and untransformed physical mortal body is still susceptible and open to demonic harassment, and because your very circumstances prey upon your soul life to create moods and feelings and emotions, there must be a constant vigilance to fight a fight of faith. Fight to be a believer. Tell yourself repeatedly, "I am a believer."[8]

John 1:1 In the beginning was the Word, and the Word was with God, and the Word was God.

Matthew 24:35 "Heaven and earth will pass away, but My words shall not pass away."

[8.] Stevens, "You're Free! Fight!," 52-53.

If we are a people of destiny, then we are here by choice, just as Christ chose to come down from an exalted place of oneness with the Father in heaven (Philippians 2:5-8). And just as Christ experienced becoming flesh, when you were born out of the spirit realm into the physical realm, you found yourself in a physical body. You are here for one reason. In your destiny, at this time, you are here to fight a fight of faith. One of the most wonderful things that you have that will help you fight that fight of faith is your physical body. Why? Because it is totally incapable of perceiving the spirit realm. Because of your physical body, you must walk by faith. You do not have to believe for that which you already see, do you? "Hope that is seen is not hope; for why does one also hope for what he sees? But if we hope for what we do not see, with perseverance we wait eagerly for it" (Romans 8:24-25). The problem is not that the Kingdom is not here; the problem is that we do not see it. Our physical senses are what stop us from seeing it. We are limited to see a certain realm or spectrum, which forces us to walk by faith. However, the fact that we do not see it does not change the reality of what exists. Your blindness to the Kingdom does not change the reality of it. The Kingdom of God exists now in the heavenly realm. The victory is won.

The realm that now exists by virtue of Christ's victory on the cross is more real than what we call reality. As we read in Hebrews 11:1 (KJV), "Now faith is the substance of things hoped for, the evidence of things not seen." The substance is already there, and faith merely becomes your eyes and ears in the spirit realm. It is not something you make up. Our concept of faith is, "I believe in that—sort of," and then we sort of pretend that it happens. We are like a child playing

---

Philippians 2:5-8 Have this attitude in yourselves which was also in Christ Jesus, [6] who, although He existed in the form of God, did not regard equality with God a thing to be grasped, [7] but emptied Himself, taking the form of a bond-servant, and being made in the likeness of men. [8] And being found in appearance as a man, He humbled Himself by becoming obedient to the point of death, even death on a cross.

with dolls, pretending to have a tea party: "Okay, let's pour the tea now." There is no tea in the teapot, but we pretend to pour the tea and drink it. That is how we, as Christians, relate to faith, but faith is not pretending. Faith becomes our new sense that allows us to perceive what really does exist. It is ludicrous to think that we can create the victory by our faith, and yet that is how we relate to it. Let's not give ourselves that much credit. Do you think that if you have faith in the Word of God, you will create the fulfillment of the Word? No way! The fulfillment of the Word already exists. Your faith becomes the eyes of your spirit by which you perceive the reality of that fulfillment. Once you have seen something by faith, then, in a sense, you do not have to have faith for it anymore, because you know it is a reality.

The existence of the fulfillment, and the reality of everything the Word has brought forth, is already physical. In a sense, you came down into this physical realm when it already existed as a completed work. But as you came down into this realm, a veil was placed on you so that you cannot see, feel, or prove what the Word has already created. So what do you do? You walk by faith. If you can see it, then it is not faith. Christ Himself could not participate with us unless He became flesh. Unless He took on flesh and blood, He was not qualified to gain our salvation (Hebrews 2:14-15). Christ had to be in the flesh and have the limitations of the flesh, because it had to be a fight of faith for Him too. You have to believe; you have to walk by faith. Faith is the substance being developed in your physical body that gives you the spiritual senses, the tactual connection with what really exists that you have been blocked from seeing. When you have that connection, it is all over. You do not waver, because you know the reality and the truth. Drop your pretend faith. This is not

---

Hebrews 2:14-15 Since then the children share in flesh and blood, He Himself likewise also partook of the same, that through death He might render powerless him who had the power of death, that is, the devil; [15] and might deliver those who through fear of death were subject to slavery all their lives.

a child's tea party; this is coming into contact with what really exists in the realm of spirit. John Stevens continues,

> You can find a devil behind every bush if you go out looking for devils. Do not fall into that trap. Even if you saw ten million devils lined up against you, you still must believe that you are more than a conqueror through Jesus Christ who loves you. Believe in your position in the Lord.
>
> The big battle is to take the promises in the Scriptures and believe them. Believe them! That is the fight of faith. Believe the Word that has been spoken over you. Believe the Word that has come over your brother. It will turn the tide. Believe it.
>
> Never judge anything by what you see. That is never the issue.[9]

It is never the issue, because it is never the truth. We have to come into a new covenant, with a new revelation of what is really going on. We have to believe in our hearts that we chose to be here, to fight this fight of faith, and that we have the most wonderful tool in our flesh. It is the veil that stops us from seeing the true reality that exists. That is why the fight has to be within the veil before it reaches out beyond the veil. We start very simply. We begin to perceive things in a different way than we have ever perceived them. Something has to break the lies and conditioning off of our thinking. Something has to open our perception so we recognize the truth about the way things are. The way we think is not the way things really are. The way we think things happen is not the way things really happen. We must reach into the Lord and start on a course of being believers. We must understand that our perception is one thing, but the reality is another. Faith can overcome our partial perception that locks us into deception, and we will see the true reality that is there. Lord,

---

[9.] Stevens, "You're Free! Fight!," 53.

set us free from believing in the way things are not. We want to have Your perception to see how things really are as we believe Your Word.

As you are trying to absorb this message, do one simple thing: say, "I will never again be sucked into fighting anything other than this fight of faith." Take two steps back from your enemy or your impasse. Those are not the issue. Take two steps back and fight the fight of faith. Then step into the situation again and see if the impasse has been removed. If not, take two steps back and fight the fight of faith again. The only purpose of those impasses is to give you a way to measure how you are doing in your fight of faith. There is no way to prove what ground you have taken unless there is an impasse. When you step back into it and it disappears, then you know that you have taken a new level of faith. If you step back into it and get into a contentious battle, then you know you are not moving in faith. You have to let God humble your spirit. When you are not humble, you pick a fight with your impasse, because you cannot admit your unbelief. It hurts to admit that the impasse did not move because you did not believe. You get really mad because you think, "I know I believed this time!" If your impasse did not move, then you did not believe.

There is no battle except the battle to believe. We will not be drawn off again into the deception that there is any fight except the fight of faith. Keep that one thought clear in your mind. You can feel, "How can I remember all these concepts?" Don't worry about it. Just keep driving away the birds of the air and let the Word take root in you (Matthew 13:3-4, 8). The Word of God is what the fight of faith is all about. We do not see it, but the Word tells us what is there. Believing

---

Matthew 13:3-4 And He spoke many things to them in parables, saying, "Behold, the sower went out to sow; ⁴ and as he sowed, some seeds fell beside the road, and the birds came and ate them up."

Matthew 13:8 "And others fell on the good soil, and yielded a crop, some a hundredfold, some sixty, and some thirty."

is simply a matter of deciding, "What do I believe? Do I believe my senses, or do I believe what the Word is telling me?" That is why we are called The Living Word Fellowship; we are a fellowship based wholly upon the Word of God. We cannot see what is on the other side through the veil of the flesh, but Christ is telling us what is there. When Christ came down to earth, He took on the blindness that we have. But by hearing the Word, He literally formed a world of reality in His heart by faith.

Why did we go to all the trouble of birthing the Living Word with John Stevens? We connected with the Word because we did not have the faculties to see reality, but if the Word is loosed, it tells us what the reality is. Now we can take all the pieces that don't appear to fit together and, by the Word, we know where each piece belongs. By virtue of the Word, we do as Christ did; we create the world out of that Word (John 1:1-3; Hebrews 11:3). In doing that, we are simply bringing the physical realm that we perceive into alignment with the spiritual truth that we know by faith. That is why you have to read the Word and listen to it, because the Word will say of you as it said of Christ, "It is written of Me" (Hebrews 10:7). This should come alive for you in this new covenant: "Lord, it is written of me that I will do what You said, and I will be what You said." When we make that connection, we will really have fulfillment. We are closing the door to the ways we have thought in the past that have excused us from being real believers. There is no valid reason for unbelief. We have the Living Word in our hands. Therefore, we can touch it, we can believe it, and we can become it.

John 1:1-3 In the beginning was the Word, and the Word was with God, and the Word was God. ² He was in the beginning with God. ³ All things came into being by Him, and apart from Him nothing came into being that has come into being.

Hebrews 11:3 By faith we understand that the worlds were prepared by the word of God, so that what is seen was not made out of things which are visible.

Hebrews 10:7 "THEN I SAID, 'BEHOLD, I HAVE COME (IN THE ROLL OF THE BOOK IT IS WRITTEN OF ME) TO DO THY WILL, O GOD.'"

CHAPTER 5

Unbelief – Your Greatest Enemy

There are times in history when not much seems to be happening in the unfolding of God's purposes and destiny. At other times, there seems to be a rapid release of His timing and destiny. For instance, the children of Israel lived for 430 years in the land of Egypt. The prophecy was that they would be enslaved for 400 years, but they left Egypt after 430 years to the very day (Genesis 15:13; Exodus 12:40-41). The difference between the prophecy and the actual events was that they were not always there as slaves. For those first thirty years in Egypt, a tremendous destiny rested on the children of Israel, and a tremendous destiny was being executed by Joseph. Then at some point they were enslaved, and many generations lived through that 400-year period of slavery. We do not read in the Scriptures of much happening during those 400

Genesis 15:13 And God said to Abram, "Know for certain that your descendants will be strangers in a land that is not theirs, where they will be enslaved and oppressed four hundred years."

Exodus 12:40-41 Now the time that the sons of Israel lived in Egypt was four hundred and thirty years. [41] And it came about at the end of four hundred and thirty years, to the very day, that all the hosts of the LORD went out from the land of Egypt.

years. We know that they lived in misery and suffering, but we do not see an open door for Israel to move into its destiny. About the only thing you can say concerning that period was that they were multiplying, which was one of the prophecies (Genesis 46:3). But at the end of that time, there arose the generation that God would deliver out of the slavery of Egypt. On that generation a tremendous destiny began to unfold. God was very engaged with them during that period. He delivered them out of Egypt, led them into the wilderness, and created them into a people.

This gives us the sense that God has a timing. Some generations may simply be sitting and waiting, while other generations find themselves in the midst of a tremendous unfolding of God's will. It is important for us to recognize that we are living in a generation of destiny and promise. Another way to say it is that we live in a generation in which there is an open door. I would say that the generation living at the time when Jesus walked the earth was definitely a generation of destiny. According to the Scriptures, Jesus Christ came in the fullness of time (Galatians 4:4). That generation had a tremendous opportunity for much to take place in their lives, and to literally see the whole course of human history change in a very short number of years. Today, you need to have the sense that you are living in a generation of destiny. You too are living in one of those time frames when God is looking for much to happen.

We read about such a time in Hebrews chapter 4, which recounts what happened with one generation of destiny. It shows us clearly what can go wrong, and what needs to happen for things to go right:

Genesis 46:3 And He said, "I am God, the God of your father; do not be afraid to go down to Egypt, for I will make you a great nation there."

Galatians 4:4 But when the fulness of the time came, God sent forth His Son, born of a woman, born under the Law.

> For if Joshua had given them rest, He would not have spoken of another day after that. There remains therefore a Sabbath rest for the people of God. For the one who has entered His rest has himself also rested from his works, as God did from His. Let us therefore be diligent to enter that rest, lest anyone fall through following the same example of disobedience. (Hebrews 4:8-11)

These verses are about the generation that died in the wilderness because of their disobedience. Therefore we have the warning, "Do not follow their example! Be diligent to enter in." In other words, if you live in a generation to whom God has offered an open door, then it behooves you to act accordingly. It is not a time to be passive. It is not a time to be waiting. It is a time to be aggressively pursuing the destiny that God has for you. Because of their disobedience, the generation in the wilderness was not able to enter in through the open door that God had provided them. God had to lay that mantle on another generation; and even then, Joshua did not really give them this rest that the Book of Hebrews speaks about. Therefore, the open door of entering into God's rest, the Kingdom of God, is still a potential in the realm of spirit. It is waiting for a generation to lay hold of it and successfully possess that land.

We must understand what this Scripture means for us right now. We are people in a generation that has an open door set before it by God. What is it that holds us back from really entering through that door? I considered titling this message "How to Irritate Jesus," because of how Jesus reacted to unbelief. When we read the Gospels and study the personality of Jesus, we find that He was very patient and forbearing in most situations. However, there was one thing that irritated and angered Jesus every time He encountered it. Do you know what that was? Unbelief. You have to face the fact that unbelief is your greatest enemy.

If you were to ask people, "What is your greatest enemy spiritually?" most would say, "The devil." But the devil is not your greatest enemy. Satan is a defeated foe, and he has already been dealt with (Revelation 12:7-9). We know that one of the things still to happen is that satan will be cast out of the earth. While that may look like our prime objective, it is not really the biggest issue that we face. In our minds, if satan or anything else is our main problem, then we are being distracted from what we really need to deal with as God's people. Our greatest enemy is the unbelief that dwells within us. We run into that wall over and over again in our walk with God. I want this message to enable us to come right up to that wall of unbelief, face it, and determine to believe. That is the one thing that will move us forward into the Kingdom of God.

I want to lay out five points that will show us how unbelief is challenging our ability to fulfill this destiny that is before us. The first three points will be very personal, showing how unbelief affects our lives. The last two points will apply more to our ministry to others and to the world. In all of these points there are scriptural examples in which Jesus corrects His disciples or other people that He is addressing. These are not compliments; Jesus is putting His finger on something. As you read these examples, do more than just recognize that unbelief is there. Really try to understand how unbelief impacts you in your personal life and in your ability to move forward in God. Study these points, see how unbelief impacts your life, and go after the areas of unbelief in your own heart until they break and something changes for you.

Revelation 12:7-9 And there was war in heaven, Michael and his angels waging war with the dragon. And the dragon and his angels waged war, [8] and they were not strong enough, and there was no longer a place found for them in heaven. [9] And the great dragon was thrown down, the serpent of old who is called the devil and Satan, who deceives the whole world; he was thrown down to the earth, and his angels were thrown down with him.

1. Understanding the Written Word (Luke 24:13-27)

We are familiar with the story of Jesus appearing to the disciples on the road to Emmaus. Jesus had gone to the cross, was resurrected, and began to walk alongside a couple of disciples who were going to Emmaus. As He walked with them, He asked, "What are you talking about?" Then they begin to tell Him their story:

> "But we were hoping that it was He who was going to redeem Israel. Indeed, besides all this, it is the third day since these things happened. But also some women among us amazed us. When they were at the tomb early in the morning, and did not find His body, they came, saying that they had also seen a vision of angels, who said that He was alive. And some of those who were with us went to the tomb and found it just exactly as the women also had said; but Him they did not see." And He said to them, "O foolish men and slow of heart to believe in all that the prophets have spoken! Was it not necessary for the Christ to suffer these things and to enter into His glory?" And beginning with Moses and with all the prophets, He explained to them the things concerning Himself in all the Scriptures. (Luke 24:21-27)

The two disciples were saying, "We were hoping He would redeem Israel, but now our dreams are shattered." To this Jesus replied, "O foolish men and slow of heart to believe!" and He began to unfold to them the *Tenakh*, the Hebrew Scriptures, and to explain what they prophesied about Him. He said, "Was it not necessary for the Christ to suffer these things to enter His glory? You should have known that when you read the *Tenakh*. You have had the Scriptures read to you from the time you were born and have studied them all of your lives, and you do not see this simple truth? Why are you so steeped in unbelief and discouraged by all that has happened? You do not see in the Scriptures the correct end to the story."

This illustrates the fact that when we are trapped in unbelief, it clouds our ability to understand the written Word. Jesus had to correct the real problem these disciples had. They had read the Scriptures, but because of their unbelief, they could not comprehend what the Scriptures said about Him and what was supposed to happen. The problem was a direct result of being slow of heart to believe. Our unbelief absolutely takes away our ability to understand what the Scriptures are saying. Jesus faced this throughout His ministry on the earth. The scribes and Pharisees simply could not recognize who He was based on their understanding of the Scriptures. When they read them, what they understood and what they believed did not reveal Jesus to be the Christ. If we are reading the Scriptures and not seeing Jesus in them, or not meeting God in them, then we have a real problem. We have a problem, not only because we are not seeing Him, but because our unbelief is literally leading us away from understanding what God is doing. That was the state of heart of those disciples who were walking with Jesus on the road to Emmaus. They literally gave up their hope that He was the Savior because they did not see it in the Scriptures. We have to realize that many of the problems in our personal lives and in our walk with God are connected to the fact that when we read the Word we do not really understand what it is saying. That is a direct result of the unbelief in our own hearts. We are not seeing the true end of the story and what God is trying to tell us is to take place. We are a people of destiny, but how do we walk in that destiny if we really cannot understand the Word of God?

2. Understanding the Lord When He Speaks (Matthew 16:5-8)

In this next point we will read from Matthew chapter 16. Jesus was in the boat with His disciples as they went to the other side of the Sea of Galilee.

> And the disciples came to the other side and had forgotten to take bread. And Jesus said to them, "Watch out and

beware of the leaven of the Pharisees and Sadducees."
And they began to discuss among themselves, saying,
"It is because we took no bread." But Jesus, aware of this,
said, "You men of little faith, why do you discuss among
yourselves that you have no bread?" (Matthew 16:5-8)

I don't know how the disciples could hear, "Beware of the leaven of
the Pharisees and Sadducees," and respond, "Oh no, we didn't bring
bread for the trip and now Jesus is upset!" Jesus' reaction seemed
almost harsh, but He went directly to the root of the problem.
He told them, in no uncertain terms, "The reason you do not
understand what I am saying is because of your unbelief." This is
troubling, because it means that when Jesus speaks to us, we will not
be able to understand what He is saying.

We put a great deal of importance on having a meeting with the
Lord, but we should put more importance on getting rid of our
unbelief. You could have that meeting with the Lord that you have
been looking for and still not understand what He says to you.
Unquestionably, the disciples had meetings with the Lord. They
were with Jesus all the time! We just read about a personal encounter
they had with Jesus where He gave them a direct Word, and a very
specific warning. That is what I would expect if I had a meeting with
the Lord. I assume I would get some personal direction for my life.
Jesus was speaking to those disciples in very plain language. There is
no question about what He was saying, but because of their unbelief
they did not understand Him. It scares me to think that the meeting
with God I have been crying out for, believing for, and praying for,
could take place and what He says to me could go right over my
head. In fact, it could confuse me to the point where it would lead
me astray. Perhaps that is why He does not speak to us more. Until
we truly deal with the unbelief in our hearts, would God speaking to
us help us or hinder us? The voice of the Lord to us personally can
literally be confusing or misunderstood as a result of the unbelief

in our own hearts. I know that we believe in waiting on the Lord, the prayer of listening. Jesus said, "My sheep hear My voice" (John 10:27). That is a promise. If I am one of His sheep, then I should expect to hear His voice. But let's do more than just ask, "Lord, I want to hear Your voice." Let's pray, "Lord, I want to get rid of my unbelief so that when You do speak to me, I clearly understand what You are saying."

3. Only Believe (Mark 5:21-42)

The next example is the story of the synagogue official whose daughter was sick. He had come to Jesus, asking Him to lay hands on his daughter to heal her. Jesus did not use the same tone as in the previous examples. He did not harshly rebuke this man.

> While He was still speaking, they came from the house of the synagogue official, saying, "Your daughter has died; why trouble the Teacher anymore?" But Jesus, overhearing what was being spoken, said to the synagogue official, "Do not be afraid any longer, only believe." (Mark 5:35-36)

What Jesus said impacts us on a very personal level, because there are many times when we are looking to the Lord to help us with something, or to do something for us. We have many areas in our personal lives where we need a real touch from God. This synagogue official was also in that place of need. His daughter was dying. He obviously believed in healing. While they were walking to his house, Jesus had healed a woman of a hemorrhage. So healing was something that was very believable to that man. But before Jesus could arrive and meet the need, the man's daughter died. Now this man and the people with him were in a realm they had never experienced before. So they were beyond any assistance that their own experience could give them. That was when Jesus said, "Do not be afraid."

Whenever we face something that is new and different, fear is usually one of the first reactions that rises up in our hearts. Jesus said to the synagogue official, "Do not be afraid; only believe." Fear and unbelief are like twins. They are very closely linked together. According to the Book of Revelation, it is the fearful and unbelieving who lead the parade into hell (Revelation 21:8, KJV). We all know the experience of walking along, believing to receive something from the Lord. Then, all of a sudden, our circumstances turn into something we've never seen before. What is our attitude when that happens? "Don't bother anymore." Isn't that what they told the synagogue official? "Don't bother the Teacher anymore. Your daughter has died. It's now beyond the boundary of what's possible." In our unbelief, we just quit asking. They probably told the Lord, "Sorry we bothered You. We don't need You anymore because the girl is dead. If she were still sick, we know You could do something about it. But because she is dead, it's too late. Nothing can happen. This is beyond Your ability." No, it is only beyond our ability to believe. Jesus had to correct that attitude by saying, "Don't be afraid. Only believe!" When He arrived at the house, He threw everyone but the parents and His companions out of the room because He did not need their unbelief. Then He prayed for her and raised her from the dead.

Jesus had told the people, "The girl is asleep." To everyone else, she was dead, but to Jesus she was merely sleeping. Many of your problems are the same to you as the death of this man's daughter was to these people. You think that your problems are in a state that is beyond any help from God. But in His eyes, it is only a temporary state, waiting for the moment of faith when you "only believe." Jesus took the young girl's father into the room with Him and he was part of the faith that raised her from the dead. Our problems are

---

Revelation 21:8, KJV   But the fearful, and unbelieving, and the abominable, and murderers, and whoremongers, and sorcerers, and idolaters, and all liars, shall have their part in the lake which burneth with fire and brimstone: which is the second death.

never beyond God's reach. Our circumstances are never beyond the bounds of what He is capable of doing. For man it is impossible, but with God all things are possible (Matthew 19:26). The only thing that is lacking in most situations is our ability to believe. It is when the situation is impossible that we should believe the most. That is when we should throw out the fear. Fear comes with the feeling, "There is no solution. There is no way out." Only believe! If we just believe, we will discover that God's capacities go far beyond anything we have ever seen or known. To Him all things are possible. He is the One who calls things into being out of that which does not exist (Hebrews 11:3). The only thing God is looking for is that we believe. Therefore, if you have a need that seems to be completely out of the realm of possibility, repent of your unbelief and believe in Him.

4. Uproot the Unbelief (Matthew 17:1-21)

This next point is about how our unbelief affects our ministry to the world. It deals with who we are as God's sons in the earth, walking in this generation of destiny. Again, this is a story we know very well. It begins with the Mount of Transfiguration. Jesus took Peter, James, and John up on the mountain. Moses and Elijah appeared to them, Jesus was transfigured, and the glory of God was manifested as a great light. Afterwards, as they were walking down the mountain, Jesus said to the three disciples, "Do not tell anyone what happened here" (Matthew 17:1-3, 9). Further down the mountain, a man came out of the crowd and said to Jesus,

---

Matthew 19:26 And looking upon them Jesus said to them, "With men this is impossible, but with God all things are possible."

Hebrews 11:3 By faith we understand that the worlds were prepared by the word of God, so that what is seen was not made out of things which are visible.

Matthew 17:1-3 And six days later Jesus took with Him Peter and James and John his brother, and brought them up to a high mountain by themselves. ² And He was transfigured before them; and His face shone like the sun, and His garments became as white as light. ³ And behold, Moses and Elijah appeared to them, talking with Him.

Matthew 17:9 And as they were coming down from the mountain, Jesus commanded them, saying, "Tell the vision to no one until the Son of Man has risen from the dead."

"Lord, have mercy on my son, for he is a lunatic, and is very ill; for he often falls into the fire, and often into the water. And I brought him to Your disciples, and they could not cure him." And Jesus answered and said, "O unbelieving and perverted generation, how long shall I be with you? How long shall I put up with you? Bring him here to Me." And Jesus rebuked him, and the demon came out of him, and the boy was cured at once. (Matthew 17:15-18)

This example is important because it shows the real frustration that Jesus had with unbelief. He was disgusted by it. Remember, this was a generation of promise. They were walking with Jesus Christ in the earth, yet He called them an unbelieving and perverted generation. This is similar to what happened with the generation that came out of Egypt into the wilderness. They tested God, and He said, "I was angry with them for forty years" (Psalm 95:8-10). When we read about God's anger and the anger and frustration of Jesus with our unbelief, it gives us a sense of how horrific our unbelief is. It is a perversion. It is something that is absolutely against everything God is, and everything He stands for.

So how does this story apply to us today? In this way: Jesus was gone. What do you do when Jesus is not around? You take your demon-possessed son to the disciples for deliverance. There was no other place to go because Jesus was not there. And the world has nowhere to go right now except to God's people. The Mount of Transfiguration was very similar to where Jesus is right now. He's gone into glory, into the presence of the Father; He is not here. So the world should be able to bring their demon-possessed sons to us, the disciples. We are the ones who must move in healing and

---

Psalm 95:8-10 Do not harden your hearts, as at Meribah, as in the day of Massah in the wilderness; ⁹ "When your fathers tested Me, they tried Me, though they had seen My work. ¹⁰ For forty years I loathed that generation, and said they are a people who err in their heart, and they do not know My ways."

deliverance. We are the ones who must have a Word from God. Like Jesus, we must be Immanuel (God with us), His presence in the earth. This story is not just about how our unbelief impacts us. This story is about how our unbelief impacts the whole world around us.

What happens if the world comes to us and we are still locked into our own unbelief? Unfortunately, when faced with the need for deliverance or healing, too often we pull the ripcord of unbelief and say, "I have never really seen God move like that before." The disciples obviously believed in deliverance. They had everything they needed to cast out this demon. They had witnessed Jesus do it time and time again. They had seen healings, resurrections, and countless miracles take place. Yet seeing it did not release them from their unbelief. As many times as they had witnessed Jesus move on every level of ministry, when the world came to their doorstep, their unbelief blocked the anointing and presence of God from moving through them. We need to stop saying, "It has been such a long time since we have seen miracles and healing ministries." We have heard stories from the outpouring at Azusa Street where people re-grew missing limbs. Still we say, "I wasn't there. I didn't see it." That is an excuse for unbelief that is unacceptable. When you see Jesus in heaven, try that excuse on Him. He will say, "Depart from Me, you worker of iniquity. I never knew you" (Matthew 7:23). Unbelief is absolutely insidious. It makes the Lord angry that we would make excuses to get out of confronting our own unbelief. It is the root cause of why things do not happen.

Interestingly, one of the verses in Matthew 17 supports this idea:

> Then the disciples came to Jesus privately and said, "Why could we not cast it out?" And He said to them, "Because of the littleness of your faith; for truly I say to you, if you have

---

Matthew 7:23 "And then I will declare to them, 'I never knew you; DEPART FROM ME, YOU WHO PRACTICE LAWLESSNESS.'"

faith as a mustard seed, you shall say to this mountain, 'Move from here to there,' and it shall move; and nothing shall be impossible to you." (Matthew 17:19-20)

Now look at verse 21: "But this kind does not go out except by prayer and fasting." Some Bibles have this verse in brackets, which means that the well-accepted Greek texts do not include this verse in the text. Literal Greek New Testaments and many Bible translations omit verse 21 altogether; the passage goes from verse 20 directly to verse 22, skipping verse 21, because it is not actually there in the Greek. This is significant because verse 21 addresses this need to find an excuse for why we cannot believe. Someone literally wrote into this passage an excuse: "This is such a big, powerful demon that the only way you can possibly cast it out is through prayer and fasting. Normally, nobody can get rid of this spirit. So don't feel bad when it doesn't work." Logically, this verse does not even make sense in the context of the story, because when the man brought his son to Jesus, Jesus simply cast out the spirit and went on with His day. There was no prayer and fasting. Obviously, that extra verse was not added to help Jesus. It was added to make the rest of us feel better when something does not work. The disciples were looking for a reason why they could not cast out the demon. And Jesus gave them the real reason. He said, "It is because of the littleness of your faith; for truly I say to you, if you have faith the size of a mustard seed, nothing shall be impossible to you." With faith, **nothing** is impossible for us.

We have faith, but only up to the point where our faith falters and our unbelief kicks in. That is the borderline between the Kingdom of God and where we are right now. When the Israelites went in to take the land of Canaan, they had to cross the Jordan River, which was the borderline. But before they could take the land, they had to be circumcised. Actually, it was a circumcision of heart, where

God rolled away the reproach of Egypt (Joshua 5:8-9). What was the reproach of Egypt? It was the unbelief that they and their parents had which God needed to remove. We have to cross our own Jordan and have the same reproach removed from us. You may ask, "How do I know the difference between the Kingdom of God and where I am now?" Discovering where your unbelief resides will show you. That is where the borderline is drawn. It is the boundary that we must cross if we are to move further into God's Kingdom. We need deliverance, but we will never get deliverance from something that we continually deny even exists. If we will not confess our unbelief, we will not even get close to seeing it removed.

When John the Baptist came preaching the Kingdom of God, he said, "Now the axe is laid to the root of the tree" (Matthew 3:10). There is something about the Kingdom of God and getting to the root of things that go hand in hand. To cross our Jordan River into the Kingdom, we need to be able to confess, to the root, how deep our unbelief really is. Otherwise, we will only be able to exercise the faith that we have, and we will continue to avoid being confronted by the unbelief that is still in our hearts. Do not go into condemnation over this; just confess it. God has set us free from condemnation so that we can hear truths like this and be delivered. "If we confess our sins, He is faithful and righteous to forgive us our sins and to cleanse us from all unrighteousness" (1 John 1:9). That means every bit of sin. He casts it into the sea of His forgetfulness, separating it

---

Joshua 5:8-9 Now it came about when they had finished circumcising all the nation, that they remained in their places in the camp until they were healed. ⁹ Then the LORD said to Joshua, "Today I have rolled away the reproach of Egypt from you." So the name of that place is called Gilgal to this day.

Matthew 3:10 "And the axe is already laid at the root of the trees; every tree therefore that does not bear good fruit is cut down and thrown into the fire."

from us as far as the east is from the west (Micah 7:19; Isaiah 43:25; Psalm 103:12).

5. Believe in the Lord's New Appearing to You (John 20:24-29)

For the final point, I want to begin with the story in John 20:24-29 about the disciple Thomas, who had a problem believing that Jesus had been resurrected. This story is significant for us because, at that moment when Jesus was appearing to the disciples, He was appearing to them and to the world in a new form. He was appearing to them in a new day, in a new epoch, and it was that new appearing that Thomas refused to believe. He said, "I will not believe it unless I can put my finger in the holes in His hands, and my hand in the wound in His side" (John 20:25). That sounds very much like the story of the children of Israel in the wilderness:

> Therefore, just as the Holy Spirit says,
>   "TODAY IF YOU HEAR HIS VOICE,
>   DO NOT HARDEN YOUR HEARTS AS WHEN THEY
>   PROVOKED ME,
>   AS IN THE DAY OF TRIAL IN THE WILDERNESS,
>   WHERE YOUR FATHERS TRIED ME BY TESTING ME,
>   AND SAW MY WORKS FOR FORTY YEARS.
>   THEREFORE I WAS ANGRY WITH THIS GENERATION,
>   AND SAID, 'THEY ALWAYS GO ASTRAY IN THEIR HEART;
>   AND THEY DID NOT KNOW MY WAYS';

Micah 7:19 He will again have compassion on us; He will tread our iniquities under foot. Yes, Thou wilt cast all their sins into the depths of the sea.

Isaiah 43:25 "I, even I, am the one who wipes out your transgressions for My own sake; and I will not remember your sins."

Psalm 103:12 As far as the east is from the west, so far has He removed our transgressions from us.

John 20:25 The other disciples therefore were saying to him, "We have seen the Lord!" But he said to them, "Unless I shall see in His hands the imprint of the nails, and put my finger into the place of the nails, and put my hand into His side, I will not believe."

As I swore in My wrath,
They shall not enter My rest."

Take care, brethren, lest there should be in any one of you
an evil, unbelieving heart, in falling away from the living
God. But encourage one another day after day, as long as
it is still called "Today," lest any one of you be hardened by
the deceitfulness of sin. (Hebrews 3:7-13)

The children of Israel kept testing God. How did they test Him? They said, "We are not going to believe unless You give us food, unless you give us water, unless you perform miracles for us." God was frustrated with them and said, "I have already done so much; how can you not believe? I am not going to keep trying to convince you. Your unbelief is challenging Me over the way I am appearing to you." The Lord appeared to those slaves in Egypt who had endured bondage for generation after generation, but they could not believe. Just like those slaves, we get tired, conditioned, and set in our ways until we also do not want to believe anymore.

Thomas' problem really was unbelief. He did not want to believe in a new and different Jesus. He wanted the old Jesus. He wanted things to be the way they were before, because he had believed in that; he could handle that. But as the apostle Paul wrote, "Even though we have known Christ according to the flesh, yet now we know Him thus no longer" (2 Corinthians 5:16). Jesus was something different to the early Church than what He was before. And, in a sense, Christ is appearing to us in another form. He is appearing to us in a way that is different than what has existed for the last 2,000 years. God is moving in another way. There is a generation in which something new and different is happening; there is an open door for a breakthrough. We cannot keep saying to God, "If You will just do this for me, I will believe." The way Thomas expressed it was, "If I can just put my hand in Your side, then I'll believe." The children of Israel had their way of expressing it: "Did You bring us out here to kill us? Just give us water!" However our unbelief is expressed,

Hebrews chapters 3 and 4 give us a very clear message: "Listen, there is a promise of entering His rest that still exists for the house of God. Do not miss out the way they did, hardened by the deceitfulness of sin, having an evil, unbelieving heart in falling away from the living God."

I believe that the door to the Kingdom of God is open. It has been kicked down through years of intercession, spiritual warfare, and faith. What could be worse than not walking through that open door because of our unbelief? If there remains a promise of entering God's rest, let's not fall short of it. We have not come this far only to fall away now. We cannot say, "This is far enough! We have enough; we do not need anything more." No, we do need something more. We need to be the generation that crosses over into Canaan and takes the land. It will only be done by a generation of faith. We read in Luke 12:27-31,

> "Consider the lilies, how they grow; they neither toil nor spin; but I tell you, even Solomon in all his glory did not clothe himself like one of these. But if God so arrays the grass in the field, which is alive today and tomorrow is thrown into the furnace, how much more will He clothe you, O men of little faith! And do not seek what you shall eat, and what you shall drink, and do not keep worrying. For all these things the nations of the world eagerly seek; but your Father knows that you need these things. But seek for His kingdom."

Jesus told us to seek for His Kingdom. For some of us, this is something we have lived for since our youth, from the moment we first heard a Living Word from God. The course of destiny for our lives is to press into the Kingdom of God, but unbelief turns us away from the intensity of that. Jesus said, "Do not be afraid, little flock, for your Father has chosen gladly to give you the kingdom" (Luke 12:32). I want to end the message with this promise, because we should not have the feeling that this is just an uphill struggle. It is God's good pleasure to give us the Kingdom. God is waiting for our faith to simply appropriate all that He, in His abundant love and grace, is pouring out upon us and beaming toward us (Ephesians 1:18-19). The challenge we face in this generation is whether or not we will allow our unbelief to cause us to fail in obtaining God's promises, and hold us back from appropriating all that God's Word has made available.

Ephesians 1:18-19 I pray that the eyes of your heart may be enlightened, so that you may know what is the hope of His calling, what are the riches of the glory of His inheritance in the saints, [19] and what is the surpassing greatness of His power toward us who believe. These are in accordance with the working of the strength of His might.

CHAPTER 6

When God Comes Down

The Feast of Tabernacles is the feast that celebrates the Lord's presence in the earth. Traditionally, Tabernacles is celebrated by building booths, or *sukkahs*, with the tops open to remind the Jewish people of the forty years in the wilderness, when the Lord camped with Israel (Leviticus 23:39-43). His presence was with them by day, and His presence was with them by night (Numbers 14:14). In our fellowship, we also have a tradition of celebrating this time of Tabernacles. Celebrating Tabernacles is one thing, but we should

---

Leviticus 23:39-43   "On exactly the fifteenth day of the seventh month, when you have gathered in the crops of the land, you shall celebrate the feast of the LORD for seven days, with a rest on the first day and a rest on the eighth day. ⁴⁰ Now on the first day you shall take for yourselves the foliage of beautiful trees, palm branches and boughs of leafy trees and willows of the brook; and you shall rejoice before the LORD your God for seven days. ⁴¹ You shall thus celebrate it as a feast to the LORD for seven days in the year. It shall be a perpetual statute throughout your generations; you shall celebrate it in the seventh month. ⁴² You shall live in booths for seven days; all the native-born in Israel shall live in booths, ⁴³ so that your generations may know that I had the sons of Israel live in booths when I brought them out from the land of Egypt. I am the LORD your God."

Numbers 14:14   And they will tell it to the inhabitants of this land. They have heard that Thou, O LORD, art in the midst of this people, for Thou, O LORD, art seen eye to eye, while Thy cloud stands over them; and Thou dost go before them in a pillar of cloud by day and in a pillar of fire by night.

do it with a deep sense of destiny that the presence of the Lord will be with us in reality. Nothing takes place without His presence; this needs to be real to you. On the surface, that sounds oversimplified, but there are actually times when the presence of God is limited. That is simply a historical reality.

Look at the 400 years before Israel's exodus from Egypt. In a very real sense, it was a time without the presence of God. I know that He is always with us, but if you are a spiritual individual walking with God, you know the difference between the times when His presence is there and the times when it is not. The 400 years of slavery in Egypt is a great example of God not being there. There is a great contrast between those 400 years of slavery and the presence of God that Israel experienced in the wilderness. They are two completely opposite realities. For 400 years they were slaves in Egypt, and there was no deliverance during that time. Two hundred years into that period of slavery, an Israelite could have woken up one morning and said, "I know that God is with us and that He is coming to deliver us. I think I will just walk out of Egypt today." That would have been one dead Israelite about 100 yards past the border of the slave camp. Deliverance did not manifest for them for another 200 years. What if you had lived during that 400-year period in Israel's history? It must have been horrible to be in a life of bondage during that time. Yet, it was not as if nothing was happening for Israel. They were moving toward the fulfillment of the prophecies, but the only thing that appeared to be happening for them was that they were multiplying. Despite all of the limitations that Egypt imposed on them, they were growing into a nation that was like the sands of the seashore (Genesis 46:2-3; 22:17). So, in a sense, the promises were

---

Genesis 46:2-3 And God spoke to Israel in visions of the night and said, "Jacob, Jacob." And he said, "Here I am." ³ And He said, "I am God, the God of your father; do not be afraid to go down to Egypt, for I will make you a great nation there."

Genesis 22:17 "Indeed I will greatly bless you, and I will greatly multiply your seed as the stars of the heavens, and as the sand which is on the seashore; and your seed shall possess the gate of their enemies."

coming to pass, but there was still so much that they did not have and so much oppression that they lived under.

There is something in this that I want us to lay hold of. John Stevens, our founder, used to pray intensely to God about the fact that there is not enough of God in the earth, at any given time, to accomplish the things that we need to accomplish. You need to have the same level of intensity in your prayer today. There is only so much of God available. There is only a limited amount of the presence of Jesus Christ in the earth right now, and it has been that way for some period of time. We have to face the truth that our ability to move in God is determined by how much of His presence we actually have. In this example of Israel in Egypt, we can see the dramatic difference between the time when God was not in the earth, and when He truly was. When God met Moses in the wilderness and spoke to him out of a burning bush, something very dynamic was about to happen for the children of Israel. God was getting ready to come down and deliver Israel out of Egypt after their 400-year dormant period.

> He said also, "I am the God of your father, the God of Abraham, the God of Isaac, and the God of Jacob." Then Moses hid his face, for he was afraid to look at God. And the LORD said, "I have surely seen the affliction of My people who are in Egypt, and have given heed to their cry because of their taskmasters, for I am aware of their sufferings. So I have come down to deliver them from the power of the Egyptians, and to bring them up from that land to a good and spacious land, to a land flowing with milk and honey, to the place of the Canaanite and the Hittite and the Amorite and the Perizzite and the Hivite and the Jebusite. And now, behold, the cry of the sons of Israel has come to Me; furthermore, I have seen the oppression with which the Egyptians are oppressing them." (Exodus 3:6-9)

You cannot say that God was not hearing their cries. God was aware of their suffering in Egypt. What you can say about Israel's time in Egypt was that God was in heaven and observing what was happening to them. Although it is very comforting to know that God saw their affliction, if I had been one of those people, I would have said, "God, why didn't You do something about this a long time ago!" Do you realize how many generations take place over 400 years, how many people lived in those circumstances with God just looking down and seeing the affliction of Israel? Yet God told Moses that He was giving heed to their cries. In other words, all their groaning and prayers were heard. God was not disengaged. But then God said to Moses, "I have come down." It was truly awesome that God's presence was there, but don't miss the significance of that statement. His presence **had** to be there in order for something to change, for the deliverance from Egypt to happen, and for them to possess the land of Canaan. It did not matter how many promises Abraham received from God; during those 400 years in Egypt, a slave could not just walk out of there and go possess the land of Canaan. Were the promises true? Of course they were. God said to Moses, "I am the God of your father, the God of Abraham, the God of Isaac, and the God of Jacob" (Exodus 3:6). All of those prophecies and promises were alive. They were real. They were available. Nothing was stopping them from happening except that there was not enough God in the earth at that time for them to happen.

When you really lay hold of this truth, it completely wipes away the reliance on doctrine. Doctrine is a belief **about** God. We can read the Bible and study **about** Jesus and miss the reality that Jesus **is** the resurrection, Jesus **is** the life, and Jesus **is** the way (John 11:25; 14:6).

John 11:25 Jesus said to her, "I am the resurrection and the life; he who believes in Me shall live even if he dies."

John 14:6 Jesus said to him, "I am the way, and the truth, and the life; no one comes to the Father, but through Me."

You can study about Jesus and God, but at some point they have to come on the scene for the promises in the Bible to be fulfilled. There will never be a fulfillment of prophecy that is not the result of the presence of God—the presence of His Son Jesus Christ—coming into our midst in the earth. At some point, God must introduce Himself into the situation. When His presence is not here, we are living in a dormant time. When His presence **is** here, the difference is obvious. When God came down to deliver the children of Israel, look at what happened and the rapidity with which it happened. After nothing happened for 400 years, suddenly, within a year of the Lord appearing to Moses, they were delivered out of Egypt and on their way to the land God had promised them. Talk about a change in lifestyle! They were no longer eating slave slop from the Egyptians; now they were being fed with manna (Deuteronomy 8:3). Now their clothes did not wear out (Deuteronomy 29:5). Why did their clothes wear out before? Because God was not there.

When we talk about futility, what are we really talking about? Futility is the lack of God's presence. When God was with the Israelites in the wilderness, they had none of the diseases of Egypt (Exodus 15:26). They were led every day; they saw the visible presence of God (Exodus 13:21). They were in motion to go in and

---

Deuteronomy 8:3 "And He humbled you and let you be hungry, and fed you with manna which you did not know, nor did your fathers know, that He might make you understand that man does not live by bread alone, but man lives by everything that proceeds out of the mouth of the Lord."

Deuteronomy 29:5 "And I have led you forty years in the wilderness; your clothes have not worn out on you, and your sandal has not worn out on your foot."

Exodus 15:26 And He said, "If you will give earnest heed to the voice of the Lord your God, and do what is right in His sight, and give ear to His commandments, and keep all His statutes, I will put none of the diseases on you which I have put on the Egyptians; for I, the Lord, am your healer."

Exodus 13:21 And the Lord was going before them in a pillar of cloud by day to lead them on the way, and in a pillar of fire by night to give them light, that they might travel by day and by night.

possess the land. God was angry with them at times, but remember the prayer of Moses: "God, if You will not go with us, then don't lead us from here (Exodus 33:15). I am not about to go through another 400 years without Your presence. That is not an option. So Your presence is staying right here with us, and only then will we move forward." As a result, God's presence moved with them and stayed with them through the entire time in the wilderness, through the possessing of the land and the building of the tabernacle. Then at some point, because of their sin, God's presence left them. The Book of Ezekiel paints a vivid picture of His presence leaving Israel. First the presence of God departed the Temple; then it departed Jerusalem; and then it departed Israel (Ezekiel 10:18-19; 11:22-23). In a sense, you could say that God returned to heaven. Now Israel was back where they had been during their bondage in Egypt. In Ezekiel's day, Judah had been taken into captivity to Babylon. They were hauled away into bondage for another period of time. What happened to them? They lost the presence of God. No matter what promises we have and what has been prophesied over us, without God they do not happen.

What we really need, as a people today, is the presence of God. It has to be real to us that this is what we are looking for. We have experienced His presence to a degree. We have the presence of Christ with us, but it is limited; we have come to the end of what

---

Exodus 33:15 Then he said to Him, "If Thy presence does not go with us, do not lead us up from here."

Ezekiel 10:18-19 Then the glory of the LORD departed from the threshold of the temple and stood over the cherubim. ¹⁹ When the cherubim departed, they lifted their wings and rose up from the earth in my sight with the wheels beside them; and they stood still at the entrance of the east gate of the LORD's house. And the glory of the God of Israel hovered over them.

Ezekiel 11:22-23 Then the cherubim lifted up their wings with the wheels beside them, and the glory of the God of Israel hovered over them. ²³ And the glory of the LORD went up from the midst of the city, and stood over the mountain which is east of the city.

we can attain by virtue of the presence of God that is available to us. Think about that. You may be very familiar with the prophecies and the promises of God, and know what is supposed to be happening. If so, then you must also be aware that there is an absolute dichotomy between what works and what does not work. We have many wonderful things that do work. We have divine order that works. We have beautiful worship that was restored during a period of God's presence. We are still living in a time when God came down to earth, going back to the outpouring of the Holy Spirit at Azusa Street and the spiritual outpourings that followed. In a very real way, we have seen God's presence come into the earth. We have a Living Word. Many of the things that we are walking in today are a result of that presence. What was behind the Azusa Street miracles and the Pentecostal outpouring? What made those things happen? God came down. God stopped being in heaven, and He brought His presence here to the earth.

To whatever degree we have God's presence with us, to that degree we walk in His promises. From those early outpourings of the Holy Spirit, we have broken through and seen God come on the scene in ways that are exceptional. We see the results of it in the gifts that people are able to move in. Do we have healings? Yes. Do we have the kind of healings we should be having? No. We have prophecies about resurrection life; however, we are not going to pray resurrection life into existence. We have prophecies about the fullness of sonship and the Kingdom of God manifesting in the earth. How will these things happen? They will be the direct result of God coming down, of His presence being here with us. When Christ's presence appears, these things will naturally come forth, because He is the resurrection and the life.

It is important to understand that the second coming of Christ and what happens by virtue of His presence with us go hand in hand. The Church has lost the understanding of Christ's second coming. Many Christians today are so busy telling others that they will be "left behind" that they forget what the Bible really says about the second coming of Christ. I hate the fact that they use fear-mongering to try to bring people to Jesus. God so **loved** the world that He gave His only begotten Son (John 3:16). It is perverse to turn the second coming of Christ into something fearful, until people have to sleep under their beds every night because they are so afraid of what is going to happen. It is a perversion of the Scriptures and a perversion of the truth. A more accurate picture is that Christ's coming is an unfolding manifestation in which more and more of His presence, and more and more of the Father's presence, returns. Jesus said, "My Father and I will come and take up our abode in you" (John 14:23). The second coming of Christ to the earth is a successive unfolding. For example, when you come to a church service, you don't just appear there. First, you leave your house, and then you go through successive steps to get there. The return of Christ is the same. We are already very much in the unfolding of the second coming of Christ. Because of that, there is a presence of the Lord that is with us.

One of the ways the Lord appears to us, in a unique manifestation, is by His Word. The Scriptures tell us that God appears in His Word (1 Samuel 3:21). Jesus appears to us as the Word of God (John 1:1, 14). And the Father has appeared to us in the Living Word that He gave us as part of this time of outpouring. The Living Word is something that we still have. The anointing is as great, or

---

John 3:16 "For God so loved the world, that He gave His only begotten Son, that whoever believes in Him should not perish, but have eternal life."

John 14:23 Jesus answered and said to him, "If anyone loves Me, he will keep My word; and My Father will love him, and We will come to him, and make Our abode with him."

1 Samuel 3:21 And the Lord appeared again at Shiloh, because the Lord revealed Himself to Samuel at Shiloh by the word of the Lord.

John 1:1 In the beginning was the Word, and the Word was with God, and the Word was God.

John 1:14 And the Word became flesh, and dwelt among us, and we beheld His glory, glory as of the only begotten from the Father, full of grace and truth.

greater, than it has ever been. So we see that whatever measure of God's presence we have, it brings us all of these wonderful fulfillments.

We must also recognize what limitations we have. It seems that the older we get, the more we recognize this fact. It is almost shocking to us when we try to move in something in God but we cannot. It is like the slave who, after 200 years of bondage, decides to go possess the land of Canaan. Everyone says, "Good luck. We're with you. We're not going with you, but we'll watch what happens from here." There are times when we have prayed intensely to break through into what we know we should have, by God's promises. By prophecy it is ours, and yet it does not work in the moment in which we are living. What are we supposed to do about it? The first thing we must do is recognize our need for God's presence. When we really get this, it changes our prayer, our intercession, and our approach to God. It takes us back into waiting on the Lord and connecting with Him, because we finally understand that the Kingdom of God is a relationship. It is a matter of Him being here with us. We must recognize that what we need is God. What we need is Jesus Christ with us in the earth. Our drive should be toward His return in this unfolding manifestation.

A verse from the Lord's Prayer came alive to me. When you do not know how to begin praying for the presence of God, pray, "Give us this day our daily bread" (Matthew 6:11). God's presence is our daily bread. Remember, the only reason the children of Israel had daily bread was because God was there with them (Deuteronomy 8:3). Jesus made it very clear that He is the bread that God sent down from heaven (John 6:33-35). So what Jesus is teaching us in the

---

John 6:33-35 "For the bread of God is that which comes down out of heaven, and gives life to the world." ³⁴ They said therefore to Him, "Lord, evermore give us this bread." ³⁵ Jesus said to them, "I am the bread of life; he who comes to Me shall not hunger, and he who believes in Me shall never thirst."

Lord's Prayer is to pray for His presence. Father, give us this day our daily bread. Release Christ into the earth! Because God so loved the world, He sent His only begotten Son into the earth (John 3:16). God knew that nothing in the world could change unless His presence was here, so He sent His Son. What was His name? Immanuel, which means "God with us" (Matthew 1:23). Jesus was not simply born in a manger; God came down again. During all the days that Jesus was in the earth, God was here. That was not the case in the days before Jesus showed up on the earth. Historically, the days before Jesus' birth were similar to the years of slavery in Egypt. The Bible describes times when there was no Word from God, no presence of God in the earth (1 Samuel 3:1; Amos 8:11-12). The period between the Old and New Testaments was very much like that. Then Jesus was born and everything changed rapidly. Immediately satan started to come against Christ, and Herod was stirred up (Matthew 2:16). In the explosion of Jesus' ministry, there were healings, signs and wonders, people's lives being touched by God, and a Living Word being spoken in the earth again. Why did all of this begin to happen? Because God's presence was here. Everything took place because of that reality, just as it did when God came down to deliver Israel out of Egypt.

Matthew 1:23 "Behold, the virgin shall be with child, and shall bear a Son, and they shall call His name Immanuel," which translated means, "God with us."

1 Samuel 3:1 Now the boy Samuel was ministering to the Lord before Eli. And word from the Lord was rare in those days, visions were infrequent.

Amos 8:11-12 "Behold, days are coming," declares the Lord God, "When I will send a famine on the land, not a famine for bread or a thirst for water, but rather for hearing the words of the Lord. 12 And people will stagger from sea to sea, and from the north even to the east; they will go to and fro to seek the word of the Lord, but they will not find it."

Matthew 2:16 Then when Herod saw that he had been tricked by the magi, he became very enraged, and sent and slew all the male children who were in Bethlehem and in all its environs, from two years old and under, according to the time which he had ascertained from the magi.

I have always thought, "I don't want to live in one of those times when God is not around. I don't want to be in a placeholder generation where we are all sitting around waiting for God to show up." Fortunately, we are not living in a time like that now. That time has ended, and we are now in the days of the Kingdom of God. The Kingdom surrounds the unfolding of God's presence; it becomes greater and greater and expands more and more. So it is time to pray for our daily bread. It is time for us to recognize our need for more of Him. We are realizing that we are at the end of what is available by virtue of the presence of God that we have had up to this point. Look back over the past thirty years; we have done a great deal with what we have received. We have seen fantastic things take place. We have a oneness today in the Body of Christ that is amazing, and there is still much more that will grow out of that. We have seen things restored that were never restored in previous generations. We are still seeing releases unfold from the anointing that we have had. There has been more and more of God's presence; but at the same time, we have come to an end of what the current manifestation can provide. It is like we have come into a cul-de-sac, and it is important that we do not get stuck where we are. We cannot become accustomed to things not working the way we want them to work. That is what happened to the Israelites in Egypt. As horrible as it was, Israel got used to being slaves. Generations of people got used to living without the presence of God. They got used to the prophecies not being fulfilled in their generation. I do not believe we have that problem; we are in the time of God's Kingdom. What we need right now is for God to come down to the earth. We need another level of Christ's presence with us. We need to pray, "Lord, we need more of You!"

You might be thinking, "I don't get this idea of there being more or less of Christ." Look at it this way: the closer He comes, the more you can see Him. Right now we may have to look at Him through binoculars: "Oh, I see. There is His presence! It is off in the distance." As we read earlier, Ezekiel described the presence of the Lord departing, but he also described the presence of the Lord returning. It returned slowly. It came back from the east, just as it had left. It descended upon Jerusalem, and then it came through the east gate, and into the inner court of the Temple (Ezekiel 43:1-5). His presence is something that is returning. The closer it gets, the stronger it is. The closer it comes, the more clearly we see it, and the more available it is to us. We need to be those who persistently cry out for the presence of the Lord. We need to have His presence here with us, just as it was with the children of Israel in the wilderness. That is why we celebrate the Feast of Tabernacles. It is a type of the Kingdom of God, and it reminds us of that time when His presence dwelt with His people. God tabernacled with them, and they had everything they needed. Yes, there were times when they murmured and complained, but remember the fantastic divine order in which they lived. All the families were camped under their fathers' banners, and they all dwelt together in peace (Numbers 2:1-2). All of Israel was one large family being fed the manna by God and experiencing His presence. Imagine living there at that time. Do you need to pray to the Lord? No, just walk outside your tent and He is right there. Are you questioning whether God is real or not? Just look out your front door. There He is! His presence was visibly real. It provided heat by night and shade by day. It provided total immunity from

---

Ezekiel 43:1-5 Then he led me to the gate, the gate facing toward the east; [2] and behold, the glory of the God of Israel was coming from the way of the east. And His voice was like the sound of many waters; and the earth shone with His glory. [3] And it was like the appearance of the vision which I saw, like the vision which I saw when He came to destroy the city. And the visions were like the vision which I saw by the river Chebar; and I fell on my face. [4] And the glory of the LORD came into the house by the way of the gate facing toward the east. [5] And the Spirit lifted me up and brought me into the inner court; and behold, the glory of the LORD filled the house.

Numbers 2:1-2 Now the LORD spoke to Moses and to Aaron, saying, [2] "The sons of Israel shall camp, each by his own standard, with the banners of their fathers' households; they shall camp around the tent of meeting at a distance."

diseases. Nations greater and mightier than they were could not overtake them. They had everything they needed.

I wish we could hold that picture in our minds. That is the image we are supposed to remember during the Feast of Tabernacles. It is the time of His presence. What happened to deliver Israel? God happened. God came down. This is what it is all about: God tabernacling—living with His people. That is to become the permanent state of our lives. The fulfillment of the Kingdom of God is the permanence of His presence abiding with us, which supplies all of our needs. Even if we lived in some kind of promised land, that alone would not be enough. If you look at the Promised Land today, the country of Israel, it is rather hilly, rocky, and barren. The land itself did not provide for God's people. What provided for them was His presence. And that is the way it should be for us. Please, do not get used to living with a limited amount of anointing and a limited amount of God's presence. Whatever we have had up to this point was fine for yesterday, but it is not enough for today. That does not mean that we have done something wrong. Quite the contrary, we have taken what presence He has made available to us and we have wrung everything out of it that we possibly could. But there is something more. We are not a people who go halfway. We are a people of the Kingdom. One of the greatest fulfillments that we are looking for, and what we have lived our lives for, is to see the manifestation of the sons of God. "So where is it?" you ask. There is not enough of God in the earth right now for the manifestation of His sons. What is the answer to releasing that manifestation? Romans chapter 8 says the sons of God will set all creation free from futility, but preceding that liberation Christ and the Father must take up Their abode in us (Romans 8:19-21, 10-11).

It is always significant when a word or a phrase is repeated in the Bible. In addition to Exodus 3:8, we find other Scriptures in which God uses the phrase "come down" about Himself. It is used again in Exodus 19:11 and in Numbers 11:17. Jesus said of Himself, "I have come down from heaven," using the exact phrase that God used (John 6:38). We read in the Book of Acts about Stephen giving his defense before the Council. When Stephen spoke, he gave a prophetic summary of the history of Israel and what God was doing. As he did so, he quoted these same verses from Exodus chapter 3 when God spoke to Moses from the burning bush: "I HAVE CERTAINLY SEEN THE OPPRESSION OF MY PEOPLE IN EGYPT, AND HAVE HEARD THEIR GROANS, AND I HAVE COME DOWN TO DELIVER THEM; COME NOW, AND I WILL SEND YOU TO EGYPT" (Acts 7:34).

One of the things that happens when God comes down is that He sends you. God moving through His people is one of the greatest manifestations of His presence (*parousia* in the Greek). The world will not see this unfolding of His presence, this *parousia* phase. It is not for their eyes, but it is for God's people who have to see it and

---

Romans 8:19-21 For the anxious longing of the creation waits eagerly for the revealing of the sons of God. [20] For the creation was subjected to futility, not of its own will, but because of Him who subjected it, in hope [21] that the creation itself also will be set free from its slavery to corruption into the freedom of the glory of the children of God.

Romans 8:10-11 And if Christ is in you, though the body is dead because of sin, yet the spirit is alive because of righteousness. [11] But if the Spirit of Him who raised Jesus from the dead dwells in you, He who raised Christ Jesus from the dead will also give life to your mortal bodies through His Spirit who indwells you.

Exodus 19:11 "And let them be ready for the third day, for on the third day the LORD will come down on Mount Sinai in the sight of all the people."

Numbers 11:17 "Then I will come down and speak with you there, and I will take of the Spirit who is upon you, and will put Him upon them; and they shall bear the burden of the people with you, so that you shall not bear it all alone."

understand it (1 Thessalonians 5:1-4; 2 Thessalonians 1:10). Again, we are talking about how the return of Christ actually manifests. The initial phase is not something that the world beholds. There is a moment when every eye shall see Him, but that does not take place in this initial phase of His Kingdom (Revelation 1:7). However, one thing that does happen in this initial phase is that God comes down and He sends you. His presence equips us as the vessels who will execute His will in the earth. That is who Jesus was. Speaking through the psalmist, He said, "I come to do Thy will, O God" (Psalm 40:8). Jesus came down, and the presence of God sent Him to fulfill God's will in the earth.

As we experience greater appearings and God coming down to the earth, we will begin to see the release of the sons of God. It is one of the great events prophesied in the Bible that is yet to take place. We have already seen many marvelous things. We have seen the restoration of the Church. We have seen divine order. We have seen miracles. Still, we have yet to see the promised manifestation of the sons of God. When God came down, He sent Moses. Moses was the anointed human vessel who executed everything that was to take place by virtue of God coming down. That is what we have lived for—to be a people that God sends. The Living Word has spoken to

---

1 Thessalonians 5:1-4 Now as to the times and the epochs, brethren, you have no need of anything to be written to you. ² For you yourselves know full well that the day of the Lord will come just like a thief in the night. ³ While they are saying, "Peace and safety!" then destruction will come upon them suddenly like birth pangs upon a woman with child; and they shall not escape. ⁴ But you, brethren, are not in darkness, that the day should overtake you like a thief.

2 Thessalonians 1:10 When He comes to be glorified in His saints on that day, and to be marveled at among all who have believed—for our testimony to you was believed.

Revelation 1:7 BEHOLD, HE IS COMING WITH THE CLOUDS, and every eye will see Him, even those who pierced Him; and all the tribes of the earth will mourn over Him. Even so. Amen.

Psalm 40:8 "I delight to do Thy will, O my God; Thy Law is within my heart."

us that we are a people God is preparing with a purpose, to be used in the end time.

We have not seen it yet, but our cry is, "Lord, come down. There is not enough of Your presence in the earth to initiate the sending forth of the sons of God; but the world is ready to see their manifestation and to have those greater works released throughout the earth." There is a deep cry in our hearts that says, "Lord, let Your presence be released. Let a new level of the unfolding of Your return begin for us now. Let enough of Your presence come that, like Moses, we are anointed and sent to be the executors of Your will in the earth today."

CHAPTER 7

The Holy Spirit Will
Descend and Remain

God is doing something in our hearts that must be clarified, and I want to work with several Scriptures that paint a picture of what we are reaching for. Why are we being gathered together as the *ekklesia*, the called out of the Lord? There is an explanation in a familiar passage from the Book of Ephesians:

> And He gave some as apostles, and some as prophets, and some as evangelists, and some as pastors and teachers, for the equipping of the saints for the work of service, to the building up of the body of Christ; until we all attain to the unity of the faith, and of the knowledge of the Son of God, to a mature man, to the measure of the stature which belongs to the fulness of Christ. (Ephesians 4:11-13)

The word "fullness" is the key. This picture of the building up of the Body of Christ means that we are to continue to grow until we reach the fullness of Christ. "For all who are being led by the Spirit of God, these are sons of God" (Romans 8:14). This is what we are looking for: the coming forth of the sons of God who are growing into the fullness of Christ. We are reaching in as sons of God to mature, and maturity means the fullness of Christ. Like the apostle Paul, we are reaching in to know Him and literally tap into the power of His resurrection (Philippians 3:10). Growing into the fullness of Christ is what the Church, the *ekklesia*, is all about. We need to understand this because we have been reaching in for an outpouring of the Lord's Spirit for some time. But that has to be more than some nebulous concept. It needs to come alive to us. There needs to be an impartation from God that releases our drive for the Holy Spirit to indwell us.

Let's read how the outpouring of the Holy Spirit happened with Christ:

> And John bore witness saying, "I have beheld the Spirit descending as a dove out of heaven, and He remained upon Him. And I did not recognize Him, but He who sent me to baptize in water [this was the Father] said to me, 'He upon whom you see the Spirit descending and remaining upon Him, this is the one who baptizes in the Holy Spirit.' And I have seen, and have borne witness that this is the Son of God." (John 1:32-34)

John the Baptist did not know who the Messiah was, but he witnessed the Holy Spirit descending like a dove and remaining on Jesus. Notice the process—descending and remaining. We are looking for an outpouring, for a descending of the Holy Spirit, but we are not looking for a flash-in-the-pan experience. We are looking for the Spirit to descend on us, and into us, and remain, because we are sons of God following the same pattern as Christ. That is the purpose of experiencing an outpouring. The pattern of Christ was that the Spirit of God, the Holy Spirit, descended upon Him and remained. Do not see this experience as a little dove coming down and sitting on Jesus' shoulder. Instead, see it as a flow coming down

---

Philippians 3:10 That I may know Him, and the power of His resurrection and the fellowship of His sufferings, being conformed to His death.

out of heaven from the Father that was constantly pouring down on Him. It was not an experience that happened one time and then stopped. It was a continual outpouring upon Him. The Holy Spirit remained descending; it was always pouring out on Christ as He walked the earth.

It is never enough to have just a momentary experience with the Father. How was it possible that Jesus always did those things that He saw the Father doing (John 5:19)? It was because the Holy Spirit descended, and kept descending upon Him. The descending remained, so that He heard what the Father was saying; He saw what the Father was doing; He went where the Father was going. That is the outpouring we want. We are not looking for a one-time breakthrough that we walk away from and say, "Wasn't that cool?" No, we are looking for God's presence to continually descend upon us. That was the testimony of John the Baptist about Jesus, who is the pattern Son. Therefore, if that is how the Spirit came upon Him, we should expect the same experience.

The church mentality is that we look at Jesus and the Father as being unreachable, and see experiences in Christ as something way out in the future. This is the mentality that makes an image of the cross, gazes upon it, and says, "This is Jesus. I am just trying to appropriate a salvation experience of the forgiveness of my sin." We know that we have received the forgiveness of our sin. But we also know that Jesus Christ was the pattern Son of God, and when the Holy Spirit descended upon Him, it continued to descend upon Him. Jesus said, "For He whom God has sent speaks the words of God; for He gives the Spirit without measure" (John 3:34). Christ received the Spirit without measure. It could not be measured since the Holy Spirit was always descending, always pouring out upon Him.

John 5:19 Jesus therefore answered and was saying to them, "Truly, truly, I say to you, the Son can do nothing of Himself, unless it is something He sees the Father doing; for whatever the Father does, these things the Son also does in like manner."

We relate to the baptism of the Holy Spirit as the moment when we receive the Holy Spirit, and by virtue of that, speak in tongues or receive other spiritual gifts. With Christ, it was not like that. With Christ it was an ongoing experience; He had the Spirit without measure. We, on the other hand, find it acceptable to have just a measure of the Spirit. We accept that as our Christian experience. Somehow we have developed the idea that Jesus had everything, and we only get a little bit of it, if we are lucky. At some point, we have to get over that way of thinking. We need to repent of these barriers in our minds that keep us from appropriating all that Christ is, and all that we are supposed to have. Jesus had the Spirit without measure, and He was the pattern for us. Therefore, we should have the Spirit without measure, and not believe that all we can have is one infilling of the Holy Spirit that we receive after tarrying at the altar for months.

We use the term "baptism of the Holy Spirit" to refer to what happened on the Day of Pentecost, but the Book of Acts uses the word "filled" (Acts 2:4). When you read about the Holy Spirit in the Book of Acts, the word "filled" is used repeatedly (Acts 4:8, 31; 9:17; 13:9, 52). They were all filled with the Spirit, not baptized. The word "baptism" conveys the idea of getting water poured over you

---

Acts 2:4   And they were all filled with the Holy Spirit and began to speak with other tongues, as the Spirit was giving them utterance.

Acts 4:8   Then Peter, filled with the Holy Spirit, said to them, "Rulers and elders of the people."

Acts 4:31   And when they had prayed, the place where they had gathered together was shaken, and they were all filled with the Holy Spirit, and began to speak the word of God with boldness.

Acts 9:17   And Ananias departed and entered the house, and after laying his hands on him said, "Brother Saul, the Lord Jesus, who appeared to you on the road by which you were coming, has sent me so that you may regain your sight, and be filled with the Holy Spirit."

Acts 13:9 But Saul, who was also known as Paul, filled with the Holy Spirit, fixed his gaze upon him.

Acts 13:52 And the disciples were continually filled with joy and with the Holy Spirit.

one time and then you are done. No, there is a fullness of the Spirit that we are looking for. We want what Jesus had: the Spirit without measure. We are not crying out for a one-time experience. We are looking for our lives to be changed because we receive the Spirit without measure, which rests upon us and continues to flow into our lives. The way we relate to church services is an example of the thinking that needs to change. In a service, when something meets us—maybe in the Word, or in the worship—we tend to say, "That was wonderful, but now it's time to go." There is something missing in that. I do not want that mentality anymore.

Being led by the Holy Spirit is still too vague to us. It is too much of a guessing game. We try to be led; we pray, "Lord, lead me." Yet, when Jesus received the Holy Spirit, the Spirit drove Him into the wilderness (Mark 1:12). Do not just pray, "Lord, lead me." Pray, "Lord, pour out Your Spirit on me in such a way that I am literally driven to do Your will." The Greek word used for "driven" in this Scripture is an intense, forceful word. Jesus was thrown, impelled into the wilderness. He did not need to pray, "Father, lead Me." He was driven by the Father to go where the Father wanted Him to go. We tend to flip that around; we go wherever we want and when we get there we say, "Now, Holy Spirit, what do You want me to do?" And He responds, "You're in the wrong place. I don't want to be here at all. Go back." We are like the priests who carry the ark of the covenant (Deuteronomy 31:9). But that does not mean we are to become the leader, deciding where God's presence goes. The priests were not the leaders; they were led by the presence of God. The Holy Spirit is the Spirit of power; He should drive us to where He wants to go. We should look to the Spirit and hand Him the reins. He should lead; we should follow.

Mark 1:12 And immediately the Spirit impelled Him to go out into the wilderness.

Deuteronomy 31:9 So Moses wrote this law and gave it to the priests, the sons of Levi who carried the ark of the covenant of the LORD, and to all the elders of Israel.

That is the relationship Christ had with the Holy Spirit. The Spirit fell on Him, "and immediately the Spirit driveth him into the wilderness," as we read in the King James translation of Mark 1:12. Mark constantly used this term "immediately," or "straightway," in his Gospel. He was captivated by the idea of Jesus being driven by the Holy Spirit, being forcefully moved from location to location, being told what to do. Why did Jesus wait for Lazarus to die (John 11:6)? If it were us, we would be in an ambulance yelling, "Get me there quick!" But Jesus waited for the Spirit. The Holy Spirit said, "Wait here for a while." When the Spirit finally said, "All right, go now," suddenly they had a resurrection on their hands (John 11:44). That is the leading of the Spirit that we are to move into, the Spirit without measure.

"For it was the Father's good pleasure for all the fulness to dwell in Him" (Colossians 1:19). In the New American Standard Bible, the marginal note on "fulness" reads, "fulness of deity." Christ is our pattern. He is not someone who is far off. He is not out of reach. We make Christ unattainable in our minds because we can never figure out how to have what He has. We say, "I will try to appropriate little experiences from Him. He can have the fullness of Deity; I can have a little baptism of the Holy Spirit. I can pray for sick people, but nothing usually happens." Jesus was God in the earth. God's Spirit was in Him without measure. He was the fullness. God could pour nothing more of Himself into Jesus, because Jesus was the fullness of Deity in the flesh of one man. No wonder things worked for Him. No wonder the demons cried out. No wonder the lame walked. And He is the pattern that we are to follow.

John 11:6 When therefore He heard that he was sick, He stayed then two days longer in the place where He was.

John 11:44 He who had died came forth, bound hand and foot with wrappings; and his face was wrapped around with a cloth. Jesus said to them, "Unbind him, and let him go."

Stop worshiping Christ from afar and continually making Him unattainable. Realize that He is not only attainable, He came to give us the example to follow. We know what He did for us: He died on the cross; He was buried and resurrected; His blood cleanses us of our sin. He did all of those things as a provision, but He also did them as a pattern so that we would not merely appropriate what He did, but also follow the pattern of what He was. In this age there will be two distinct groups of people: those who appropriate all that He did, and those who follow the pattern of what He did. Of course, in following the pattern, you have to appropriate all of His provision. However, appropriating that provision while you are using His strength to do the very things that He did is quite different than seeing Him as an unattainable God no one will ever be like. You can thank the Lord from afar and say, "Let's appropriate salvation, healings, resurrection," or you can walk in the pattern of Christ. We repent for letting ourselves off the hook by simply appropriating His provision and using it for less than the purpose for which it was given.

Christ's provision is what strengthens us to walk the way that He walked. Jesus became a Son; He was made perfect by the things which He suffered (Hebrews 2:10; 5:8). He did that all by the Holy Spirit. It started at the River Jordan when the Holy Spirit came upon Him. This is the baptism that we are still looking for. What is the point of having an outpouring of the Spirit in the first place? Is it so that we can write a book about another outpouring? No, it is so that we can start walking as Jesus did on the earth (1 John 4:17).

Hebrews 2:10 For it was fitting for Him, for whom are all things, and through whom are all things, in bringing many sons to glory, to perfect the author of their salvation through sufferings.

Hebrews 5:8 Although He was a Son, He learned obedience from the things which He suffered.

1 John 4:17 By this, love is perfected with us, that we may have confidence in the day of judgment; because as He is, so also are we in this world.

Where are we going to go? Where the Spirit drives us. What are we going to do? What we see the Father doing by the Spirit. What are we going to say? What we hear the Spirit saying. We will do these things because there will be a continuous outpouring of God's Spirit upon us, just as there was with Christ, our example. If we do not follow that example, are we not, in a sense, being disobedient to our calling? Jesus did not shed His blood just so we could come to church, use the Communion to wipe away our sins, and then go back to sinning all over again. We are not to be a blackboard on which we chalk up our problems, and then Jesus comes and erases them with His blood. His provision is far greater than that. His provision is the strength of God to enable us to walk as He walked; it was not given to use as a crutch. His blood is not an anti-condemnation drug: "If I take this I will feel much better. Then I can go back to my old way of life." From the moment Jesus received the outpouring of the Holy Spirit, He never went back to His old life. You cannot read much about Jesus' life before that moment, but you sure can read a lot about what happened after He received the Spirit, and that is the pattern for us today. We are to walk in the fullness of the Holy Spirit. We see this in the Book of Colossians:

> See to it that no one takes you captive through philosophy and empty deception, according to the tradition of men, according to the elementary principles of the world, rather than according to Christ. For in Him all the fulness of Deity dwells in bodily form, and in Him you have been made complete, and He is the head over all rule and authority; and in Him you were also circumcised with a circumcision made without hands, in the removal of the body of the flesh by the circumcision of Christ. (Colossians 2:8-11)

"In Him all the fulness of Deity dwells in bodily form, and in Him you have been made complete." We have to face the fact that we have a complete provision. I know it feels like we can never get there, that we can never see it duplicated in us. We repent of our unbelief, because the Word says that in Christ we have been made complete. In Him, the provision has already been given. It has been handed to us so we can walk in the same way that the pattern Son walked, in **all** that He walked in. We may suffer some things, but so did Christ. It was out of those sufferings that He was made perfect (Hebrews 2:10). Christ had all of the attributes of Deity, but He was completely and fully man. All that He did, He did by the Holy Spirit that descended and kept on descending upon Him. That is all He had, and yet it is so hard for us to believe that He was not God when He arrived on the earth.

We believe that all Deity dwelt in Christ, but we believe that it dwelt in Him when He was born into the flesh. Therefore, we excuse ourselves from the responsibility to walk as He walked. "Of course we can't walk as Jesus walked; He was divine from the moment of His birth." No, He laid that Deity aside (Philippians 2:5-7). This is a crucial issue of faith, because if we do not believe Jesus was human, just like us, then we have no hope. We will always have some excuse. Repent of your excuses. Repent of giving Jesus a special advantage that you do not have. The Lord has given us everything we need. Through our salvation, Christ has put His resurrected Spirit within us. God has given us the Holy Spirit. Right now, we have a tremendous amount to work with. By the Spirit we can cry, "Abba! Father!" (Romans 8:15). By it we can walk by faith. By it we can ask, and keep on asking, until we receive the fullness of the

---

Philippians 2:5-7 Have this attitude in yourselves which was also in Christ Jesus, [6] who, although He existed in the form of God, did not regard equality with God a thing to be grasped, [7] but emptied Himself, taking the form of a bond-servant, and being made in the likeness of men.

Romans 8:15 For you have not received a spirit of slavery leading to fear again, but you have received a spirit of adoption as sons by which we cry out, "Abba! Father!"

outpouring (Luke 11:9). In the Book of Ephesians, the apostle Paul describes what we have:

> I pray that the eyes of your heart may be enlightened, so that you may know what is the hope of His calling, what are the riches of the glory of His inheritance in the saints, and what is the surpassing greatness of His power toward us who believe. These are in accordance with the working of the strength of His might which He brought about in Christ, when He raised Him from the dead, and seated Him at His right hand in the heavenly places, far above all rule and authority and power and dominion, and every name that is named, not only in this age, but also in the one to come. And He put all things in subjection under His feet, and gave Him as head over all things to the church [*ekklesia*], which is His body, the fulness of Him who fills all in all. (Ephesians 1:18-23)

Christ was the fullness of God, the fullness of Deity in bodily form. Now He is seated at the right hand of the Father, and He is the head of the Body of Christ, which we are. We are to be the fullness of Christ, who is the fullness of God in bodily form on this earth. This is the hope of His calling. Jesus Christ called you, and the Father chose you with a hope that you will follow the pattern. We repent of our unbelief. This is not impossible to obtain, because His Word proclaims it. Not only that, the surpassing greatness of God's power is directed toward us who believe. This is not a passive thing that He is doing. We think we want an outpouring, but God wants an outpouring more than we can imagine. His power is being aimed at us to see a people break through into this fulfillment. Christ is the head and we are His Body, the fullness of Him who fills all things. That is where this all leads. It is important that we sweep away the

---

Luke 11:9 "And I say to you, ask, and it shall be given to you; seek, and you shall find; knock, and it shall be opened to you."

clutter, the confusion, and any other purpose that we think we are here for. The Body of Christ is not here for any purpose other than the fullness of the Godhead dwelling in us. There is no other purpose. This is not a social club. This is not a church, as defined by current standards. This is the remnant, the called out. This is Christ's Body in formation, the sons of God reaching for the outpouring of the Spirit until the fullness of Christ and the fullness of the Father are continually poured out upon us in bodily form.

No matter what comes against me, I refuse to back off from this point. This is what the Word of God says to me. This is what my apostolic father imparted to my heart, and I cannot get rid of it. We are not here to play church; we are not here to be a social club. We are here to break through to Him who is reaching toward us with great power, saying, "You, in bodily form, will be My fullness in the earth." Church, as we know it, will never bring about the manifestation of the Kingdom of God in the earth, but this drive will. If we follow the pattern of Christ, we will recognize that He was able to do all that He did by the Holy Spirit. He did not have anything else. There were no aces up His sleeve, nor was He doing tricks using smoke and mirrors. Unlike so much in the Church today, what Jesus did was not a performance. It was a living reality that He accomplished by the Holy Spirit that was within Him.

That is how we will do it also. We will do it by the Holy Spirit that is in us. Paul wrote that we were sealed with the Holy Spirit of promise, which is a pledge of our inheritance (Ephesians 1:13-14). This means that we have the down payment. That should encourage us, because a down payment is the guarantee that the deal will be followed through to completion. We have the earnest of our inheritance, and

---

Ephesians 1:13-14 In Him, you also, after listening to the message of truth, the gospel of your salvation—having also believed, you were sealed in Him with the Holy Spirit of promise, [14] who is given as a pledge of our inheritance, with a view to the redemption of God's own possession, to the praise of His glory.

therefore we cry out to the Lord because an earnest is not enough. If we think, "This is all we need; this is all the Bible talks about; this is all we are going to get," then we are deceiving ourselves. When you make a down payment on a house, it goes into escrow. You do not say, "That is enough. It is just too hard to go through and fulfill the escrow." No, you want to take possession of your house! That is why we are crying out to the Lord to meet us. This spark of the Spirit, the earnest of our inheritance within us, is crying out, "Abba! Father! We need Your fullness!" We confess that we cannot follow the pattern with what little we have. We must have the Spirit without measure, as Christ had. That is the only thing that will allow us to follow in the footsteps of the pattern Son of God.

This message is not based on Scriptures that vaguely allude to a concept we hope is the truth. The Word of God hammers away, over and over again, on the fact that this is what Jesus did, and this is what we will do. We read in the Book of Ephesians,

> For this reason, I bow my knees before the Father, from whom every family in heaven and on earth derives its name, that He would grant you, according to the riches of His glory, to be strengthened with power through His Spirit in the inner man; so that Christ may dwell in your hearts through faith; and that you, being rooted and grounded in love, may be able to comprehend with all the saints what is the breadth and length and height and depth, and to know the love of Christ which surpasses knowledge, that you may be filled up to all the fulness of God. Now to Him who is able to do exceeding abundantly beyond all that we ask or think, according to the power that works within us. (Ephesians 3:14-20)

There is little room to question what this Scripture is describing. If we missed it in all the other Scriptures, this one is beyond clear. To know the love of God—that is the new covenant we read about in

Jeremiah 31:33-34. In this new covenant, God says, "They shall all know Me, from the least of them to the greatest." This is a guarantee. He is giving you a down payment in which He says, "I promised there would be a new covenant and I would forgive your sins. And the new covenant is that you will know Me and you will be filled with My Spirit." We will "know the love of Christ which surpasses knowledge." God is giving us something that no human can obtain, "that you may be filled up to all the fulness of God." God is able to do this "according to the power that works within us." What is that power? It is the Holy Spirit that we already have within us. By the Spirit, by this down payment, God "is able to do exceeding abundantly beyond all that we ask or think," or can even imagine. We have what we need to trigger the outpouring of His Spirit. We have what we need for that down payment experience to literally become an unceasing outpouring of His fullness. We read in Romans 8,

> And we know that God causes all things to work together for good to those who love God, to those who are called according to His purpose. For whom He foreknew, He also predestined to become conformed to the image of His Son, that He might be the first-born among many brethren; and whom He predestined, these He also called; and whom He called, these He also justified; and whom He justified, these He also glorified. What then shall we say to these things? If God is for us, who is against us? He who did not spare His own Son, but delivered Him up for us all, how will He not also with Him [or by Him] freely give us all things? (Romans 8:28-32)

Jeremiah 31:33-34 "But this is the covenant which I will make with the house of Israel after those days," declares the LORD, "I will put My law within them, and on their heart I will write it; and I will be their God, and they shall be My people. 34 And they shall not teach again, each man his neighbor and each man his brother, saying, 'Know the LORD,' for they shall all know Me, from the least of them to the greatest of them," declares the LORD, "for I will forgive their iniquity, and their sin I will remember no more."

The fullness of Christ is not some unattainable illusion. Christ was the firstborn Son of God who was given as our example. He was also the One who paved the way, who paid the price for us to walk as He walked. He is the way, the truth, and the life (John 14:6). What are we doing on this earth? We are walking in the Way. What is the Way? It is walking as Christ walked, following Him as the example. He was the firstborn Son, and God has predestined us to be conformed to His exact image. We are to be like Him. He is the Savior, but He is also the firstborn among many brethren (Romans 8:29). He is the pattern Son, and He paid the price so that we can follow that pattern. Because He made it, we can make it—by the grace of God, by the Holy Spirit that is in us, and by the predetermined knowledge of God. This is so powerful. God has **predetermined** that we will make it! Do not give up. Do not be discouraged. Do not say, "I don't have anything backing me." You literally have the power and the strength of Almighty God reaching down, focused on you while you are here in the earth crying out to Him. He has already done it once; He gave us Christ, and the path has already been made. He is the way, and we can do it.

Read these Scriptures over and over. I want you to understand that this is our purpose; this is our goal; this is what we are all about. Get rid of any residue of unbelief. Get rid of every bit of resistance within you. Get rid of the lies and false doctrines that say, "Jesus was God-man when He got here." Get rid of all the reasons why you think you cannot walk as He walked. We repent of everything that would distract us from this path of walking as our pattern walked, of doing what our pattern was able to do. I am not looking for just a regular repentance in this; I am looking for the Lord to rewire

---

John 14:6 Jesus said to him, "I am the way, and the truth, and the life; no one comes to the Father, but through Me."

Romans 8:29 For whom He foreknew, He also predestined to become conformed to the image of His Son, that He might be the first-born among many brethren.

our brains! Lord, give us the mind of Christ (1 Corinthians 2:16). We have the same Holy Spirit Christ had, we have the same Father as Christ, and now we have Christ seated at the Father's right hand interceding for us day and night (Romans 8:34). How can we miss it? We take authority over every discouragement. We take authority over everything that would lie to our hearts and say that this is impossible. We take authority over satan's plan to trip us up. Paul said, "I press on to lay hold of the thing for which God laid hold of me, and that is to be like Jesus Christ, the pattern Son" (Philippians 3:12). Sometimes you just have to get mad in your repentance. You need an anger that literally throws off the things that are stopping you. Throw off everything that would turn you aside from crying out to the Lord. Father, we claim that we will receive Your Spirit without measure! That is what will turn the tide. That is what will move us from the Church Age into the Kingdom. There is only one Body of Christ, and that is the fullness of Him that fills all things. We move into that fullness, in the name of the Lord.

---

1 Corinthians 2:16 FOR WHO HAS KNOWN THE MIND OF THE LORD, THAT HE SHOULD INSTRUCT HIM? But we have the mind of Christ.

Romans 8:34 Who is the one who condemns? Christ Jesus is He who died, yes, rather who was raised, who is at the right hand of God, who also intercedes for us.

Philippians 3:12 Not that I have already obtained it, or have already become perfect, but I press on in order that I may lay hold of that for which also I was laid hold of by Christ Jesus.

CHAPTER 8

We Wear the
Mantle of Christ

In the process of the Kingdom of God coming to the earth, the Lord has to deal with that which supplants the Kingdom in every realm. In our prophecies, we have named the realms of Government, Religion, the Arts, Finance, Science, Education, and Health, as well as others. In all of these areas there is that which has supplanted God's Kingdom. When Adam gave up his authority, satan was able to supplant Adam and make himself the ruler over all the earth. Satan has usurped that authority. As we bring satan down, we will not do it in a general way. We will pursue him specifically into all these realms with a determination to uproot him and his supplanters out of every area where they are entrenched. The establishment of God's Kingdom is not just something that happens in a moment, in one day. There may be an instant when every eye will see Him, but the coming of the Kingdom is a process of the Lord taking over all of the earth (Revelation 1:7; 11:15). "The earth is the LORD's,

---

Revelation 1:7 BEHOLD, HE IS COMING WITH THE CLOUDS, and every eye will see Him, even those who pierced Him; and all the tribes of the earth will mourn over Him. Even so. Amen.

Revelation 11:15 And the seventh angel sounded; and there arose loud voices in heaven, saying, "The kingdom of the world has become the kingdom of our Lord, and of His Christ; and He will reign forever and ever."

and the fulness thereof" (Psalm 24:1, KJV). And He has been in the process of bringing His Kingdom to the earth ever since John the Baptist and Jesus preached, "Repent, for the kingdom of heaven is at hand" (Matthew 11:12; 3:2). The Kingdom comes in a way that is similar to a steamroller moving down a road. It does not compact the entire road at once, but it rolls steadily along, and in the process flattens everything that gets in its way. That was the ministry of John the Baptist. His purpose was to raise up the valleys, bring down the mountains, and get everything out of the way for the King (Matthew 3:3; Isaiah 40:3-4). More and more, as we see the coming of the Kingdom of God, we will see our part in this same anointing. That is where prophecy comes in. It frames the ages by the Word. It brings into the visible that which is now invisible (Hebrews 11:3).

It is important for us to understand this principle of the anointing, and I want to go into some of the details of how it works. 2 Kings chapter 2 tells the story of Elijah's mantle falling on Elisha. The Hebrew word for "mantle" is *adderet*, which means the outer cloak or garment that people wore; but it is also translated as "glory." Often the Lord will use a natural term to explain something spiritual, and that is the case when we talk about the mantle. A mantle is obviously something that is worn as a garment, but spiritually it is a glory, or an anointing that is put on. We are talking about receiving an anointing

---

Matthew 11:12 "And from the days of John the Baptist until now the kingdom of heaven suffers violence, and violent men take it by force."

Matthew 3:3 For this is the one referred to by Isaiah the prophet, saying, "THE VOICE OF ONE CRYING IN THE WILDERNESS, 'MAKE READY THE WAY OF THE LORD, MAKE HIS PATHS STRAIGHT!'"

Isaiah 40:3-4 A voice is calling, "Clear the way for the LORD in the wilderness; make smooth in the desert a highway for our God. 4 Let every valley be lifted up, and every mountain and hill be made low; and let the rough ground become a plain, and the rugged terrain a broad valley."

Hebrews 11:3 By faith we understand that the worlds were prepared by the word of God, so that what is seen was not made out of things which are visible.

from God that is passed on, just as Elijah's mantle was passed on to Elisha (2 Kings 2:13-15). I want you to see what is meant by the mantle, and what happens by virtue of the mantle being passed on, because this principle did not die with Elijah and Elisha. It greatly impacts our lives today.

Let's read from the 17th chapter of John. This is Jesus' prayer before He was crucified, and although He was praying to the Father, He was also teaching and explaining things to those who were around Him. We need this teaching very much and we need to trust that this prayer by the Lord will have its fulfillment.

> "As Thou didst send Me into the world, I also have sent them into the world. And for their sakes I sanctify Myself, that they themselves also may be sanctified in truth. I do not ask in behalf of these alone, but for those also who believe in Me through their word; that they may all be one; even as Thou, Father, art in Me, and I in Thee, that they also may be in Us; that the world may believe that Thou didst send Me. And the glory which Thou hast given Me I have given to them, that they may be one, just as We are one; I in them, and Thou in Me, that they may be perfected in unity, that the world may know that Thou didst send Me, and didst love them, even as Thou didst love Me. Father, I desire that they also, whom Thou hast given Me, be with Me where I am, in order that they may behold My glory, which Thou hast given Me; for Thou didst love Me before the foundation of the world." (John 17:18-24)

---

2 Kings 2:13-15 He also took up the mantle of Elijah that fell from him, and returned and stood by the bank of the Jordan. [14] And he took the mantle of Elijah that fell from him, and struck the waters and said, "Where is the LORD, the God of Elijah?" And when he also had struck the waters, they were divided here and there; and Elisha crossed over. [15] Now when the sons of the prophets who were at Jericho opposite him saw him, they said, "The spirit of Elijah rests on Elisha." And they came to meet him and bowed themselves to the ground before him.

In many Bible schools and seminaries it is taught that Christ's anointing only applied to the twelve apostles. But that is refuted in this very prayer, because Jesus said, "I do not ask in behalf of these alone, but for those also who believe in Me through their word" (John 17:20). The prayer to the Father that Jesus was voicing was not only for those who were there listening to Him. He explained specifically who else the prayer was for. If you have believed in Jesus Christ through the Gospel, then this prayer applies to you. It is for those in any generation who believe by virtue of the witness about Jesus. It is important for us to know that what He is saying is ours. "That they may all be one; even as Thou, Father, art in Me, and I in Thee, that they also may be in Us" (John 17:21). Jesus is including all of us in what He and the Father have. He and the Father were already one, and He prayed that we would be one just as they are.

Then Jesus said, "And the glory which Thou hast given Me I have given to them" (John 17:22). We can word that a little differently: "And the **mantle** which Thou hast given Me I have given to them." The things that we are to move in will not happen because we try hard or work things up in ourselves. They will happen by virtue of the mantle. The mantle that passed from Elijah to Elisha was the glory that had rested on Elijah. It was not just a cloak or a coat. So when Jesus said, "The glory which Thou hast given Me I have given to them," He was describing a process that had come to its conclusion, but was also to continue. He was announcing to the disciples, "I am putting something on you that you have not had up to this point." He was talking about something new. Jesus Himself was getting ready to move into a new level, to receive a new glory at the right hand of the Father, and something had to happen with the mantle that He carried while He was on the earth (Acts 2:33). It could not just be thrown away. Elijah did not just throw away

---

Acts 2:33 "Therefore having been exalted to the right hand of God, and having received from the Father the promise of the Holy Spirit, He has poured forth this which you both see and hear."

his mantle, saying, "I've got to get out from under this old mantle, this old anointing!" No, he threw it on Elisha. Jesus was doing the same thing. Having come as the Son of God manifested in the flesh, crucified, resurrected, and ascending to the Father, Jesus could not just drop what He had established on the earth. He had established the mantle of being the Son of God, Christ in the flesh, carrying the glory of the Father on Himself as a human vessel. He could not just discard that mantle and say, "It's finished! I'm done, and now I will return to the right hand of the Father." No, He had to pass on that mantle. He had to do something with that glory.

The Scriptures tell us that there are different glories. "There is one glory of the sun, and another glory of the moon, and another glory of the stars; for star differs from star in glory" (1 Corinthians 15:41). There are levels of glory, and the different glories are necessary because we grow and become by virtue of going from one glory to another (2 Corinthians 3:18). The disciples had moved in much already, but now Jesus was giving them something new. He gave them His mantle, because He was about to get a new one. While Jesus was on the earth, He was perfected (Hebrews 5:8-9). Part of His mantle, the glory that rested on Him, was His perfection as the Son of God in the flesh on the earth. Now He was sending the disciples just as the Father had sent Him. He was giving them His glory. So He prayed, "Father, I desire that they also, whom Thou hast given Me, be with Me where I am, in order that they may behold My glory, which Thou hast given Me" (John 17:24). Jesus was getting ready to receive another glory, which was His manifestation at the right hand of the Father, so He asked the Father for something else. Not

---

2 Corinthians 3:18 But we all, with unveiled face beholding as in a mirror the glory of the Lord, are being transformed into the same image from glory to glory, just as from the Lord, the Spirit.

Hebrews 5:8-9 Although He was a Son, He learned obedience from the things which He suffered. 9 And having been made perfect, He became to all those who obey Him the source of eternal salvation.

only was He putting His current mantle, or glory, on the disciples and on successive generations who would believe by virtue of the Gospel, but He also wanted them to see the glory that He would receive as His new mantle. Therefore He said, "Father, I do not want them to only be aware of what they have now. I want them to see the glory that I am receiving, because someday that will be theirs also."

Jesus had promised them, saying, "I will not leave you as orphans," yet He also said, "It is better for you if I go" (John 14:18; 16:7). Why? Because only by His going to the Father are we able to receive the glory that was on Him. We could not receive Christ's glory until He was able to divest Himself of it and move into the next level of glory. Now we have received His glory; however, there is still something missing in our thinking. When we think of the manifestation of glory, we think of something that comes and goes, but that is not the way it is with a mantle. You have to put on a mantle. You wear it! The glory did not come and go from Jesus. It was a mantle that He wore. The Holy Spirit descended on Him and remained on Him (John 1:32-33). It was by virtue of the Holy Spirit that He was filled with all the fullness of God and manifested everything He did on earth (Colossians 1:19). This same mantle has been imparted to us. When the Holy Spirit fell on the Day of Pentecost, we saw the literal fulfillment of Christ's prayer to the Father. At that point, Jesus had been crucified and resurrected, and had ascended to the right hand of God. Without question He had moved into the next glory, and the Holy Spirit, which was the mantle that rested on Him, had fallen

---

John 14:18 "I will not leave you as orphans; I will come to you."

John 16:7 "But I tell you the truth, it is to your advantage that I go away; for if I do not go away, the Helper shall not come to you; but if I go, I will send Him to you."

John 1:32-33 And John bore witness saying, "I have beheld the Spirit descending as a dove out of heaven, and He remained upon Him. 33 And I did not recognize Him, but He who sent me to baptize in water said to me, 'He upon whom you see the Spirit descending and remaining upon Him, this is the one who baptizes in the Holy Spirit.'"

Colossians 1:19 For it was the Father's good pleasure for all the fulness to dwell in Him.

out of heaven onto those who had gathered on that day. When Peter described this event, quoting from the prophet Joel, he said,

> "For these men are not drunk, as you suppose, for it is only the third hour of the day; but this is what was spoken of through the prophet Joel:
>> 'AND IT SHALL BE IN THE LAST DAYS,' God says,
>> 'THAT I WILL POUR FORTH OF MY SPIRIT UPON ALL MANKIND;
>> AND YOUR SONS AND YOUR DAUGHTERS SHALL PROPHESY,
>> AND YOUR YOUNG MEN SHALL SEE VISIONS,
>> AND YOUR OLD MEN SHALL DREAM DREAMS;
>> EVEN UPON MY BONDSLAVES, BOTH MEN AND WOMEN,
>> I WILL IN THOSE DAYS POUR FORTH OF MY SPIRIT
> And they shall prophesy.'" (Acts 2:15-18)

The pouring forth of the Spirit was the falling of the mantle that had rested upon Jesus while He walked on the earth as the Son of Man, carrying the presence of God. He was Immanuel, God with us, by virtue of the anointing of the Holy Spirit and the mantle that rested upon Him (Matthew 1:22-23). This mantle was taken off of Christ and fell on those who believed, so that they would carry it. In theory, the earth was never left without this mantle remaining on the believers. It was given to every generation, to all who would believe, not only to those who were sitting there listening to Jesus pray. The anointing, the glory, and the presence of God that rested upon Jesus as the Son of Man in the flesh, was divested and imparted to the believers. It should rest upon us today as the continuation of those who believe by His Word. That outpouring of the Holy Spirit

---

Matthew 1:22-23   Now all this took place that what was spoken by the Lord through the prophet might be fulfilled, saying, [23] "BEHOLD, THE VIRGIN SHALL BE WITH CHILD, AND SHALL BEAR A SON, AND THEY SHALL CALL HIS NAME IMMANUEL," which translated means, "GOD WITH US."

was not to be an end in itself. Peter emphasized this when he said, "For the promise is for you and your children, and for all who are far off, as many as the Lord our God shall call to Himself" (Acts 2:39). In other words, we can have this experience today.

This tremendous outpouring of the Spirit, and the mantle that was on Jesus, is what Joel spoke of: "And it will come about after this that I will pour out My Spirit on all mankind; and your sons and daughters will prophesy" (Joel 2:28). What is the manifestation of Christ's mantle? It is prophecy. As the anointing rests upon us, it has this expression of prophetic utterance. It is the proof of the anointing. It is not something that we make up. Peter wrote, "For no prophecy was ever made by an act of human will, but men moved by the Holy Spirit spoke from God" (2 Peter 1:21). Jesus said, "My Words are spirit and they are life" (John 6:63). He spoke from the glory, by this anointing, to preach and bring forth the Kingdom of God on the earth. That is why, when this mantle of anointing falls, believers begin to prophesy; prophecy is the first manifestation of Christ's appearing in our human flesh. So I expect prophecy to come out of our mouths as the response to this mantle resting on us. If we missed that gift somewhere and do not have it, then we can appropriate it because it has been poured out upon us.

As Peter spoke on the Day of Pentecost, he continued to quote from the prophet Joel: "AND I WILL GRANT WONDERS IN THE SKY ABOVE, AND SIGNS ON THE EARTH BENEATH, BLOOD, AND FIRE, AND VAPOR OF SMOKE" (Acts 2:19). When Peter voiced this prophecy he went beyond what was manifesting right there for them and he spoke about the judgments and manifestations of the Kingdom. He was speaking about that which is invisible beginning to manifest in the realm of the visible. How? Through the spirit of prophecy. That is what Jesus did. He said, "Why do you ask Me to show you the Father?

John 6:63 "It is the Spirit who gives life; the flesh profits nothing; the words that I have spoken to you are spirit and are life."

If you have seen Me, you have seen the Father" (John 14:9). By virtue of the anointing, He was manifesting that which was invisible. That is where the healings and miracles came from. I almost hate to call them miracles, because they were manifestations of what exists in the Kingdom of God. When we see a miracle in this realm it simply means that we are seeing the Kingdom of God manifested among us; it becomes evident where before it was not. In everything Jesus did, whether He healed someone or cast out demons, He proclaimed, "This is being done by the Spirit of God; therefore the Kingdom of God has come near to you" (Luke 10:9; Matthew 12:28).

I understand that seeing wonders in the heavens above and signs in the earth beneath—blood, fire, and smoke—can seem scary, but don't be afraid of these end-time manifestations. Keep your eyes on the Kingdom. The important thing that is happening is not the judgments, or the smoke, or this or that beast with ten horns (Revelation 13:1). If you get your eyes on those things, you are getting your eyes off of Christ coming as the King of kings and Lord of lords, manifesting the Kingdom of God (Revelation 19:16). We read in Joel chapter 2 about a mighty people. It is like the Garden of Eden before

---

John 14:9 Jesus said to him, "Have I been so long with you, and yet you have not come to know Me, Philip? He who has seen Me has seen the Father; how do you say, 'Show us the Father'?"

Luke 10:9 "And heal those in it who are sick, and say to them, 'The kingdom of God has come near to you.'"

Matthew 12:28 "But if I cast out demons by the Spirit of God, then the kingdom of God has come upon you."

Revelation 13:1 And he stood on the sand of the seashore. And I saw a beast coming up out of the sea, having ten horns and seven heads, and on his horns were ten diadems, and on his heads were blasphemous names.

Revelation 19:16 And on His robe and on His thigh He has a name written, "KING OF KINGS, AND LORD OF LORDS."

them and behind them a desolate wilderness (Joel 2:2-3). This is a positive picture because it is the coming forth of the Kingdom. All of these other manifestations happen while God removes that which is standing in the way of His Kingdom. Not everyone is happy about that. Not everyone was happy about John the Baptist; he raised a few problems here and there. But don't look at the problems. We are those who are looking for and manifesting the Kingdom of God in the earth. I dislike the way that so many people make the coming of the Kingdom of God such a negative and fearful thing. That is why Christians start calling for a "rapture": "I don't want to go through this. Get me out of here!" My thinking is different. I want to be here because I want to manifest the Kingdom of God in the earth through this anointing of prophecy, by virtue of this mantle that Christ left us, which is the same mantle that He carried when He was here.

That anointing is Christ, from the Greek word *christos*, which is carried over from the Hebrew word *mashiach*, or Messiah, meaning "the anointed." That is the mantle. It is the glory. Jesus did not take that anointing with Him; He gave it to us. We have the feeling, "Jesus is gone. Where is He? We want Him back!" But the anointing, the *christos*, has never left. People recognized that reality when they started calling the believers Christians, or "the anointed ones" (Acts 11:26). They acknowledged that Jesus had moved into a new glory, and the glory that had been on Him in the earth was now resting on His people. Therefore, the work of Jesus would continue.

Joel 2:2-3   A day of darkness and gloom, a day of clouds and thick darkness. As the dawn is spread over the mountains, so there is a great and mighty people; there has never been anything like it, nor will there be again after it to the years of many generations. ³ A fire consumes before them, and behind them a flame burns. The land is like the garden of Eden before them, but a desolate wilderness behind them, and nothing at all escapes them.

Acts 11:26   And when he had found him, he brought him to Antioch. And it came about that for an entire year they met with the church, and taught considerable numbers; and the disciples were first called Christians in Antioch.

We are to be the Christ, the anointing from God the Father in the earth right now. And we had better pick up that mantle as Elisha did, smite the waters, and say, "Where is the power, the authority, the ability to move as God's people in the earth?" (2 Kings 2:14). Jesus has a new mantle, a new anointing, and He is doing what He needs to be doing. We have to make sure that the mantle He has given us is not dropped.

Unfortunately, that is what happened. Not long after Jesus left, the mantle of Christ was dropped. Sure, occasionally individuals have picked it up. Once in a while someone like Smith Wigglesworth or John Stevens comes on the scene; but we have not seen the consistent ministry of Christ's anointing as we should have it in the earth. John Stevens talked about us being Christ in the flesh. The mantle was the anointing on the flesh of man; Christ was the Word made flesh (John 1:14). The mantle that Christ established was never supposed to leave the earth. So why do we live in a world that is devoid of the anointing? That is the biggest robbery and deception that the Church has ever seen, and we have allowed it to happen. The believers were to simply carry on what Christ walked in as He went on into something greater.

"The gifts and calling of God are without repentance" (Romans 11:29, KJV). That means that the anointing He puts on you never goes away. So why do we allow there to be no anointing in the earth? Jesus finished what He was supposed to do as the Anointed, as the Messiah, but when He left, we were supposed to pick up that mantle so that the anointing of Christ in the earth would never go away. How has the Church missed the point that what God started with Christ, with the anointing, with the mantle, was never supposed to

---

John 1:14   And the Word became flesh, and dwelt among us, and we beheld His glory, glory as of the only begotten from the Father, full of grace and truth.

go away? When God took Elijah, his mantle had to stay here on the earth. That mantle of prophetic anointing did stay on the earth because it is a ministry to the earth. Elijah did not need to be that prophet after he was translated. Christ is now seated at the right hand of the Father. He is the King of kings and Lord of lords. He has transitioned into another ministry, into wearing another mantle. When the Holy Spirit fell, that was the mantle of the *christos*, the Messiah, remaining in the earth where it belongs because it is a ministry to the earth.

Now we can understand why it is better that Jesus went away, because for us and for the world the mantle has been extended to all believers (John 16:7). Before Jesus left, He commissioned the seventy to go out, but when they returned, the mantle returned as well (Luke 10:1). This was just a taste of what was to come, because at some point the mantle of the Holy Spirit was to descend and remain on the disciples, as it had descended and remained on Jesus. That should be the place the Body of Christ starts from, because God's plan for us is to keep moving from glory to glory. Jesus said, "I go to prepare a place for you" (John 14:2). He moved into another glory; that is the next step that we should enter into. As we are perfected in oneness, the world will believe because God's glory is resting on us. We still wonder, "Why doesn't the world believe; why does everything seem to disintegrate?" The answer to that question is, because the Body of Christ does not wear this mantle. If they did, the world would believe.

Luke 10:1 Now after this the Lord appointed seventy others, and sent them two and two ahead of Him to every city and place where He Himself was going to come.

John 14:2 "In My Father's house are many dwelling places; if it were not so, I would have told you; for I go to prepare a place for you."

The mantle that Christianity is wearing today is actually the first mantle in the story of Elijah and Elisha (1 Kings 19:19-21). Elisha put on the mantle and served the man of God. We still see ourselves as servants: "I just want to be a servant. I want to serve Jesus." We are serving, but we are serving with no anointing. There is no power in our serving. Jesus was not in the earth without power. He was not lacking in anointing. He was the Anointed One. He was the Christ. He was the Messiah. Whatever term you use, that is what He was all about. He said, "I can do nothing of Myself" (John 5:19). He served the Father, but He served Him in the anointing. The Body of Christ should not just be servants of Jesus doing a lot of good works. We should be anointed with the same mantle that Jesus wore, the mantle that turns water into wine, speaks and the wind ceases, speaks Words of spirit and life, heals the sick, casts out demons, and gives life to the dead. Jesus said, "In My name, you will do many mighty works" (Mark 16:17-18). But we cannot do those works without His anointing, without His mantle. We are to be the *christos*, to wear the anointing, to wear the mantle. Then we can move as the servants of God. That was what happened for the 120 on the Day of Pentecost. We read in the Book of Acts how

---

1 Kings 19:19-21 So he departed from there and found Elisha the son of Shaphat, while he was plowing with twelve pairs of oxen before him, and he with the twelfth. And Elijah passed over to him and threw his mantle on him. ²⁰ And he left the oxen and ran after Elijah and said, "Please let me kiss my father and my mother, then I will follow you." And he said to him, "Go back again, for what have I done to you?" ²¹ So he returned from following him, and took the pair of oxen and sacrificed them and boiled their flesh with the implements of the oxen, and gave it to the people and they ate. Then he arose and followed Elijah and ministered to him.

John 5:19 Jesus therefore answered and was saying to them, "Truly, truly, I say to you, the Son can do nothing of Himself, unless it is something He sees the Father doing; for whatever the Father does, these things the Son also does in like manner."

Mark 16:17-18 "And these signs will accompany those who have believed: in My name they will cast out demons, they will speak with new tongues; ¹⁸ they will pick up serpents, and if they drink any deadly poison, it shall not hurt them; they will lay hands on the sick, and they will recover."

they moved in power and in miracles. Peter's shadow healed the sick (Acts 5:12-16). They spoke the Word of God with all boldness (Acts 4:31). Why did those things happen? Because they were moving in the anointing. Where did we lose that in Christianity? When did we as believers remove Christ's mantle and start being unanointed servants? That is not what the story of Elijah and Elisha teaches us. That is not what Jesus prayed for in John chapter 17. That is not who we are.

Let's take up the mantle that Jesus gave us when He baptized us in His Holy Spirit. The mantle is the glory that He carried when He was here, and we are the continuation of that glory in the earth. God did not bring that glory simply to take it away and have the earth devoid of His glory. The manifestation of that glory by Jesus was the first step in the manifestation of the Kingdom of God in the earth. Now we are to do that. The mantle brings about the prophetic flow that will progressively uproot all that has displaced God's Kingdom in every realm, and replace it with the Kingdom of God. It is important for you to take stock of where you are in God, what you have, and what you do not have. Ask yourself, "What am I doing as a believer? What am I moving in? Am I just trying to be a humble servant of Jesus without any anointing?" We repent. Repentance means to turn away. We must turn away from how we

---

Acts 5:12-16 And at the hands of the apostles many signs and wonders were taking place among the people; and they were all with one accord in Solomon's portico. [13] But none of the rest dared to associate with them; however, the people held them in high esteem. [14] And all the more believers in the Lord, multitudes of men and women, were constantly added to their number; [15] to such an extent that they even carried the sick out into the streets, and laid them on cots and pallets, so that when Peter came by, at least his shadow might fall on any one of them. [16] And also the people from the cities in the vicinity of Jerusalem were coming together, bringing people who were sick or afflicted with unclean spirits; and they were all being healed.

Acts 4:31 And when they had prayed, the place where they had gathered together was shaken, and they were all filled with the Holy Spirit, and began to speak the word of God with boldness.

have approached serving the Lord. Go back and pick up the mantle. Put on the mantle and become God's anointed, standing as Christ stood in the flesh. Just move in it. Believe it, do it, and become it!

CHAPTER 9

Atonement: Our Promise of Sanctification

I want us to lay hold of something about the Day of Atonement. It is one of the feasts of the Lord that we have studied for many years in our fellowship. God commanded His people to come together three times a year and appear before Him (Exodus 23:14). It was during these appointed times that seven feasts were celebrated, and each of these feasts has had a fulfillment, or is yet to have a fulfillment. Many of them have already been fulfilled, but one feast in particular has not, and we have put a great deal of emphasis on believing for its fulfillment. That is the Feast of Tabernacles. We are anticipating the time when the Lord will inhabit, or tabernacle with, His people. We also have not seen the complete fulfillment of the Day of Atonement, and its fulfillment is actually necessary to the fulfillment of Tabernacles.

First of all, let's summarize the feasts and how each one has been fulfilled in the generation of the Church. The first feast is the Feast of Passover, where each household in Israel killed a lamb in

Exodus 23:14 "Three times a year you shall celebrate a feast to Me."

remembrance of the time they escaped judgment by the blood of the lamb (Exodus 12:4, 13). Christ our Passover Lamb, who was slain for us, is the fulfillment in the Church Age of the Feast of Passover (1 Corinthians 5:7). Immediately after Passover, the Feast of Unleavened Bread was observed for seven days (Leviticus 23:6). In the Feast of Unleavened Bread we see the beginning of the Church's new relationship with Christ. Because of His crucifixion at Passover, the disciples were forced to break their bonds with the Lord Himself. It was during the Feast of Unleavened Bread that the disciples, who had known Christ after the flesh, knew Him thus no longer (2 Corinthians 5:16). The Feast of Unleavened Bread is a new start, a new beginning. Once Christ is resurrected and comes and finishes His work, we have to relate to everything anew. The leaven of our old thoughts, ways, and concepts has to be swept out so that we are a new lump of dough (1 Corinthians 5:7). God makes us relate to Christ, and to one another in the Body of Christ, in an entirely new way.

During the seven days of unleavened bread is the Feast of the First Fruits. On this feast day, the priest waved a sheaf of the first

---

Exodus 12:4 "Now if the household is too small for a lamb, then he and his neighbor nearest to his house are to take one according to the number of persons in them; according to what each man should eat, you are to divide the lamb."

Exodus 12:13 "And the blood shall be a sign for you on the houses where you live; and when I see the blood I will pass over you, and no plague will befall you to destroy you when I strike the land of Egypt."

1 Corinthians 5:7 Clean out the old leaven, that you may be a new lump, just as you are in fact unleavened. For Christ our Passover also has been sacrificed.

Leviticus 23:6 "Then on the fifteenth day of the same month there is the Feast of Unleavened Bread to the LORD; for seven days you shall eat unleavened bread."

2 Corinthians 5:16 Therefore from now on we recognize no man according to the flesh; even though we have known Christ according to the flesh, yet now we know Him thus no longer.

fruits of the barley harvest before the Lord (Leviticus 23:9-11). Again we see the fulfillment in Christ who is the first fruits of the resurrection (1 Corinthians 15:20). In fact, the priest would have stood in the Temple waving the sheaf of the first fruits at the time when Christ was resurrected. And so the Feast of the First Fruits is extremely significant for us. It is always speaking about the resurrected Lord. Then we come to the Feast of Pentecost, which we know was the beginning of the Church (Leviticus 23:15-16; Acts 2:1-4). It was literally the formation of the Body of Christ by the Holy Spirit. The Spirit was poured out upon the Church with power, so that we might be His Body and His witnesses in all the earth (Acts 1:8). The next feast is the Feast of Trumpets, and the Church has seen wonderful fulfillments of this feast (Leviticus 23:23-24). The fulfillment of the Feast of Trumpets is still unfolding, because

---

Leviticus 23:9-11 Then the LORD spoke to Moses, saying, [10] "Speak to the sons of Israel, and say to them, 'When you enter the land which I am going to give to you and reap its harvest, then you shall bring in the sheaf of the first fruits of your harvest to the priest. [11] And he shall wave the sheaf before the LORD for you to be accepted; on the day after the sabbath the priest shall wave it.'"

1 Corinthians 15:20 But now Christ has been raised from the dead, the first fruits of those who are asleep.

Leviticus 23:15-16 "You shall also count for yourselves from the day after the sabbath, from the day when you brought in the sheaf of the wave offering; there shall be seven complete sabbaths. [16] You shall count fifty days to the day after the seventh sabbath; then you shall present a new grain offering to the LORD."

Acts 2:1-4 And when the day of Pentecost had come, they were all together in one place. [2] And suddenly there came from heaven a noise like a violent, rushing wind, and it filled the whole house where they were sitting. [3] And there appeared to them tongues as of fire distributing themselves, and they rested on each one of them. [4] And they were all filled with the Holy Spirit and began to speak with other tongues, as the Spirit was giving them utterance.

Acts 1:8 "But you shall receive power when the Holy Spirit has come upon you; and you shall be My witnesses both in Jerusalem, and in all Judea and Samaria, and even to the remotest part of the earth."

Leviticus 23:23-24 Again the LORD spoke to Moses, saying, [24] "Speak to the sons of Israel, saying, 'In the seventh month on the first of the month, you shall have a rest, a reminder by blowing of trumpets, a holy convocation.'"

it is always moving to a higher level. The spiritual outpourings that occurred at the end of the nineteenth and beginning of the twentieth centuries saw the release of the gifts and ministries of the Holy Spirit. One of the greatest manifestations from that time, which continues to unfold, is the ability to speak a Living Word from God. This is our fulfillment of the Feast of Trumpets: the manifestation of speaking the Word of God.

Now we come to the Day of Atonement (Leviticus 23:26-27). On the Day of Atonement one goat was sacrificed for the sanctification of the people, the tent of meeting, and the priests, which is reminiscent of what was done at Passover. However, there was a second goat, which exists nowhere else in the Law concerning sacrifices, and is unique to the Day of Atonement. This second goat is the goat of removal (the scapegoat or *azazel*), upon which the high priest laid his hands, literally imparting to it the sins of the people. The sacrifice of the first goat cleansed them of their actions of sin and iniquity. Then the second goat, the goat of removal, removed the very nature of sin (Leviticus 16:15-16, 20-22). In Christ's sacrifice on the cross, He forgave our acts of sin and iniquity, but He also

---

Leviticus 23:26-27   And the LORD spoke to Moses, saying, [27] "On exactly the tenth day of this seventh month is the day of atonement; it shall be a holy convocation for you, and you shall humble your souls and present an offering by fire to the LORD."

Leviticus 16:15-16   "Then he shall slaughter the goat of the sin offering which is for the people, and bring its blood inside the veil, and do with its blood as he did with the blood of the bull, and sprinkle it on the mercy seat and in front of the mercy seat. [16] And he shall make atonement for the holy place, because of the impurities of the sons of Israel, and because of their transgressions, in regard to all their sins; and thus he shall do for the tent of meeting which abides with them in the midst of their impurities."

Leviticus 16:20-22   "When he finishes atoning for the holy place, and the tent of meeting and the altar, he shall offer the live goat. [21] Then Aaron shall lay both of his hands on the head of the live goat, and confess over it all the iniquities of the sons of Israel, and all their transgressions in regard to all their sins; and he shall lay them on the head of the goat and send it away into the wilderness by the hand of a man who stands in readiness. [22] And the goat shall bear on itself all their iniquities to a solitary land; and he shall release the goat in the wilderness."

removed the nature of sin. All of our sin and iniquity was placed on Him (Isaiah 53:6). In a very real way Christ is the goat of removal who carries all of our iniquity outside the camp (Hebrews 13:12-13). Christ subsequently put that iniquity on satan, sending him to the abyss along with our sin nature, thus getting rid of it. Then, in His resurrection Christ returns to the camp to dwell with His people (Leviticus 16:27-28).

The Day of Atonement leads into the Feast of Tabernacles, the seventh feast of the year (Leviticus 23:39, 42-43). We know that we are yet to see the fulfillment of Tabernacles, but what about the Day of Atonement? We have not seen the complete fulfillment of that feast either. Our emphasis has been almost entirely on the fulfillment of Tabernacles, but we need to back up and realize that the Church, as the Body of Christ, is in desperate need of the fulfillment of the Day of Atonement. We know this is possible by looking at what God has done in all the other feasts. What He has done is not just a fulfillment; it is exceedingly, abundantly above all that we could

---

Isaiah 53:6 All of us like sheep have gone astray, each of us has turned to his own way; but the LORD has caused the iniquity of us all to fall on Him.

Hebrews 13:12-13 Therefore Jesus also, that He might sanctify the people through His own blood, suffered outside the gate. [13] Hence, let us go out to Him outside the camp, bearing His reproach.

Leviticus 16:27-28 "But the bull of the sin offering and the goat of the sin offering, whose blood was brought in to make atonement in the holy place, shall be taken outside the camp, and they shall burn their hides, their flesh, and their refuse in the fire. [28] Then the one who burns them shall wash his clothes and bathe his body with water, then afterward he shall come into the camp."

Leviticus 23:39 "On exactly the fifteenth day of the seventh month, when you have gathered in the crops of the land, you shall celebrate the feast of the LORD for seven days, with a rest on the first day and a rest on the eighth day."

Leviticus 23:42-43 "You shall live in booths for seven days; all the native-born in Israel shall live in booths, [43] so that your generations may know that I had the sons of Israel live in booths when I brought them out from the land of Egypt. I am the LORD your God."

ask or think (Ephesians 3:20). Who would have ever dreamed of the salvation experience that was to come in Passover? What Christ did in bringing about our salvation is far beyond what our minds are able to conceive. It is also amazing what we have in Pentecost in the availability of the Holy Spirit to us. Each one of these feasts is a building block in the restoration of the Church, and what God is doing in our generation. Now we are ready for Him to add this building block of Atonement, because we really need it.

What is the Day of Atonement dealing with? Atonement deals with the elimination of the nature of sin in the believer. The Church has put way too much emphasis on the acts of sin. Christians are so hung up with thinking, "If you do that sin, it is really bad," then other sins are deemed to be not so bad. We completely miss the point when we think that way. The acts or manifestations of sin that we have are like leaves and branches on a tree, but the root is the nature of sin that exists in man. The nature of sin has to be dealt with, and that is what the Day of Atonement is all about. I wish that we could become very wholehearted and intense about this, because this is absolutely the next step for the Body of Christ. This is not something we can be passive about. When we really get ahold of this concept of the sin nature that exists, and removing that nature from the believer, it doesn't take long to understand why we skip over Atonement and jump right into Tabernacles. At Tabernacles, we are believing for the Lord to appear. That is easy to believe for. All He has to do is walk through the wall or descend in a cloud. It is easy to believe for because we know He is so capable of doing it. But Atonement deals with what needs to transpire in us. More than that, it is the prelude to Tabernacles, His presence dwelling with us.

Atonement is something that has been identified and recognized for a long time in the history of the Church. It is not some strange

---

Ephesians 3:20 Now to Him who is able to do exceeding abundantly beyond all that we ask or think, according to the power that works within us.

doctrine that I made up. There is a tremendous history behind the recognition that in Christ there is the work of justification and the work of sanctification. Salvation is our justification in Christ, the forgiveness of our sin; but there is also the experience of sanctification, which is the removing of the nature of sin so that the believer no longer lives a sinful life. Doctrinally, people have recognized and grappled with this in the Church for a long time. The man who is at the very center of this issue is John Wesley. He is literally the father of all modern theology and doctrine about sanctification, which is what Atonement is all about. Let's read from an article about John Wesley in *The International Standard Bible Encyclopedia*:

> John Wesley (1703–1791), who must be regarded as the father of virtually all modern teaching on personal holiness or sanctification and specifically of the teaching concerning "entire sanctification in this life.".…
>
> Following the pattern of orthodox Protestantism, Wesley maintained a strict distinction between justification and sanctification. According to Wesley justification is an objective act of God by which human beings are forgiven their sins, delivered from guilt, and restored to favor with God. But sanctification is a subjective and inward change, a genuine renewal of an individual beginning in the new birth. …Thus Wesley could argue that although justification and the beginning of sanctification "are joined together in point of time, yet they are of wholly distinct natures" (*Standard Sermons*, I, 299f; cf. p. 119). …
>
> According to Wesley full or "entire" sanctification, perfect holiness, is possible in this life. No Christian who has

experienced conversion and divine forgiveness can fail to desire perfection and strive for it.[10]

Everyone who has walked with God for any period of time realizes that when you receive salvation from the Lord, you are immediately thrown into a conflict. You realize that there is still the sin nature living in you. That does not take away your eternal salvation. It does not take away from the fact that God loves you, that Christ died for you, His blood cleanses you, and that you will live with Christ forever. All of those things are in place where justification is concerned. What is missing is our sanctification, the deliverance from the sin nature that is in us. Let's read what the apostle Paul had to say about this:

> For we know that the Law is spiritual; but I am of flesh, sold into bondage to sin. For that which I am doing, I do not understand; for I am not practicing what I would like to do, but I am doing the very thing I hate. But if I do the very thing I do not wish to do, I agree with the Law, confessing that it is good. So now, no longer am I the one doing it, but sin which indwells me. For I know that nothing good dwells in me, that is, in my flesh; for the wishing is present in me, but the doing of the good is not. (Romans 7:14-18)

Paul is not frustrated here; he is speaking from his spirit. He is describing how the spirit, which is redeemed in the justification and salvation of Jesus Christ, wars against the nature of sin from Adam that still remains following that experience. We are believing for the fulfillment of Tabernacles. We are drawing the indwelling of Jesus Christ and the indwelling of the Father into our being. As Jesus said,

---

[10.] R.A. Muller, "Sanctification," in *The International Standard Bible Encyclopedia, Revised*, ed. Geoffrey W. Bromiley (Grand Rapids, MI: William B. Eerdmans Publishing Company, 1979-1988), 4:330.

"My Father and I will take up Our abode in you" (John 14:2ɔ).
God cannot abide with sin, can He? So we have a problem. We have
to get rid of these squatters before the owner can move back into
the house. We face this dilemma. Anyone who is a believer, who
has received salvation, who has walked with God, and tells you that
this is not the case is lying to you. Down through the ages, people
have denied the reality of this conflict because it was too difficult
to confront. John Wesley faced the same conflict, but rather than
explain it away, he chose to believe for something that Christians
had not experienced before—real sanctification. The Methodist
revival, the Holiness movement, and a lot of the Pentecostal
movements were all literally ushered in through Wesley's faith in
sanctification. To usher in something new, Wesley had to be one of
those who pushed against a wall of unbelief and said, "By faith we
have it." Maybe they did not get that wall to move, but they stood
with their noses pressed up against it, and they stood there for a
very long time.

Let me give you an example of this. John Wesley was influenced and
inspired by the Moravians, who were absolutely amazing when it
came to prayer. They had two groups of twenty-four people each,
one group of women and one group of men. Each person in the
group would pray one hour a day, so that by the time everyone
in the group prayed, they had prayed for twenty-four hours. As a
result, there were two groups of people praying twenty-four hours
a day all the time. Would you like to know how long they did that?
They did it for a hundred years, nonstop! So if we think that we have
really been into intercession, and now we're discouraged because
we prayed for a couple of months and nothing happened—these
people prayed for a hundred years! Their prayers literally initiated
and ignited the great revivals of the nineteenth century, which were

---

John 14:23 Jesus answered and said to him, "If anyone loves Me, he will keep My word;
and My Father will love him, and We will come to him, and make Our abode with him."

inspired by John Wesley. This led to the hungering and thirsting for holiness that sparked the outpourings of the twentieth century. I wish we could get the spirit of that, because that is the kind of drive it will take to initiate and experience the Day of Atonement. I loose us to be that hungry. The churches in our fellowship were started by people who were hungry, and who sought the Lord for the new things that God was about to do. I loose us to have the same drive that existed in those who said, "It doesn't matter that this has never happened before. If it is in the Word, then it is ours!"

Having this kind of drive is not necessarily easy or fun. That is why many have turned to doctrines like dispensationalism, which teaches that what God is doing is dependent on the age, or dispensation, you live in. Whenever you cannot get something from God, all you have to do is declare that it is not for this time and therefore it cannot happen. If you cannot receive the Holy Spirit, you can say, "The baptism of the Holy Spirit is not for this age." I have heard that said for just about every one of the New Testament experiences: "There are no more apostles and prophets. There are no more outpourings of the Holy Spirit. There are no more healings and miracles." When it comes to certain beliefs in the Church, some say there is just about no more of anything! I am not trying to criticize; I am just recognizing what man does when confronted with some of these difficult issues in the Word of God. When you read in the Bible what God says He will do for His people, and then after all your prayer and believing it doesn't seem to happen, the natural response is to back away and say that God stopped doing that at some point.

Religion is pretty good at identifying where God stopped doing something. But there is another course of action, and that is to be the ones who drive into the impossible. Everything that is the truth about Jesus Christ and God is impossible for man. If you don't think that is true, go back to Christ's advent and try to work up a virgin birth. God always makes the foundations of our walk with Him things that we cannot do in ourselves. None of us could have gone to the cross and died for humanity. It would be impossible. So when it happened, we know the Lord is the One who did it. And when we look at the Day of Atonement, someone has to rise up in faith and say, "What God has said can happen is going to happen." Let's recognize that, by the very institution of the Day of Atonement, we have the promise that it will happen. It is our promise of sanctification.

Each feast is a promise that God instituted, a guarantee of something that is going to happen for the Body of Christ. Passover, Unleavened Bread, the Feast of the First Fruits, Pentecost, Trumpets, Atonement, and Tabernacles are all very purposeful, very distinct and different from one another. That is why it can be confusing when there seems to be an overlap. Passover deals with sin and salvation. Then we come to Atonement, and it seems to be dealing with sin and salvation all over again. We think, "Why are there two feasts that deal with our salvation?" Passover represents the blood of Christ that covers us, just as the children of Israel were covered by the blood of the Passover lamb. They were delivered from their bondage and their oppressors. Moses boldly said to Pharaoh, "Let us go that we may worship the Lord. We have to take everything with us. Not one hoof can be left behind. We have to get as far away from you as we can because, if you saw the way we are going to worship, you would probably want to kill us" (Exodus 8:25-27; 10:24-26). Then, when they went out into the wilderness, what happened? Instead of going

---

Exodus 8:25-27   And Pharaoh called for Moses and Aaron and said, "Go, sacrifice to your God within the land." 26 But Moses said, "It is not right to do so, for we shall sacrifice to the LORD our God what is an abomination to the Egyptians. If we sacrifice what is an abomination to the Egyptians before their eyes, will they not then stone us? 27 We must go a three days' journey into the wilderness and sacrifice to the LORD our God as He commands us."

Exodus 10:24-26   Then Pharaoh called to Moses, and said, "Go, serve the LORD; only let your flocks and your herds be detained. Even your little ones may go with you." 25 But Moses said, "You must also let us have sacrifices and burnt offerings, that we may sacrifice them to the LORD our God. 26 Therefore, our livestock, too, will go with us; not a hoof will be left behind, for we shall take some of them to serve the LORD our God. And until we arrive there, we ourselves do not know with what we shall serve the LORD."

out and worshiping, they went out murmuring and complaining (Exodus 15:23-24). They faced the same reality that we face; the sin nature was still there. At Passover we receive justification through the blood of Jesus Christ, but there is still more that we need. We need the Day of Atonement to drive out the sin nature.

As we read in the article about John Wesley, "Sanctification is a subjective and inward change, a genuine renewal of an individual beginning in the new birth." Wesley was quoted as saying, "By justification we are saved from the guilt of sin, and restored to the favour of God; by sanctification we are saved from the power and root of sin, and restored to the image of God."[11] One of the problems that we see in the Church today is the misuse of the term "born again," because being born again deals more with the experience of sanctification than of justification. Sanctification is what Christ was referring to when He said, "Unless one is born of water and the Spirit, he cannot enter into the kingdom of God. That which is born of the flesh is flesh, and that which is born of the Spirit is spirit" (John 3:5-6). "Flesh and blood cannot inherit the kingdom of God" (1 Corinthians 15:50). There must be a spiritual rebirth because the Kingdom will not be filled with believers who still have the sin nature resident within them. You may say, "But I'm not doing anything wrong." It doesn't matter; the sin nature has to go. Let's read one more Scripture to seal this:

> Beloved, now we are children of God, and it has not appeared as yet what we shall be. We know that, when He

---

Exodus 15:23-24 And when they came to Marah, they could not drink the waters of Marah, for they were bitter; therefore it was named Marah. 24 So the people grumbled at Moses, saying, "What shall we drink?"

1 Corinthians 15:50 Now I say this, brethren, that flesh and blood cannot inherit the kingdom of God; nor does the perishable inherit the imperishable.

11. John Wesley, "Sermon 85: On Working Out Our Own Salvation," in *Sermons, on Several Occasions* (Oak Harbor, WA: Logos Research Systems, Inc., 1999).

appears, we shall be like Him, because we shall see Him just as He is. And everyone who has this hope fixed on Him purifies himself, just as He is pure. Everyone who practices sin also practices lawlessness; and sin is lawlessness. And you know that He appeared in order to take away sins; and in Him there is no sin. No one who abides in Him sins; no one who sins has seen Him or knows Him. Little children, let no one deceive you; the one who practices righteousness is righteous, just as He is righteous; the one who practices sin is of the devil; for the devil has sinned from the beginning. The Son of God appeared for this purpose, that He might destroy the works of the devil. No one who is born of God practices sin, because His seed abides in him; and he cannot sin, because he is born of God. (1 John 3:2-9)

Let's not forget that "the Son of God appeared for this purpose, that He might destroy the works of the devil." Therefore, do not think that He will allow this adamic nature, which was born from the infusion of satan himself, to exist in us. Christ came to destroy it. Thank God! I'm done with it! I am ready for the Atonement experience to become our reality. As we read, John Wesley believed that "no Christian who has experienced conversion and divine forgiveness can fail to desire perfection and strive for it."[12] Atonement is our striving for perfection. It is not a work that we can do ourselves, but we can come before God and say, "Lord, the Day of Atonement is the time for You to remove from me this conflict of natures, this sin that indwells me." Do you walk around with an awareness that it is literally impossible for you to sin? How often do you say, "I really tried to sin today, but I just couldn't pull it off"? We all know that we are in the same dilemma that Paul described in Romans chapter 7; we try not to sin but we cannot help falling into it. But think about

---

[12.] Muller, "Sanctification," 4:330.

reversing that reality. I know it is hard for our minds to imagine, but the truth is that the reversal is already happening, because the seed of the Word of God that has been planted in us is coming to maturity. In the Atonement experience, there is the crucifixion of the adamic nature until it is not possible to sin. That is a radical change.

The Day of Atonement is about this change, and it is the time for it. This is the day and the hour for it to happen. According to your faith be it done unto you (Matthew 9:29). I bless you to experience Atonement and the freedom from the sin nature. We reach in with faith for the complete fulfillment of the Day of Atonement, in the name of the Lord.

Matthew 9:29 Then He touched their eyes, saying, "Be it done to you according to your faith."

CHAPTER 10

A Personal Experience
With the Word of God

I want to teach you about the Bible in a way that you have never heard before. We call it the Bible, but it is the Word of God, and the Word of God has to be an experience for you. Every experience that we have in God can increase, grow, and abound. We do not have just one salvation experience in Christ. We meet Him multiple times, and that salvation experience grows. We do not have just one baptism of the Holy Spirit and then it's all over. We find that we are baptized many times in the Holy Spirit. That is the reality with most of the sacraments. I believe that the experience of water baptism can grow. According to the Scriptures, if you really experience being baptized in water, you come out of the water in resurrection life (Romans 6:3-5). So if you did not receive that the first time you were baptized, why not try again? Why not see if your faith has

---

Romans 6:3-5 Or do you not know that all of us who have been baptized into Christ Jesus have been baptized into His death? ⁴ Therefore we have been buried with Him through baptism into death, in order that as Christ was raised from the dead through the glory of the Father, so we too might walk in newness of life. ⁵ For if we have become united with Him in the likeness of His death, certainly we shall be also in the likeness of His resurrection.

increased to the point where something can happen for you that has never happened before? In the same way, no matter what your revelation of the Bible is now, it is something that can grow and expand even more. The key element of the power of God that is missing from the Body of Christ is not the revelation of Jesus; it is not the understanding of God the Father or the Holy Spirit. It is the lack of revelation of the Bible that leaves us without the power we need to act on the other experiences we have received from God.

I want to read something from Smith Wigglesworth. He was very much a part of the foundation of this fellowship, because our father in the Gospel, John Stevens, was connected to him and received impartation from his ministry. Smith Wigglesworth is a real part of the genetics and anointing of The Living Word Fellowship. A portion of his spirit is imparted to us in every Word that we hear and in everything that we do. Smith Wigglesworth raised the dead. He healed the sick. Probably the greatest miracles that have been seen in centuries came through his hands. We need to understand how the power of God moved through this man in many ways that were witnessed and written down time and time again. These manifestations of God's power did not happen 2,000 years ago; they happened literally within John's generation, and very much in the time frame of our history. Everything that was done in the power of God through this man came from his revelation of the Bible. The source of all that he did was his revelation of the Scriptures as the Word of God. Let's read what Smith Wigglesworth wrote about the Scriptures in his book *Faith That Prevails*. This is from a chapter titled "Like Precious Faith":

> "Never compare this Book with other books. Comparisons are dangerous. Never think or never say that this Book contains the Word of God. It is the Word of God. It is supernatural in origin, eternal in duration, inexpressible in value, infinite in scope, regenerative in power, infallible

in authority, universal in interest, personal in application, inspired in totality. Read it through. Write it down. Pray it in. Work it out. And then pass it on."[13]

Smith Wigglesworth is telling us to pray the Word into existence, to work it out in our lives. To him, the Bible was not a collection of writings; it was a revelation. And by virtue of that revelation he moved in what he did. People have taken the Bible, studied all the concepts, and tried to argue them through. That is where the modernists went with the Bible. But in that approach there is no power to deal with all the things that we face in our own lives and in the world today. If you do not have a revelation that the Bible is the Word of God, then you do not have a leg to stand on. Everything that we are, everything that we believe, stems and grows from the reality that the Scriptures are the Word of God.

We live in an age when there is so much controversy about God. The complaint is, "It's too difficult to believe in God the Father, or to relate to Jesus the Son, or to understand the Holy Spirit because they are all invisible." It can become an excuse: "They are all invisible!" But God has given us something visible in the Bible, something that we can pick up, handle, read, and relate to. Some people's response to that is, "It's too human. It's too natural. It can't be from God!" First, they say they cannot relate to God because He is invisible, but then they say they cannot relate to the Bible because it is visible. It doesn't matter what you give to man, he will always find a way around believing God. Jesus faced this reality when He walked among us.

> "And from the days of John the Baptist until now the kingdom of heaven suffers violence, and violent men take it by force. For all the prophets and the Law prophesied

---

13. Smith Wigglesworth, "Like Precious Faith," in *Faith That Prevails* (Springfield, MO: Gospel Publishing House, 1924).

until John. And if you care to accept it, he himself is Elijah, who was to come. He who has ears to hear, let him hear. But to what shall I compare this generation? It is like children sitting in the market places, who call out to the other children, and say, 'We played the flute for you, and you did not dance; we sang a dirge, and you did not mourn.' For John came neither eating nor drinking, and they say, 'He has a demon!' The Son of Man came eating and drinking, and they say, 'Behold, a gluttonous man and a drunkard, a friend of tax-gatherers and sinners!' Yet wisdom is vindicated by her deeds." (Matthew 11:12-19)

God always gives two witnesses (Deuteronomy 19:15). He gives a witness in the spirit and a witness in the natural. He gives us the Holy Spirit and Christ within us, the hope of glory, and all of the spiritual realities that come with our faith (Colossians 1:27). But He does more than that; He also gives us the physical, written Word of God. Nevertheless, people will always find something wrong: "It is just too hard to relate to God. It's too spiritual! And this Bible—I just find too many problems with it!" Isn't that exactly what Jesus was saying? God sent John the Baptist, who was under the vow of a Nazirite, never cutting his hair or beard, living in the wilderness, constantly fasting and not drinking. It was easy to look at him and say that he had a demon. Then you look at Jesus and He appears to be a glutton and a drunkard. People will always find some reason if they do not want to believe. Refuse to contend with that spirit. It is the way that satan comes to block your faith and keep you from moving in the power of God. Smith Wigglesworth overcame that

---

Deuteronomy 19:15 "A single witness shall not rise up against a man on account of any iniquity or any sin which he has committed; on the evidence of two or three witnesses a matter shall be confirmed."

Colossians 1:27 To whom God willed to make known what is the riches of the glory of this mystery among the Gentiles, which is Christ in you, the hope of glory.

problem. He definitely understood what the Word of God is. He had a relationship with the Word.

The Bible is not a book. It is a living, breathing reality. It is alive. Hebrews chapter 4 talks about those in the wilderness who were not able to enter God's rest, and that there remains a promise of entering that rest (Hebrews 4:1). This promise of entering the Sabbath rest, that even Joshua could not bring them into, is directly connected with our understanding of the Word of God. "For the word of God is living and active and sharper than any two-edged sword, and piercing as far as the division of soul and spirit, of both joints and marrow, and able to judge the thoughts and intentions of the heart" (Hebrews 4:12). This should speak to us. The logo of The Living Word Fellowship is a Bible with a sword through it, with these words surrounding it: "The Word of God is living and powerful." This is the very root of who we are and where this fellowship came from, because it was John Stevens' foundation. He literally became the Word made flesh because he had such a revelation of the Bible as the Word of God.

The Bible is not some ancient book with ancient stories; it is the Living Word of God, and it is speaking to our generation. As much as you have had an experience with Christ as your Savior, you need to have an experience with the Bible as the Word of God to you. If the Bible is not that to you, then the power and authority will always be drained away from it. There will always be some excuse or reason why it does not work in your life. Why did it work for Smith Wigglesworth? He read that Jesus raised the dead, and that we will do greater works than these, so he went out and raised the

---

Hebrews 4:1 Therefore, let us fear lest, while a promise remains of entering His rest, any one of you should seem to have come short of it.

dead (Mark 5:39-42; John 14:12). There has to be a source in your life where the power of God comes from. Something has to tell you that all things are possible (Mark 9:23). It is part of human nature to not have this awareness in ourselves. People thought it was impossible to run a four-minute mile, until someone finally did it. Once that happened, many could do it because now it was believable. In the same way, the Bible has to be a reality to you.

God wants you to have a meeting with Him and an experience with His Word. It has to be the Word of God to **you**. It is not enough for you to know Jesus Christ. You do not know who He is unless the Bible is the Word of God to you. You do not know who the Father is unless the Bible is the Word of God to you. When it is the Word of God to you, it tells you all that Christ and the Father are. It reveals to you their personalities; it shows you their attributes; it tells you how they live and the way they move. It gives you everything you need. The Bible is the portal between the spirit world and the natural world that we see with our eyes. "By faith we understand that the worlds were prepared by the word of God, so that what is seen was not made out of things which are visible" (Hebrews 11:3). That Scripture applies to the Word itself—by faith we understand that the Bible was prepared through a Word from God, so that what is seen in this Book was not made out of things which are seen. The Bible is the invisible becoming visible, tangible, and real. It is something

---

Mark 5:39-42   And entering in, He said to them, "Why make a commotion and weep? The child has not died, but is asleep." [40] And they began laughing at Him. But putting them all out, He took along the child's father and mother and His own companions, and entered the room where the child was. [41] And taking the child by the hand, He said to her, "Talitha kum!" (which translated means, "Little girl, I say to you, arise!"). [42] And immediately the girl rose and began to walk; for she was twelve years old. And immediately they were completely astounded.

John 14:12   "Truly, truly, I say to you, he who believes in Me, the works that I do shall he do also; and greater works than these shall he do; because I go to the Father."

Mark 9:23   And Jesus said to him, "'If You can!' All things are possible to him who believes."

you can touch and feel, and by it the Father, the Son, and the Holy Spirit can begin to speak to you.

There is no greater experience than when the Word comes alive to you. You can read the Bible and nothing happens; that is called unbelief. On the other hand, you can read the Bible and the author's words come off the page. You can read the Bible and Christ materializes before you. He comes out of the invisible realm and is transformed into the visible. The Bible is the portal. It is the door through the veil, and through the veil the Father comes into your life. Through the veil the Holy Spirit comes so that the invisible, intangible realm becomes a reality by the Word of God. The Word then becomes the power in you to heal, to resurrect, to prophesy, to create, and to speak things into existence.

Prophecy is speaking the Word of God, but you cannot really believe in prophecy unless the Bible is the Word of God to you. The Bible is not a religious text; it is what gives us the authority to speak the Word. It tells me that my mouth can be as His mouth, and I can speak the Word of God (Jeremiah 15:19, KJV). Therefore, I reach into that. Likewise, the Bible gives me the ability to see Christ as a transformational force in my life. It tells me to put on the mind of Christ (Romans 12:2; 1 Corinthians 2:16). That is available to me because the Bible is the Word of God, not just a book. The Bible has to be the Word of God to you personally. It does not matter if it is the Word of God to me; it has to be that to you. God has to meet you in it. You have to cry out to God until you know it as the Word

---

Jeremiah 15:19, KJV Therefore thus saith the Lord, If thou return, then will I bring thee again, and thou shalt stand before me: and if thou take forth the precious from the vile, thou shalt be as my mouth: let them return unto thee; but return not thou unto them.

Romans 12:2 And do not be conformed to this world, but be transformed by the renewing of your mind, that you may prove what the will of God is, that which is good and acceptable and perfect.

1 Corinthians 2:16 For who has known the mind of the Lord, that he should instruct Him? But we have the mind of Christ.

of God. When that happens, it will come out of your mouth with impartation and authority. The Word of God is living and powerful, but it has to come out of your mouth as a living, breathing reality, like a two-edged sword that pierces to the heart.

Knowing the Bible as the Word of God will be the next experience that we renew in our faith. I am not saying that you do not know these things, or that you have not experienced them. I am trying to pull you up by faith into another level, to where this is a constant reality in your life, and you know that it works because the power of God is there. That is what we have waited for. John Stevens talked to us about speaking a power Word from God. This revelation that the Bible is the Word of God is where that comes from. We are looking for many things, and this is where it starts. As much as you can relate to your salvation experience with Jesus Christ, you can have the same experience with the Word. We come to know Christ; He introduces us to the Father, and the Holy Spirit teaches us all things (John 14:26). But I guarantee you that it will be out of this Book that He will teach us all things. By the Holy Spirit, this Book will come alive. It will speak to you, change your heart, and show you things which eye has not seen and ear has not heard, neither have they entered into the heart of man (1 Corinthians 2:9). As you believe for God to speak to you out of His Word, it will come alive to you as you read it; you will know what it is that you are reading. I want this for us. I want the living relationship that Jesus had with the Word. Jesus said, "I do not say anything but what I hear the Father say. I do not do anything but what I see the

---

John 14:26 "But the Helper, the Holy Spirit, whom the Father will send in My name, He will teach you all things, and bring to your remembrance all that I said to you."

1 Corinthians 2:9 But just as it is written, "THINGS WHICH EYE HAS NOT SEEN AND EAR HAS NOT HEARD, AND WHICH HAVE NOT ENTERED THE HEART OF MAN, ALL THAT GOD HAS PREPARED FOR THOSE WHO LOVE HIM."

Father do" (John 12:49; 5:19). That is not because He was psychic and saw visions. He was talking about the Word of God. How many times in the Gospels do you read about Jesus quoting from the Hebrew Scriptures? That was how the Father spoke to Him. The Father spoke to Him out of the Word of God, and those things Jesus spoke because the Scriptures were the Words of His Father to Him. Let's read what Jesus thought about the Word of God:

> "Let your light shine before men in such a way that they may see your good works, and glorify your Father who is in heaven. Do not think that I came to abolish the Law or the Prophets; I did not come to abolish, but to fulfill. For truly I say to you, until heaven and earth pass away, not the smallest letter or stroke shall pass away from the Law, until all is accomplished. Whoever then annuls one of the least of these commandments, and so teaches others, shall be called least in the kingdom of heaven; but whoever keeps and teaches them, he shall be called great in the kingdom of heaven." (Matthew 5:16-19)

Jesus is speaking here about the *Tanakh*, the Hebrew Scriptures. The phrase "the smallest letter" is a translation of the Greek word *iota*, which corresponds to the Hebrew letter *yodh*. "Stroke" is the Greek word *keraia*, which could be translated in English as "serif." Each character in a font is categorized as either having serifs or being sans serif, which means "without serifs." A serif is a small line or stroke that comes off the edges of a letter. So what was Jesus talking about? When you look at the smallest letter in the Hebrew language, the *yodh*, ׳, you can see that it is like a half letter. This is "the smallest

---

John 12:49 "For I did not speak on My own initiative, but the Father Himself who sent Me has given Me commandment, what to say, and what to speak."

John 5:19 Jesus therefore answered and was saying to them, "Truly, truly, I say to you, the Son can do nothing of Himself, unless it is something He sees the Father doing; for whatever the Father does, these things the Son also does in like manner."

letter" that Jesus was referring to. Then, when you look at the Hebrew word for "lips," שָׂפָה, you can see a curved line, like a small hook, on the tips of each letter. That is the serif, or "stroke." Jesus was saying that not even the smallest letter or stroke of a letter in the Word will disappear.

When God spoke creation into existence, He did it in the Hebrew language. In the Hebrew tradition, God made the visible creation with the *tav,* the last letter of the Hebrew language, and He made the invisible creation with the *yodh*. It is very significant that Jesus picked the *yodh* for His example. All of the other letters can be divided into parts as you form them in writing. However, you cannot do that with the *yodh*. It cannot be divided, so it is recognized by Hebrew scholars as representing God. Not only is it the smallest letter, but because God is One, it is also seen as being God Himself. *Shema Yisrael, Adonai eloheinu, Adonai echad.* "Hear, O Israel! The Lord is our God, the Lord is one" (Deuteronomy 6:4)! The name of God in Hebrew is *yodh he waw he,* יהוה. Notice what letter is at the beginning (on the right)—God's name begins with *yodh*. So Jesus was saying that the smallest letter, the *yodh*, will never pass away, just as God Himself will never pass away. It is also significant that the names Jacob, Israel, and Judah all begin with *yodh*. Every aspect of God, and the whole family that He brought forth, begins with this letter.

The meaning in Jesus' reference to the *yodh* is deeper than what is readily apparent. He was stating that not even the smallest part of God's Word will pass away until all is accomplished. Every Word must be fulfilled, and God will not allow even one of the smallest strokes of a letter to be lost. Did Jesus believe that the Scriptures were the Word of God? He absolutely believed it! He respected the Scriptures. He held them in the highest esteem. This revelation of the Word that Jesus was talking about also relates to the testimony that we are to have. We are as a city set on a hill. We are to be a lamp that is lit and not hidden (Matthew 5:14-16). The testimony will come out of us, and through us, in the power of God as we experience a true revelation of the Word of God in our lives. "In the beginning was the Word, and the Word was with God, and the Word was God" (John 1:1). "And the Word became flesh, and dwelt among us" (John 1:14). You cannot separate God from His Word. When you have a revelation of that, you will experience a living, tangible relationship with the Bible as the Word of God. God will no longer be invisible to you. He will become tangible. He will become relatable. Jesus was the Word made flesh, and for us, the Word of God is the portal from the spirit realm into the physical realm.

The Father is Spirit; He is invisible in heaven (John 4:24). Christ is at the right hand of the Father in heaven, in a resurrected body that is, by and large, invisible to us. He is preparing His Kingdom in the spirit realm, which does not impact the physical realm in which we live. That is our job; it is our anointing to impact the physical realm. So, if we are to know God and Christ, and if we are to move in the earth as we are supposed to, then we must have a revelation of the Scriptures as the Word of God. If we do not, then there is no platform for us to work from. There is no foundation. Nothing that we say or do will have the power behind it that we need. I know that we are coming to know the Lord. That is a promise, and it is very important that we do that. However, there is no way to know the Lord without believing that the Word is from Him, and without taking what He says as law and forming our lives around it. We must make sure that if anything says something different than the Word, we are not moved by it—whether that be satan or demons or circumstances or our neighbor. We must only be moved by the Word. When the

---

Matthew 5:14-16 "You are the light of the world. A city set on a hill cannot be hidden. [15] Nor do men light a lamp, and put it under the peck-measure, but on the lampstand; and it gives light to all who are in the house. [16] Let your light shine before men in such a way that they may see your good works, and glorify your Father who is in heaven."

John 4:24 "God is spirit, and those who worship Him must worship in spirit and truth."

Word of God is what moves us, then we will become immovable, because nothing else can move us.

Before Christ came to earth, He was with the Father. He was invisible. He was in the world of spirit, but through the Word He became visible and was manifested in the flesh. That same process can take place every minute of every day when the Bible is the Word of God to you. The Word can once again become flesh in you. That is what the earth is waiting for right now, for the Word to be made flesh and dwell among us in this generation. But we cannot become the Word made flesh if we do not know what the Word is. Do not confuse the Scriptures with the modern day word of prophecy, word of revelation, word of wisdom, or word of knowledge. None of that can replace the Bible, and none of those gifts can work correctly without the Bible being the foundation of them. The Word has to be planted in your heart, in your mind, and in your spirit in order for you to grow and make progress. You cannot jump over the Bible directly into the Living Word from John Stevens. People have said, "All I really relate to is John, because he spoke a Living Word." That is true, but you cannot understand John's Word if you do not understand the Bible. John's Word is a light on the Scriptures that shows you the path, and makes them more alive in your life than they have ever been. But you are missing something if you only have John's Word without having a revelation of the Scriptures.

The Word was everything to John. He believed the Scriptures; he spoke that Word, and he became that Word. From the beginning, the Word is what made him what he was, and all through his life that foundation never left him. The Scriptures were the plumb line to everything John saw, everything he heard, and everything he said. But something is still missing from us in a way that leaves us vulnerable. We need to have a meeting with the Lord about the Word of God, until it means to us what it meant to Christ, what it meant to John, so that we can bring that same anointing to our generation. John Stevens had a unique anointing; he was able to take the Scriptures and make them alive and applicable to his generation. When people read or listen to a message from John, many say, "That is what the Scriptures are saying! That is what they really mean." John's gift made the Word come alive so that it became God speaking to you. That ability is something you can only do through God's anointing. Now we are faced with the fact that we need that anointing also. We need to take the Scriptures by revelation and make them alive, real, and applicable to our generation.

We need something more. We need something deeper. This has to be a reality to us. I guarantee that satan will throw everything at you to prevent you from getting this, because when you do get it, it is all over as far as he is concerned; satan is done. If we know that the Bible is the Word of God, then everything else falls into place. The ability to move in the power of God is turned loose for us. Paul wrote, "For I am not ashamed of the gospel, for it is the power of God for salvation to everyone who believes, to the Jew first and also to the Greek" (Romans 1:16). Paul understood that the Gospel is the power of God. Do you ever wonder, "Where is the power of God in my life?" It is in the revelation of the Word in your life. When the Bible is really the Word of God to you, then everything will be different in those areas where it just didn't work before. If you say, "I read the prophecies over me and they have never come to pass," you are getting the cart before the horse. The prophecies that you have will never have the power until first the Bible is the Word of God to you. Whatever prophecies we have in this generation, whatever messages we call the Living Word, they are only Words from God because this Book is the Word of God.

Those other Words can never have greater power, anointing, or veracity in your life than the Scriptures have. The Word of God is the source; it is the wellspring. Everything comes from that. Christ is manifested on the earth through the Scriptures. That is where

He came from. It is the portal. The Scriptures will transport you to be seated at God's right hand in the heavenly places. They will also transport the Father, Son, and Holy Spirit to your right hand to live, breathe, and move with you, in you, and through you. What the world needs is the power of God manifested in a people, not doctrines or more messages. The world needs to see the undeniable power of God. Jesus had that power, because He knew the Father. To Him, the Scriptures were the Father, and they were the Words of the Father to Him personally. They were so real to Him that they worked. We have to honestly accept that the reason things do not work for us is because the Word is not that real to us. Don't take that negatively; let it focus your attention. Don't just deal with the leaves and branches and say, "I'm a horrible person; I don't have faith." No, say, "Lord, give me a revelation of Your Word!" Seek God for that revelation. Then, when you get it, seek Him for a greater revelation. Go after it with all your heart. Just as you sought God for your initial salvation experience, and just as you sought Him for the baptism of the Holy Spirit, go after this. "For the word of the cross is to those who are perishing foolishness, but to us who are being saved it is the power of God" (1 Corinthians 1:18). God, release Your power!

When people came and challenged Jesus, He said, "You have a problem. You do not understand the Scriptures or the power of God. That is why you are confused" (Matthew 22:29). The Body of Christ needs to get out of its confusion. We, as a people and as individuals, need to get out of the confusion in our own hearts. Something has to be turned loose in us. I don't care how long you have been in this fellowship; something can happen for you today. I loose it to happen right now in your heart and in your spirit. Holy Spirit, meet this people and let the Word, the *Logos*, become alive and real to them. Let it be living and powerful in the lives of Your people. Let it be a

---

Matthew 22:29   But Jesus answered and said to them, "You are mistaken, not understanding the Scriptures, or the power of God."

new revelation to us. Let it be something that spreads through the Body of Christ like a wildfire of revelation. Whatever we have had, we need more and we reach for it. We reach in by faith to know that we know that the Bible is the Word of God. As real as it was to John Stevens, as real as it was to Smith Wigglesworth, as real as it was to Jesus Himself, let it be that real to us. As it was to Christ the power of God that moved through Him, let it be the power of God in us. We cannot just have beliefs and doctrines, preachers and sermons, churches and denominations; we must have the power of God. If the world needed it in the time of Christ, they certainly need it now. More than any generation, this generation needs it. Can you feel the sense of responsibility? Are you willing for the Scriptures to become so alive and real to you that your whole life is transformed? They will change your way of life. Everything will change, just like it did for Jesus when He was driven by the Holy Spirit into the presence of God (Mark 1:12). This revelation will drive us into the will of God to bring forth His Kingdom in the earth.

Mark 1:12 And immediately the Spirit impelled Him to go out into the wilderness.

CHAPTER 11

When the Word Becomes Flesh

"And the Word became flesh, and dwelt among us, and we beheld His glory, glory as of the only begotten from the Father, full of grace and truth" (John 1:14). The whole concept of Christ, the Messiah, is the idea of God manifesting Himself by the Holy Spirit in the flesh of a man. I am very concerned about our acceptance of that concept, because we are believing for an outpouring of the Holy Spirit. Every outpouring of the Holy Spirit in history has been generated by some event you could point to where people came together to seek God. The great outpourings of the Spirit, these miraculous events on the earth, were absolutely divine manifestations. However, they were also absolutely initiated by the faith of believers who prayed, interceded, and cried out to God until those events transpired. So when we say that we are looking for an outpouring of the Holy Spirit, or a global event that is initiated through the Holy Spirit, let's back up and understand exactly what we are asking for. How does the Holy Spirit work? The Holy Spirit works through man. We are filled with the Holy Spirit. All of the gifts and attributes of the Holy Spirit work through human vessels. We seek to manifest the fruit of the Spirit; we want to have love, joy, and peace (Galatians 5:22-23). All of those are attributes of God's personality that are being transmitted via the Holy Spirit to indwell man, and through man to manifest in the earth. Therefore, when we say that we are believing for an outpouring of the Holy Spirit, we must rephrase that to say we are believing for the outpouring of God into the earth through human vessels.

There is a misconception about the return of Christ and the events of the end times as they are currently being taught. People teach that they are wholly divine events; I believe that the events that transpire will have far more of a human element and human involvement to them than anyone is anticipating. One of the great burdens of my heart is that a people be prepared for the true expression of God in the earth through human vessels once again. When Jesus came to the earth, He was the Word made flesh dwelling among us. He was God in the earth. One of the names given to Him in Hebrew is Immanuel, God with us (Matthew 1:23). God was in the earth, but He moved through a man, and He appeared to a specific group of people. Jesus said, "I was sent to the lost sheep of Israel. I was not sent to those outside" (Matthew 15:24). We know that He died on the cross and accomplished salvation for all of mankind, but He came as God in the flesh to minister to Israel, God's chosen people. He came to the believers at that time. He came to the synagogue, to the Church, if you will. In that day in Israel, everyone was taught the Torah. Everyone was raised with a far greater observance of the Scriptures than we have now. So God did not come to those who were not looking for Him. When He manifested Himself in

---

Galatians 5:22-23   But the fruit of the Spirit is love, joy, peace, patience, kindness, goodness, faithfulness, 23 gentleness, self-control; against such things there is no law.

Matthew 1:23   "BEHOLD, THE VIRGIN SHALL BE WITH CHILD, AND SHALL BEAR A SON, AND THEY SHALL CALL HIS NAME IMMANUEL," which translated means, "GOD WITH US."

Matthew 15:24   But He answered and said, "I was sent only to the lost sheep of the house of Israel."

Christ His Son, He appeared to His chosen people, to those who loved Him, and to those who sought to walk with Him. They were a people who had a messianic hope.

Today, when we talk about the Messiah and the messianic hope, we are referring to the man Jesus Christ as a singular appearance some 2,000 years ago. What the Jewish people were believing for was something more than just a singular appearance. If you study the messianic hope in Second Temple Judaism, up to three Messiahs were to appear. The idea of the appearing of a Messiah was not a singular event to them, because it was to be a threefold expression of the messianic prophet, priest, and king. Therefore, it was very dramatic that God sent John the Baptist and Jesus at the same time. Together they fulfilled what Judaism was looking for in the messianic appearance of a priest of the order of Aaron, and a king who was of the lineage of David. The Jews had a prophecy that they would never be left without someone on the throne of David's lineage, and so they were looking for a human manifestation, someone coming as a king (1 Kings 2:1-4). They did not have the thinking we have today in terms of only a divine, spiritual fulfillment. They were looking for the fulfillment to be on a natural level in a man, and they were believing that it would not happen only once. They believed that it would happen three times, whether that was three different manifestations or three simultaneous manifestations.

There probably were differing opinions about it, but the point is that they had a tremendous anticipation. They had a messianic hope for a man to come in each of these different anointings as an answer

---

1 Kings 2:1-4 As David's time to die drew near, he charged Solomon his son, saying, [2] "I am going the way of all the earth. Be strong, therefore, and show yourself a man. [3] And keep the charge of the LORD your God, to walk in His ways, to keep His statutes, His commandments, His ordinances, and His testimonies, according to what is written in the law of Moses, that you may succeed in all that you do and wherever you turn, [4] so that the LORD may carry out His promise which He spoke concerning me, saying, 'If your sons are careful of their way, to walk before Me in truth with all their heart and with all their soul, you shall not lack a man on the throne of Israel.'"

for Israel. So it is heart-wrenching that they missed it; and they did not miss it because they did not expect it. They were expecting it and they missed it. Today, the Body of Christ is not even expecting the physical manifestation and expression of the Kingdom of God. If we are not expecting that, but they were and they missed it, how tenuous is our positioning? This is something that warrants our attention. If God once again manifests Himself in human vessels, if once again the Kingdom of God begins with the Word made flesh, with God among us, with the Holy Spirit descending, remaining, and moving through a people, I am afraid that we are not ready for it. Doctrinally, this idea has been preached to us over and over again, but we are not really braced for the reality of it. More than that, I want us to initiate it, because we know that the outpouring of the Spirit can be initiated by those who are driven to make it happen. Do you believe that we can literally, by the way we walk in our relationships, in our expression of love, faith, submission, and connection, release the Holy Spirit to move through one another?

We should not have a passive attitude of believing that somehow it will just happen, but we don't really know how. We need to get out of this mode of waiting for something to happen because we have a Word that it will happen. The Lord gave us a warning in the parable of the foolish virgins who fell asleep and let their lamps go out (Matthew 25:1-13). In their waiting, they let down their

---

Matthew 25:1-13 "Then the kingdom of heaven will be comparable to ten virgins, who took their lamps, and went out to meet the bridegroom. [2] And five of them were foolish, and five were prudent. [3] For when the foolish took their lamps, they took no oil with them, [4] but the prudent took oil in flasks along with their lamps. [5] Now while the bridegroom was delaying, they all got drowsy and began to sleep. [6] But at midnight there was a shout, 'Behold, the bridegroom! Come out to meet him.' [7] Then all those virgins rose, and trimmed their lamps. [8] And the foolish said to the prudent, 'Give us some of your oil, for our lamps are going out.' [9] But the prudent answered, saying, 'No, there will not be enough for us and you too; go instead to the dealers and buy some for yourselves.' [10] And while they were going away to make the purchase, the bridegroom came, and those who were ready went in with him to the wedding feast; and the door was shut. [11] And later the other virgins also came, saying, 'Lord, lord, open up for us.' [12] But he answered and said, 'Truly I say to you, I do not know you.' [13] Be on the alert then, for you do not know the day nor the hour."

anticipation of what was to take place, and they ran out of the oil, or anointing, that they had. So waiting is not a good thing. In waiting, you can become sleepy. You do not tend to stay sharp when you are waiting. We should understand what the Word and the prophecies really mean to us. The way we function and work together, all of the things that we are doing should literally be like intercession. The creating of authority in the Body of Christ, having leadership, pastors and shepherds, is not just to have a human organization. We must relate to those in authority with a demand that the Holy Spirit fill them, that they be Christ in the flesh in the earth and not just move on a human level.

It has to start somewhere. Jesus started as a baby. Maybe when we started we were 100 percent in the flesh, but hopefully now we have some mixture of the Spirit. We all start very much on a human level, dealing with the problems and issues of the flesh, but we eventually grow out of that. Therefore, our flesh cannot be an excuse for passivity; we should aggressively relate to what God is doing in us. If we are believing for the outpouring of the Holy Spirit and we understand that means God dwelling in man, the Word becoming flesh once again, then we should start initiating that. This means that I should look at you according to what God says you are. Even if you are having a hard time with it, I should start being a force to you to believe who you are by the Word of God, because if I do that, I may be able to get through to you. Perhaps I can have enough force and faith behind my relating to you that I can literally impact your thinking. This is something we all need, because the hardest thing about believing this is to believe that God is coming forth in yourself. The hardest thing about forgiveness is really knowing that God forgave me. The hardest thing about sanctification is knowing that God is cleansing me. So I may not be the one initiating this for myself; you may be the one doing that for me. As a spiritual father, I am not trying to relate to the pastors and leaders as though they are a finished work. But I do want to relate to them according to what

God said they are, because I need to impact their thinking about themselves. Transformation comes by the renewing of the mind (Romans 12:2). That is where transformation takes place. At some point you have to believe it, you have to know it, and you have to understand it.

There is a force in doing this for one another, but we have allowed ourselves to become lazy. We have not done this aggressively, and it has become acceptable to criticize, mock, put one another down, and go back to relating in the flesh. Even if we take out that negative aspect of relating, we're still only on a human level. Even if I know that Jesus dwells in you and that the Holy Spirit is in you, I still only relate to you as human. I only see you as human, and we fellowship together as humans. I don't think that is what we should be doing. When we come into the family of God, we should be exercising the faith to create one another. If we believe that we can pray and initiate the outpouring of the Holy Spirit, then why can't we relate to one another in such a way that we demand that the Holy Spirit come forth in human flesh? Maybe it is not there today, maybe it will not be there tomorrow, but when do I have the right to give up? When do I quit? What is the trigger that causes me to say, "It will never happen for this person"? One of the greatest things we can do is really grasp this principle of confessing our faults. "If we confess our sins, He is faithful and righteous to forgive us our sins and to cleanse us from all unrighteousness" (1 John 1:9). I want you to be able to see what is wrong in yourself and confess it, because I want you to be forgiven and cleansed. I want to see created in you, by the Holy Spirit, the vessel that God is looking for in the earth.

We have to aggressively go after this. I know we have believed in this, but we have only believed it doctrinally, and I think we use

---

Romans 12:2   And do not be conformed to this world, but be transformed by the renewing of your mind, that you may prove what the will of God is, that which is good and acceptable and perfect.

that to excuse ourselves from actually doing it. There has to be a commitment in our leadership to walk in this. If you wonder what Marilyn and I are doing in working with those in leadership, this is what we are demanding. It cannot only be us relating to them this way; they have to be doing this with one another. I want this spirit to be in those who are in leadership over the fellowship, and in the leaders in every church, because if the leaders have it, the Body will have it. Like shepherd, like sheep. You will take on the same qualities that are in your leaders. We are demanding that there be an absolute determination for Christ to come forth right here in us. I know that there is a Father in heaven, and I know that Jesus Christ is seated at His right hand (Acts 2:33). I absolutely know that there is a singular Jesus, but I also know the prayer that Jesus made: "That they may all be one; even as Thou, Father, art in Me, and I in Thee, that they also may be in Us" (John 17:21). Jesus also said, "My Father and I are coming to make Our abode in you" (John 14:23). Consequently, it is wrong for me to continue to reject you and say, "You have problems, weaknesses, and issues in the flesh, so I am only going to relate to God in the sky!"

It is so easy for us to say, "I'm just going to go to my closet to pray. I don't need a human vessel. When I need something, all I have to do is pray to Jesus and the Father, and they will give me what I need." God is going to answer that kind of prayer less and less. There is a joke about a man who was caught in a flood, and he kept praying, "God save me!" Someone came along and yelled to him, "Let me throw you this rope!" The man said, "No, I prayed to God and I'm waiting for Him to save me." Then people in a boat came by and offered their help. "No," he said, "God is going to save me." Then a helicopter

---

Acts 2:33 "Therefore having been exalted to the right hand of God, and having received from the Father the promise of the Holy Spirit, He has poured forth this which you both see and hear."

John 14:23 Jesus answered and said to him, "If anyone loves Me, he will keep My word; and My Father will love him, and We will come to him, and make Our abode with him."

came along to rescue him and he said again, "No, God is going to save me." Finally the poor man drowned. When he got to heaven he was so mad at God he could hardly talk straight. He asked God, "Why didn't You save me?" God said, "I sent you a man with a rope, and a boat, and finally a helicopter. What happened?" That may be a joke, but it is a true expression of this generation. Are we going to demand that we will only receive help from God in heaven and from Jesus at His right hand, and not through any human vessel? Or will we realize that more and more, as the Kingdom unfolds, it is manifesting first and foremost right here in His people? He is coming to be glorified in His saints and to be admired in all those who believe (2 Thessalonians 1:10). Our answers are coming in each other. God is providing them, but I have to see Him in you. Otherwise, when you talk I will not hear the answer; I will only hear you.

The Holy Spirit only moves through human instruments. That is His function. Christ was the fullness of God manifested bodily in the earth because He was filled with the Holy Spirit (Colossians 2:9). The Holy Spirit rested on Him and never departed (John 1:32-33). Then, when He came to a people who were absolutely expecting the answer in a human vessel, they rejected Him. Today we feel like that time period is over. In our Christian thinking, that all happened in the past, and now we are waiting for the glorious appearing of Jesus

---

2 Thessalonians 1:10 When He comes to be glorified in His saints on that day, and to be marveled at among all who have believed—for our testimony to you was believed.

Colossians 2:9 For in Him all the fulness of Deity dwells in bodily form.

John 1:32-33 And John bore witness saying, "I have beheld the Spirit descending as a dove out of heaven, and He remained upon Him. [33] And I did not recognize Him, but He who sent me to baptize in water said to me, 'He upon whom you see the Spirit descending and remaining upon Him, this is the one who baptizes in the Holy Spirit.'"

in the sky, when every eye sees Him (Revelation 1:7). But that is not necessarily the first event of His coming in the Kingdom. If you just think about it, why would God treat this generation any differently than He has treated every other generation? After the children of Israel had been slaves for 400 years, God sent a man to deliver them (Exodus 12:40-41; 3:9-10). The first thing they had to do was submit to Moses, and in their early dealings with him, the elders of Israel became very angry and rejected him (Exodus 5:19-21). You have to remember that Moses was raised in Pharaoh's palace as the son of Pharaoh's daughter (Exodus 2:10). As far as they could discern, Moses was the enemy, and now he comes to them and says, "Trust me. God sent me." That was a major test for them, and it

---

Revelation 1:7 BEHOLD, HE IS COMING WITH THE CLOUDS, and every eye will see Him, even those who pierced Him; and all the tribes of the earth will mourn over Him. Even so. Amen.

Exodus 12:40-41 Now the time that the sons of Israel lived in Egypt was four hundred and thirty years. [41] And it came about at the end of four hundred and thirty years, to the very day, that all the hosts of the LORD went out from the land of Egypt.

Exodus 3:9-10 "And now, behold, the cry of the sons of Israel has come to Me; furthermore, I have seen the oppression with which the Egyptians are oppressing them. [10] Therefore, come now, and I will send you to Pharaoh, so that you may bring My people, the sons of Israel, out of Egypt."

Exodus 5:19-21 And the foremen of the sons of Israel saw that they were in trouble because they were told, "You must not reduce your daily amount of bricks." [20] When they left Pharaoh's presence, they met Moses and Aaron as they were waiting for them. [21] And they said to them, "May the LORD look upon you and judge you, for you have made us odious in Pharaoh's sight and in the sight of his servants, to put a sword in their hand to kill us."

Exodus 2:10 And the child grew, and she brought him to Pharaoh's daughter, and he became her son. And she named him Moses, and said, "Because I drew him out of the water."

was a test that kept on going. Out in the wilderness they murmured against Moses and Aaron continually (Exodus 14:11; 15:24; 16:2).

Relating to Moses was the test Israel had to go through. When God sent deliverance for them, He sent it in a human vessel. If they did not give themselves to Moses, submit to him, and believe that he was their answer, they did not get their deliverance. God was serious enough about this point that the ground opened up and swallowed thousands of them because of their rebellion against Moses (Numbers 16:1-2, 31-32). When Jesus came, He talked to those who believed in God and believed in the Messiah's coming, and told them that they were no different than their fathers who had refused the Lord's appearing:

> "Woe to you, scribes and Pharisees, hypocrites! For you are like whitewashed tombs which on the outside appear beautiful, but inside they are full of dead men's bones and all uncleanness. Even so you too outwardly appear righteous to men, but inwardly you are full of hypocrisy and lawlessness. Woe to you, scribes and Pharisees, hypocrites! For you build the tombs of the prophets and

---

Exodus 14:11 Then they said to Moses, "Is it because there were no graves in Egypt that you have taken us away to die in the wilderness? Why have you dealt with us in this way, bringing us out of Egypt?"

Exodus 15:24 So the people grumbled at Moses, saying, "What shall we drink?"

Exodus 16:2 And the whole congregation of the sons of Israel grumbled against Moses and Aaron in the wilderness.

Numbers 16:1-2 Now Korah the son of Izhar, the son of Kohath, the son of Levi, with Dathan and Abiram, the sons of Eliab, and On the son of Peleth, sons of Reuben, took action, ² and they rose up before Moses, together with some of the sons of Israel, two hundred and fifty leaders of the congregation, chosen in the assembly, men of renown.

Numbers 16:31-32 Then it came about as he finished speaking all these words, that the ground that was under them split open; ³² and the earth opened its mouth and swallowed them up, and their households, and all the men who belonged to Korah, with their possessions.

adorn the monuments of the righteous, and say, 'If we had been living in the days of our fathers, we would not have been partners with them in shedding the blood of the prophets.' Consequently you bear witness against yourselves, that you are sons of those who murdered the prophets. Fill up then the measure of the guilt of your fathers." (Matthew 23:27-32)

This is the mantra of Christianity today: "If we had been there in the days of Jesus, we would not have been like those legalistic Jews that Jesus chastised." Don't kid yourself. Your flesh is no better than anyone else's flesh. The flesh has a major problem receiving the manifestation of God in the flesh of another person. It is the challenge. The generations who heard Moses and who heard Jesus both rejected God's answer through man. However, we expect that everything will be easy in this generation. We won't have to put any energy into it. All we have to do is receive salvation, and we will be caught up to be with the Lord and everything will be fine. There won't be any challenge during the end time. There won't be any testing of our spirits. God will come down with His Son and set up His Kingdom on the earth, and everything will be so easy and so wonderful. We can't wait for that to happen. Let's read what another Scripture tells us:

> "You men who are stiff-necked and uncircumcised in heart and ears are always resisting the Holy Spirit; you are doing just as your fathers did. Which one of the prophets did your fathers not persecute? And they killed those who had previously announced the coming of the Righteous One, whose betrayers and murderers you have now become; you who received the law as ordained by angels, and yet did not keep it." (Acts 7:51-53)

Here the disciple Stephen directly ties the resistance against the Holy Spirit to the rejection of the prophets. Again we would all say,

"I am open to the Holy Spirit. Come, Holy Spirit; fill me, lead me, direct me." As long as the Spirit is coming and talking directly to me, I am convinced that I am absolutely open to the leading of the Holy Spirit. But when He starts moving through someone else, and talking to me through that person, then it's a different story! Jesus said the Holy Spirit will teach us all things, but He did not say that He will only do that in our own heads (John 14:26). The Holy Spirit will lead us into all the truth, but that does not mean He will only do it in the privacy of our prayer closets. If that is how the Holy Spirit moved, we would all be very open to Him. It is when the Holy Spirit comes and leads me through someone else that I have a problem. It is when He speaks to me through someone else that I start to bristle, "What do you mean? Who are you to tell me anything?"

We talk a lot about the great manifestation of the Holy Spirit at Azusa Street, and it just so happened that the Holy Spirit moved through an African-American man named William Seymour. Boy, did the established religious denominations of that day have a hard time with that! Seymour had to sneak into the prayer meetings on Bonnie Brae Street with the women who had prayed the outpouring into existence, because a black man could not come into that neighborhood at night, and he certainly could not meet with white women. Why does God do things like that? Not only was He addressing the believers of that day; He was addressing their society. So why would we think that in our day God would make things acceptable and easy for us? Do you think that He will only come in perfect people that no one can find fault with or be offended by?

Are we open to the Holy Spirit in this generation? It is something we need to work on because it is a learned skill. When the Holy Spirit speaks to you through someone and you react, what should you do? Confess your sin. He is faithful and just to forgive you and

---

John 14:26 "But the Helper, the Holy Spirit, whom the Father will send in My name, He will teach you all things, and bring to your remembrance all that I said to you."

cleanse you. It does not have to be a big problem. Deal with your reaction and get it out of your spirit. Then say, "Okay, Lord. I'm ready for the next wave of the Holy Spirit. Come and speak to me." We read in Revelation chapter 3 what the Lord said to the church at Philadelphia:

> "Because you have kept the word of My perseverance, I also will keep you from the hour of testing, that hour which is about to come upon the whole world, to test those who dwell upon the earth. I am coming quickly; hold fast what you have, in order that no one take your crown." (Revelation 3:10-11)

In these end times in which we live, before the return of the Lord, there will be a testing that will come upon the whole world. Many people believe in the concept of a "rapture"—being caught up to the Lord out of the world. I do believe we will be caught up to meet the Lord when He comes back to the earth (1 Thessalonians 4:17). The question is not if this event will happen, but when it will happen in the progression of the Lord's return and the establishment of His Kingdom. These verses from the Book of Revelation tell us that a great testing is coming on the entire earth, which we are certainly a part of. Even in Egypt, the Israelites were very much affected by the first stages of the judgments. What the Lord was saying to the church in Philadelphia was that they would have an immunity from the testing. However, that immunity is predicated on something. It does not just happen for everyone who is a believer. It happens because you have kept the Word. Remember, this was speaking to a specific group of people, not to all the Church.

What I am driven for is that we as a body of people walk in the Word that we have received. Our only immunity will be in walking in the

---

1 Thessalonians 4:17 Then we who are alive and remain shall be caught up together with them in the clouds to meet the Lord in the air, and thus we shall always be with the Lord.

Word before the testing happens. In that way we will be prepared for what is about to take place and it will not overcome us. Jesus taught us, "Do not let the day of the Lord come upon you like a thief in the night" (Matthew 24:42-44). The imagery of a thief in the night represents our unawareness, and I refuse for you to be unaware. That is why I am working so intensely with you. Someday in the Kingdom you may look back on me like that old math teacher who you hated, but when you got out of school and had to manage your own finances, you were very thankful for all that math teacher put you through. So just think of me in that way. I can handle it, but I refuse for you to be caught unaware. I refuse for the Kingdom of God to unfold on this fellowship like a thief in the night, where we don't understand or are shocked by what's going on. We had better learn the lessons.

Everything people went through in the Bible happened for our example (1 Corinthians 10:11). It happened as a lesson for us. When I read about those who were expecting the messianic appearing in a human vessel, but still could not receive Jesus, I think, "We have some homework to do." What we are doing in working with these leaders is serious. This is not about church administration or making sure that we do everything properly. This is about how we function together as a body, our coming together as a family. We say that we want to be a prophetic community. What that means to me is that we will not be unaware. It means that by the Holy Spirit, we will be a company of prophets who know what God is going to do. The promise is that before God does anything He will reveal

---

Matthew 24:42-44 "Therefore be on the alert, for you do not know which day your Lord is coming. ⁴³ But be sure of this, that if the head of the house had known at what time of the night the thief was coming, he would have been on the alert and would not have allowed his house to be broken into. ⁴⁴ For this reason you be ready too; for the Son of Man is coming at an hour when you do not think He will."

1 Corinthians 10:11 Now these things happened to them as an example, and they were written for our instruction, upon whom the ends of the ages have come.

it to His servants the prophets (Amos 3:7). I want that to be you. I want the Body of Christ to wake up and become the prophetic community that sees what will happen and is already prepared for it. As we read in the parable, there were five wise virgins who had the oil. There were those who were prepared. They knew what was going on. They were not caught unaware; they had what they needed to walk through the door at that moment. If I have anything to do with it, you will have what you need in your spirit to make it through the door at this moment.

This goes far beyond church and services and all the minor relationship issues and minutia that we get caught up in. We must not miss the Kingdom because we are so absorbed in the drama of our human relationships. Something has to goad you until you reach into something greater. The coming of the Kingdom is a testing that will happen to the whole earth, and the only people who will be preserved through it are those who have been prepared by the Word. However we want to interpret the end-time events and put them in order, we know for certain what Jesus Himself said: "Be careful because the day of the Lord comes like a thief in the night." Even in the Old Testament we read, "Behold, I will do a new thing; will you be aware of it?" (Isaiah 43:19). Our awareness is everything. We must become a prophetic community. We must be aware. We must be preserved through this time of testing. The only way that will happen is by our faithfulness to walk daily in the Word that He has given us, to press in with all of our hearts, and to know that the Lord is returning. Anticipate it!

Every time I look at you I want to anticipate the coming of the Lord. I want to anticipate the Word of the Lord. I want to anticipate

---

Amos 3:7 Surely the LORD God does nothing unless He reveals His secret counsel to His servants the prophets.

Isaiah 43:19 "Behold, I will do something new, now it will spring forth; will you not be aware of it? I will even make a roadway in the wilderness, rivers in the desert."

Kingdom administration, Kingdom creativity, and Kingdom answers coming from you. I want to anticipate the authority to rule and to reign coming from you. We too are anticipating a prophet, priest, and king manifestation at the coming of the Lord, and it will come through us. There is a testing coming on the whole earth. What will it be? Don't be afraid of the dragons, false prophets, and everything else described in the Book of Revelation. Just worry about one thing: "Will I know Him when He appears, or will I be like those in the days of Moses or Jesus? When my answer comes housed in a human vessel filled with the Holy Spirit, will I be able to recognize it, or will I also miss it? Will I persecute the one through whom the Word comes? Will I refuse the one Word to my heart that is my answer? Will I refuse the one Word of direction that could be my salvation?"

I don't want us to miss it. Jesus said that the only sin that cannot be forgiven is blasphemy against the Holy Spirit (Matthew 12:31-32). It is the only thing that you cannot get around. And we blaspheme the Holy Spirit if He moves through a human vessel and we call it man, or as they did with Christ, call the works of the Holy Spirit the works of satan (Matthew 9:32-34). Jesus sat on the Mount of Olives and wept, "I would have saved you. I would have taken you in My arms. I would have preserved you through this time if you would have just come to Me. I would have been like a mother hen protecting her little chicks. I came because God the Father so loved the world that He sent Me to gather you, to care for you, but you would not.

Matthew 12:31-32 "Therefore I say to you, any sin and blasphemy shall be forgiven men, but blasphemy against the Spirit shall not be forgiven. ³² And whoever shall speak a word against the Son of Man, it shall be forgiven him; but whoever shall speak against the Holy Spirit, it shall not be forgiven him, either in this age, or in the age to come."

Matthew 9:32-34 And as they were going out, behold, a dumb man, demon-possessed, was brought to Him. ³³ And after the demon was cast out, the dumb man spoke; and the multitudes marveled, saying, "Nothing like this was ever seen in Israel." ³⁴ But the Pharisees were saying, "He casts out the demons by the ruler of the demons."

WHEN THE WORD BECOMES FLESH | 181

Now your house is left to you desolate" (Luke 19:41; 13:34-35). The fulfillment of that prophecy came in 70 AD, because they had refused the Holy Spirit moving in a human vessel. Jerusalem was burned to the ground and thousands were crucified until they ran out of space to put up crosses. Someone, in some generation, is going to pass this test. If we are praying for an outpouring of the Holy Spirit, this is what we are praying for. Our prayer for the outpouring of the Holy Spirit is the initiation of this test that will come on the whole world. Will you accept God in man, or will you reject Him again in this generation? If we truly have a global outpouring of the Holy Spirit, the hearts of men in our generation will be tested just as they were tested by God's moving in the past.

Father, we receive Your Word. We do not pray for ourselves alone; give grace to the Body of Christ. Let us not be as those in Christ's generation, having eyes but not seeing, having ears but not hearing, having hearts that were not open. Lord, prepare us for what we will face. Give us the ability to see You coming forth in each one. Pour out Your Spirit, as Joel prophesied, on all flesh (Joel 2:28). Move through flesh in this generation, as You moved through Christ in His. We ask this, maybe with more fear and trembling than we have ever asked, but we refuse to back down from this prayer: Father, pour out Your Spirit on all flesh. Let Your Holy Spirit come into this earth. Let it fill Your people. Let it minister to the Body of Christ. Let us be filled with Your grace to open up to Your moving through

---

Luke 19:41 And when He approached, He saw the city and wept over it.

Luke 13:34-35 "O Jerusalem, Jerusalem, the city that kills the prophets and stones those sent to her! How often I wanted to gather your children together, just as a hen gathers her brood under her wings, and you would not have it! [35] Behold, your house is left to you desolate; and I say to you, you shall not see Me until the time comes when you say, 'BLESSED IS HE WHO COMES IN THE NAME OF THE LORD!'"

Joel 2:28 "And it will come about after this that I will pour out My Spirit on all mankind; and your sons and daughters will prophesy, your old men will dream dreams, your young men will see visions."

man. The Word became flesh and dwelt among us; let that happen again in our generation. Only this time, let Your people be the salvation of every generation, not only for ourselves but for all those who have gone before us, because You have prepared something better for us (Hebrews 11:39-40). We give our hearts to walk in this, in the name of the Lord.

Hebrews 11:39-40   And all these, having gained approval through their faith, did not receive what was promised, [40] because God had provided something better for us, so that apart from us they should not be made perfect.

CHAPTER 12

Do You Really
Believe in Life?

I want to teach about faith. In particular, I want to teach about resurrection life and why we believe in it. It is one of the greatest expressions of faith in the Scriptures that you can have. Our faith is based on the Word of God and on what the Word says. What God says is true, and our job is to believe what He says. We need to understand the meaning of the Bible and simply believe it. There are fancy theological words, such as "hermeneutics" and "exegesis," used for the process of getting the meaning out of the Scriptures, but one of the simplest principles is this: what the author of the Bible passage wrote is exactly what he meant. You simply accept, at face value, the text that you are reading.

Obviously, if you are reading a poetic passage you do not necessarily take that at face value. Poetry is trying to make you think about what is actually behind what is written. You also cannot read apocalyptic passages at face value, like those found in the Book of Revelation, because there is something more that the author is trying to get you to think about through all the imagery and symbolism. Similarly, when Jesus taught in parables, He was trying to get people to reach for something more. But, for the most part, the Bible is simply saying what it is saying. This is true of Hebrews chapter 10. This is not a parable; it is not a poetic passage; it is not an apocalyptic passage. It is Paul writing in very clear Greek. When we read it in English, it comes through the same way. In these verses, it may be difficult to tell who is speaking and who is being spoken of, but once you understand that, you realize that what the author is saying is exactly what he meant. To interpret the text, you can read it at face value. There is no mystery about it, and you do not need to be a biblical scholar or have a PhD in literature to understand it.

> For the Law, since it has only a shadow of the good things to come and not the very form of things, can never by the same sacrifices year by year, which they offer continually, make perfect those who draw near. Otherwise, would they not have ceased to be offered, because the worshipers, having once been cleansed, would no longer have had consciousness of sins? But in those sacrifices there is a reminder of sins year by year. For it is impossible for the blood of bulls and goats to take away sins. Therefore, when He comes into the world, He says,
> "SACRIFICE AND OFFERING THOU HAST NOT DESIRED,
> BUT A BODY THOU HAST PREPARED FOR ME;
> IN WHOLE BURNT OFFERINGS AND sacrifices FOR SIN
> THOU HAST TAKEN NO PLEASURE.
> THEN I SAID, 'BEHOLD, I HAVE COME
> (IN THE ROLL OF THE BOOK IT IS WRITTEN OF ME)
> TO DO THY WILL, O GOD.'" (Hebrews 10:1-7)

> Then He said, "BEHOLD, I HAVE COME TO DO THY WILL."…
> By this will we have been sanctified through the offering of the body of Jesus Christ once for all. (Hebrews 10:9-10)

There is certainly no mystery to what is being said here. The animal sacrifices described in the Old Testament had to take place

continually, day after day, year after year, because the sacrifices did
not really perfect or remove the sin nature of those for whom they
were sacrificed. They were only the type of something that was yet
to take place. "Otherwise, would they not have ceased to be offered,
because the worshipers, having once been cleansed, would no longer
have had consciousness of sins" (Hebrews 10:2)? Again, this is very
simple and straightforward. If sacrificing an animal would have
perfectly cleansed the worshiper who brought the sacrifice, there
would have been no need to come back and bring another animal
to sacrifice; it would have been finished. The worshiper, having been
perfectly cleansed, would literally forget to come back to the Temple
and sacrifice again. That person would not have any consciousness
of sin. Consciousness means having knowledge of something. If you
have no consciousness of sin, then you have no knowledge of sin, no
thought of sin. You literally forget about it. What a beautiful picture.

> For it is impossible for the blood of bulls and goats to take
> away sins. Therefore, when He comes into the world, He
> says,
>> "SACRIFICE AND OFFERING THOU HAST NOT DESIRED,
>> BUT A BODY THOU HAST PREPARED FOR ME;
>> IN WHOLE BURNT OFFERINGS AND sacrifices FOR SIN
>>> THOU HAST TAKEN NO PLEASURE. (Hebrews 10:4-6)

This is speaking of the Messiah standing before the Father, saying,
"You did not want all of these offerings, because You were looking
for perfect sanctification." The Father was looking for the perfect
act of sanctification—not a form, not something partial, not
something in which we are constantly reminded of sin. So when
the Messiah comes, He says, "I HAVE COME TO DO THY WILL," and
He brings this sanctification. "He takes away the first in order to
establish the second" (Hebrews 10:9). Something new is established,
removing what was done in the past because it was incomplete, and
establishing that which is complete as a new day. And He does this

by His will, by the motivation He has to do the will of God. God is able to use that motivation to sanctify us.

We read in verse 10, "By this will we have been sanctified through the offering of the body of Jesus Christ once for all." This is a key verse. Circle it in your Bible or make a note of it because it is important. I want to challenge you with this verse, because this is where we really start talking about faith. We have to ask ourselves, are we really walking with the Father according to this second sacrifice of complete cleansing, or are we still in the old worship of making sacrifice after sacrifice? Remember, not only is it impossible for those sacrifices to take away sin; they actually remind you of your lack of perfection. Now, be honest. How much of what you do in your worship and your walk with God is a reminder of your problems? How much of it brings a consciousness of sin? When the perfect comes, there is no consciousness, or awareness, of sin. But those former sacrifices did not remove the consciousness of sin. How much of what you do religiously is literally a reminder to your conscious mind of your imperfection, or of your lack of what God has promised?

Most people take Communion as a reminder of what they have done wrong and how much they need to be forgiven. People take Communion when they have the consciousness of a problem, and they look to be absolved of the sin that they are conscious of. So in a very real sense, we still experience the dichotomy between the old worship, which is the consciousness of sin and lack of sanctification, and the new worship, which is the pure, complete sanctification because the perfect has now come. Let me repeat that: the perfect has now come! By this will, by this motivation of Christ, we have been sanctified through the offering of the body of Jesus Christ once for all. That is pure, simple English and it is easy to recognize that this statement is in the past tense. It means that sanctification is already a reality. We are not reaching for something; we are to live in what we already have.

The Greek word for "sanctification" used in this passage is *hagiazo*. The word *hagiazo* was not a secular term in Greek; it came into the language purely as a biblical term. It is a Greek word that was created for the Septuagint translation of the Bible to translate the Hebrew word *kiddush,* meaning "sanctify" or "make holy." They literally had to invent new words to express what God provided for us! "By this will we have been sanctified" (Hebrews 10:10). We almost need to invent a brand new concept to describe the fact that we have been sanctified by God!

What is the basis of resurrection life? Resurrection life is directly related to this sanctification. It is based on the fact that Jesus Christ came into the world and, by His will, was accepted by God as the sacrifice for our sins. In obedience He went to the cross, died as the Lamb of God for our sins, and was resurrected by the Father. That was the process of our sanctification. Sanctification means, first of all, making us like the Father. That means that our sin is removed and therefore death is removed. In contrast, one of the greatest belief systems we see in Christianity today is the belief in death. Christians believe that we are all to die. It has been taught for centuries that our reward is in heaven, that the outcome of what Jesus did on the cross is something that we receive after we die. The Church almost glorifies death. We are taught that after death there is something better than this life. When Christians die, they go to a better place. There is a truth to that. However, when Christ died and was resurrected, our eternal bodies were formed. They already exist:

> For we know that if the earthly tent which is our house is torn down, we have a building from God, a house not made with hands, eternal in the heavens. For indeed in this house we groan, longing to be clothed with our dwelling from heaven; inasmuch as we, having put it on, shall not be found naked. For indeed while we are in this tent, we groan, being burdened, because we do not want

> to be unclothed, but to be clothed, in order that what is mortal may be swallowed up by life. (2 Corinthians 5:1-4)

It's like having a new pair of shoes that you leave in the box in your closet; you haven't worn them yet because they're for a very important occasion. When Christ was resurrected, there were those who literally came out of their graves and walked the streets of Jerusalem (Matthew 27:50-53). The first resurrection was at Christ's resurrection. He was the first to be resurrected. Then instantly, as Christ was resurrected, others were resurrected as well. Since the first resurrection has taken place and opened the door to resurrection life, Paul says, "We do not want to be unclothed, but to be clothed, in order that what is mortal may be swallowed up by life" (2 Corinthians 5:4). Paul was not looking to die in order to obtain resurrection; he believed to be clothed in his new dwelling while he was still alive.

There is no time frame or timeline for resurrection life. Resurrection life is simply putting on the new body of life which does not die. This seems so radical to people. But the only thing radical about it is that it confronts us, because we have never seen it before. It is not within the scope of our experience. Therefore it is deemed heresy, just as almost everything that Jesus said was deemed heresy because no one had ever seen it before. Everything that came out of His mouth confronted people about their unbelief in the simplicity of what the Word of God says. That is why it is important to understand that this passage in Hebrews chapter 10 is written in clear, unambiguous language. It is saying what it means, and it means what it says. And what it says is that you have been sanctified. Holiness is not a term; it is the Father. He is holiness. He is sanctification. It is His personality.

Matthew 27:50-53   And Jesus cried out again with a loud voice, and yielded up His spirit. [51] And behold, the veil of the temple was torn in two from top to bottom, and the earth shook; and the rocks were split, [52] and the tombs were opened; and many bodies of the saints who had fallen asleep were raised; [53] and coming out of the tombs after His resurrection they entered the holy city and appeared to many.

Jesus said, "I am the way, and the truth, and the life" (John 14:6). He was not just a man who walked in the earth. He was far beyond that; He was the expression of God. You have to get this picture that God Himself **is** sanctification. Therefore, when He says, "My name is Holy; My name is *Kiddush*," that means we have been sanctified, we have been brought into the holy state of the Father. Where does the Father live? What was the promise that Jesus spoke? "My Father and I will come and take up Our abode with you" (John 14:23). What happens when that takes place? "If the Spirit of Him who raised Jesus from the dead dwells in you, He who raised Christ Jesus from the dead will also give life to your mortal bodies" (Romans 8:11). The Spirit who raised Jesus from the dead is the Father, and when He dwells in us, He gives life to our mortal bodies.

Come on, live! Quit dying! What are you dying for? What are you believing that is killing you? Do you believe in death? Are you cleaving to death, or do you believe in life? If the Father—whose name is Holy, whose name is Sanctification, whose name is Righteousness—dwells in you, He will give life to your mortal body. Don't tell me that we are weird for believing in resurrection life. Don't call us a cult because that's your way of continuing in your unbelief, just because you will not believe the simplicity of what God is saying to you. He is not hiding this in apocalyptic passages, He is not hiding it in poetic verses, and He is not trying to tell you a parable. This is no parable. God is speaking explicitly, saying, "When Jesus Christ died on the cross, and I, the Father, received Him as the sacrifice for your sin, your sin was wiped away and you became sanctified through the body of Jesus Christ. And because the wages of sin is death, therefore death goes away when the price

---

John 14:6 Jesus said to him, "I am the way, and the truth, and the life; no one comes to the Father, but through Me."

John 14:23 Jesus answered and said to him, "If anyone loves Me, he will keep My word; and My Father will love him, and We will come to him, and make Our abode with him."

is paid" (Romans 6:23). To me, continuing to pay the wages of death is blasphemy. It is blasphemy to say, "Jesus' blood was not good enough for me, so I have to die my own death because I reject His death for me." If that is not blasphemy and unbelief, then tell me, what in the world is it?

The Father says that He will dwell in us. That is not a subtle nuance of what we call the New Testament; it was the reality of the Hebrew Scriptures. God not only dwells on high, but also with the contrite and lowly, with the little people who make up the Body of Christ (Isaiah 57:15). And "if the Spirit of Him who raised Jesus from the dead dwells in you, He who raised Christ Jesus from the dead will also give life to your mortal bodies" (Romans 8:11). There is a transformation, a real change. Jesus said, "Unless you are born again you cannot see the Kingdom of God. You must be born again!" (John 3:3, 7). God wants us to believe what He says. Is our unbelief just a trivial thing? I think it is a travesty. I think we had better stop reasoning away what God says. I don't care if we have never seen resurrection life before. I realize that we live in a generation that is 2,000 years after Christ's crucifixion and resurrection, but that is not the point. The point is that we either believe it or we don't. The Bible is either the truth of God to you in your life or it is not. Much of our focus in the Church is for our nation, and for this age, to accept the truth. What about us as believers accepting the truth? We must not close our hearts to the truth or override the truth or create new doctrines that get rid of the truth just because no one has ever done

---

Romans 6:23 For the wages of sin is death, but the free gift of God is eternal life in Christ Jesus our Lord.

Isaiah 57:15 For thus says the high and exalted One who lives forever, whose name is Holy, "I dwell on a high and holy place, and also with the contrite and lowly of spirit in order to revive the spirit of the lowly and to revive the heart of the contrite."

John 3:3 Jesus answered and said to him, "Truly, truly, I say to you, unless one is born again, he cannot see the kingdom of God."

John 3:7 "Do not marvel that I said to you, 'You must be born again.'"

this before. I don't care if no one has ever done it before! Let God be true and every man a liar (Romans 3:4). We should be in this fellowship because we believe what the Word says, whether we have experienced it or not. We do not need to put a spin on the Word or create a doctrine to excuse what we do not have. The fact that I do not have something this minute does not mean that I will not have it the next minute! But one thing I do know: if I let go of this truth I will never have it. Not only will I never have it, but I will be guilty of the blood of Jesus Christ. We must be believers in Christ's blood, the sacrifice that He made, and what was accomplished by that sacrifice (Hebrews 10:26-29).

As disciples, what will we have therefore (Matthew 19:27)? We will have a resurrection body. That is what Jesus promised. He promised sanctification. He promised us liberation from sin. He promised us freedom from our consciousness of sin. But in place of that, we have created a religion built around our continual awareness of sin and trying to deal with that, rather than being those who are pressing in to see the manifestation of every Word that God has spoken. Every promise from the Lord must have its fulfillment. When people did not believe what God said in the days of Moses, they were taken out and stoned to death. And God is warning us today. We do not have to live in the old concept of sacrifice when it has been replaced by a

---

Romans 3:4 May it never be! Rather, let God be found true, though every man be found a liar, as it is written, "That Thou mightest be justified in Thy words, and mightest prevail when Thou art judged."

Hebrews 10:26-29 For if we go on sinning willfully after receiving the knowledge of the truth, there no longer remains a sacrifice for sins, ²⁷ but a certain terrifying expectation of judgment, and the fury of a fire which will consume the adversaries. ²⁸ Anyone who has set aside the Law of Moses dies without mercy on the testimony of two or three witnesses. ²⁹ How much severer punishment do you think he will deserve who has trampled under foot the Son of God, and has regarded as unclean the blood of the covenant by which he was sanctified, and has insulted the Spirit of grace?

Matthew 19:27 Then Peter answered and said to Him, "Behold, we have left everything and followed You; what then will there be for us?"

new way in Christ. And yet we still have a consciousness of sin, and we trample underfoot the blood of Jesus Christ that was provided for us.

What has the blood of Christ provided for us? Sanctification. What is sanctification? It is the personality of the Father. And when the Father and His personality dwell in us, we have resurrection life. Our mortal body is quickened into the likeness of Christ's resurrected body. We do not have to wait for a doctrinal "first resurrection" off in the future. That must be emphasized, because many believers have the expectation that all we can experience is to be born, live a natural life, and then die. But they think, "Oh, how wonderful will be my reward in heaven if I serve the Lord all my life!" I could not care less about a reward in heaven, because I am here right now! I do not need a reward in heaven; I need God's presence here right now. I need to have a contrite spirit in which He dwells. I need to have His life dwelling within me. Jesus said, "I am the resurrection and the life" (John 11:25). He is these things right now, and He has to be these things in your life. You must believe. You must read the Word of God until it becomes greater in your mind, in your heart, and in your spirit than anything else around you, including what you see when you look at yourself in the mirror. Death came into the world as the wages of sin, and sickness is the road to death. Aging also is part of the road to death, and we accept and embrace that all too willingly. We should not do that! The first thing you should do when you get up in the morning is look in the mirror and prophesy against being another day older; prophesy against the deteriorating of your body. Those things are evidence that you are still living under something that has already been dealt with; you are still accepting something that the blood of Jesus Christ has taken away.

John 11:25 Jesus said to her, "I am the resurrection and the life; he who believes in Me shall live even if he dies."

Do you say, "That is too much for me to believe"? If you cannot believe in the total work of the cross, then it is really too much for you to believe that God took away your sin. You cannot separate sin from death; one is the result of the other. If you believe in Jesus Christ and that His blood took away your sin, then you have to believe that He also took away any sickness that is a result of that sin. You have to believe that when Christ was resurrected, He created a resurrection body for you. A body of life was created for each one of us; it is like a garment hanging on a hook right now in the spirit realm, waiting for us to put it on. But we will never put it on in unbelief. We put it on only when we simply take this Scripture at face value as the reality of what has happened for us: "By this will we have been sanctified through the offering of the body of Jesus Christ once for all" (Hebrews 10:10). If you are waiting for the resurrection, can you explain to me what you are waiting for? What event, in your mind, triggers healing and resurrection? Christ's sacrifice on the cross was the event that happened once for all. It already happened historically, and that is the only event that is necessary for us to have His life. There is no other event.

> And every priest stands daily ministering and offering time after time the same sacrifices, which can never take away sins; but He, having offered one sacrifice for sins for all time, SAT DOWN AT THE RIGHT HAND OF GOD, waiting from that time onward UNTIL HIS ENEMIES BE MADE A FOOTSTOOL FOR HIS FEET. (Hebrews 10:11-13)

Christ offered one sacrifice for sin for all time. If you don't believe it now, how will you believe it tomorrow? You say, "I'm waiting for the coming of the Lord." He is waiting until His enemies are made a footstool for His feet. He is waiting for your sickness, unbelief, depression, or disease, or any problem that you are dealing with, to be made a footstool for His feet. We can take every aspect of our life and, by our faith, make it a footstool for His feet right now. You can say to those things, "You were conquered by the blood of Christ back at the cross. You have no right to exist in my life. He made you His footstool. He is waiting for me to exercise His victory, to wake up and proclaim it, to enforce that which has already been won." This law is already on the books. All you have to do is be the one who enforces it.

> For by one offering He has perfected for all time those who are sanctified. And the Holy Spirit also bears witness to us; for after saying,
> "THIS IS THE COVENANT THAT I WILL MAKE WITH THEM
> AFTER THOSE DAYS, SAYS THE LORD:
> I WILL PUT MY LAWS UPON THEIR HEART,
> AND UPON THEIR MIND I WILL WRITE THEM,"
> He then says,
> "AND THEIR SINS AND THEIR LAWLESS DEEDS
> I WILL REMEMBER NO MORE."
> Now where there is forgiveness of these things, there is no longer any offering for sin. (Hebrews 10:14-18)

By one offering that was made 2,000 years ago, God has forever perfected those who are sanctified. There is nothing to wait for. You are believing a lie when you allow time to pass without appropriating what He has already accomplished. We repent on our face before God for allowing one more day to go by without receiving what He has done for us. You say, "I've never seen it." No, but it has happened. People have reached into it. Enoch did it before the cross (Hebrews 11:5). It has taken place. "Where there is forgiveness of these things, there is no longer any offering for sin." There is nothing that you can do or offer that will bring you into this. You simply

---

Hebrews 11:5 By faith Enoch was taken up so that he should not see death; AND HE WAS NOT FOUND BECAUSE GOD TOOK HIM UP; for he obtained the witness that before his being taken up he was pleasing to God.

must believe that it has already been done, that it is right here, and that you can have it. We believe in resurrection life, but in the same breath, I would include several other things that we believe in. We believe in the manifestation of the sons of God, but we have never seen them before. We could make a long list of everything that we, in this fellowship, have believed for a long time and have never seen. We can either become discouraged and buy into a lie, or we can become a people of faith who absolutely stand up against every delay, every lie, and every deception in the spirit realm that holds us back from knowing the truth. What happens when you know the truth? It sets you free (John 8:32).

Lord, set us free by knowing the truth. This is the truth about the Word of God. This is the truth about our sanctification. This is the truth about resurrection life. Open your heart to the truth, and accept what Christ's blood won for you as the sacrifice already accepted by the Father. Accept the fact that once for all time you have been sanctified by the offering of His blood that sweeps away every sin, every disease, and every challenge that you face. We literally put on Christ (Romans 13:14). We put on the presence of the Father like a garment, and as that happens we put on life. In our hearts there has to be a commitment to life, and we have to stop excusing our unbelief. We do not need an excuse. We do not need to excuse why we don't have it yet. We do not have to explain it away. We do not have to think anything about it except, as Paul said, "I am pressing on to know the Lord." And what else was he pressing on to know? He was pressing on to know the power of Christ's resurrection—the life of Christ that was triggered at the moment of His

---

John 8:32 "And you shall know the truth, and the truth shall make you free."

Romans 13:14 But put on the Lord Jesus Christ, and make no provision for the flesh in regard to its lusts.

resurrection (Philippians 3:7-11). That power is ours. It is the power of the Holy Spirit. It is that power that heals us. The Holy Spirit dwelling in you is life, and how can life and death dwell together? They cannot.

Lord, deliver the Body of Christ from the deception of unbelief about Your Word, and about what You have done for us. We refuse to demean the sacrifice of Christ into just having a few gifts, ministries, and fruits of the Spirit. No, it should be the transformation of our life. It is the impartation of life to us. As the Father indwells us, He is sanctification. And we cannot live in His presence without likewise being those who are sanctified. Refuse death! Refuse disease! What about those who have passed on? I believe that they can walk back into our midst, because they already have resurrection life (1 Thessalonians 4:14-16). I believe that those who die at this time, especially with this faith and this drive, do not go into purgatory or float around as disembodied spirits. They put on

---

Philippians 3:7-11 But whatever things were gain to me, those things I have counted as loss for the sake of Christ. [8] More than that, I count all things to be loss in view of the surpassing value of knowing Christ Jesus my Lord, for whom I have suffered the loss of all things, and count them but rubbish in order that I may gain Christ, [9] and may be found in Him, not having a righteousness of my own derived from the Law, but that which is through faith in Christ, the righteousness which comes from God on the basis of faith, [10] that I may know Him, and the power of His resurrection and the fellowship of His sufferings, being conformed to His death; [11] in order that I may attain to the resurrection from the dead.

1 Thessalonians 4:14-16 For if we believe that Jesus died and rose again, even so God will bring with Him those who have fallen asleep in Jesus. [15] For this we say to you by the word of the Lord, that we who are alive, and remain until the coming of the Lord, shall not precede those who have fallen asleep. [16] For the Lord Himself will descend from heaven with a shout, with the voice of the archangel, and with the trumpet of God; and the dead in Christ shall rise first.

life (2 Corinthians 5:1-3). And I bet the first thing they do is scream, "Oh my God, I have been ripped off! I could have had this long ago."

The purpose of the cloud of witnesses that is surrounding us, in resurrection life, is to help us (Hebrews 12:1). We say, "All right, help us!" We want to be delivered from the consciousness of sin, the consciousness of failure, and the deception that holds us back. God loose us. I declare, be healed! Just as Jesus said, according to your faith be it unto you (Matthew 9:29). Do you believe in the blood of Christ? Do you believe in His sacrifice? Do you believe in the power of the Father that reached down, pulled Christ out of the grave, resurrected Him, and gave Him life? The power of the Father is doing that same thing in you, if you will not reject it (Ephesians 1:18-20). Lord, we do not reject it. We open our hearts to it. We believe Your Word until there are no sick among us and we come into resurrection life!

---

2 Corinthians 5:1-3 For we know that if the earthly tent which is our house is torn down, we have a building from God, a house not made with hands, eternal in the heavens. ² For indeed in this house we groan, longing to be clothed with our dwelling from heaven; ³ inasmuch as we, having put it on, shall not be found naked.

Hebrews 12:1 Therefore, since we have so great a cloud of witnesses surrounding us, let us also lay aside every encumbrance, and the sin which so easily entangles us, and let us run with endurance the race that is set before us.

Matthew 9:29 Then He touched their eyes, saying, "Be it done to you according to your faith."

Ephesians 1:18-20 I pray that the eyes of your heart may be enlightened, so that you may know what is the hope of His calling, what are the riches of the glory of His inheritance in the saints, ¹⁹ and what is the surpassing greatness of His power toward us who believe. These are in accordance with the working of the strength of His might ²⁰ which He brought about in Christ, when He raised Him from the dead, and seated Him at His right hand in the heavenly places.

CHAPTER 13

Lord, I Believe in Your Resurrection – Help My Unbelief

As believers in Christ, we understand the importance of the death of Jesus on the cross, and what it means to our salvation. There has been a great deal of teaching about the work of the cross in our lives. In this message, I want to focus on the resurrection of Jesus Christ because we need a greater understanding of it. It was Christ's resurrection and ascension that triggered the outpouring of the Holy Spirit on the Day of Pentecost (Acts 2:1-4). You cannot separate the outpouring of the Holy Spirit from the events that took place, from Christ's resurrection up to the Day of Pentecost. The Lord Himself said, "The Spirit will not come until I have been resurrected and go to the Father" (John 16:7).

Acts 2:1-4 And when the day of Pentecost had come, they were all together in one place. ² And suddenly there came from heaven a noise like a violent, rushing wind, and it filled the whole house where they were sitting. ³ And there appeared to them tongues as of fire distributing themselves, and they rested on each one of them. ⁴ And they were all filled with the Holy Spirit and began to speak with other tongues, as the Spirit was giving them utterance.

John 16:7 "But I tell you the truth, it is to your advantage that I go away; for if I do not go away, the Helper shall not come to you; but if I go, I will send Him to you."

To me, the resurrection of Jesus Christ is the centerpiece of the universe. The cross without the resurrection is ineffective. What makes it effective is not simply that Jesus died on the cross, but that He was resurrected. Without the resurrection, we have nothing. We tend to lose the awareness of that in our lives. There is so much more for us to see about the reality of the resurrection of Jesus. I personally believe that the greatest expenditure of energy that has ever taken place in the universe was when God reached down and raised Jesus from the dead (Ephesians 1:19-20). In my opinion, there was more power and energy in that event than when He created the world, because it was through the resurrection of Jesus that the Father broke the bondage of death (Hebrews 2:14-15). The bondage of death was created when man relinquished his authority in the Garden by his disobedience to the Father (Genesis 2:16-17). It took the mighty power of God to resurrect Jesus from the dead. Therefore, you cannot overstate what the resurrection was and what it means to us today. We really need to press in with our spirits, and in our faith, to appropriate more of the power of the resurrection of Christ in our lives.

The heritage of our churches, going back many years, began with the Pentecostal movement. Therefore, we believe in the baptism of the Holy Spirit; we believe in signs and wonders; we believe in speaking in tongues and in exercising all of the fruit and the gifts of the Spirit.

Ephesians 1:19-20   And what is the surpassing greatness of His power toward us who believe. These are in accordance with the working of the strength of His might [20] which He brought about in Christ, when He raised Him from the dead, and seated Him at His right hand in the heavenly places.

Hebrews 2:14-15   Since then the children share in flesh and blood, He Himself likewise also partook of the same, that through death He might render powerless him who had the power of death, that is, the devil; [15] and might deliver those who through fear of death were subject to slavery all their lives.

Genesis 2:16-17   And the LORD God commanded the man, saying, "From any tree of the garden you may eat freely; [17] but from the tree of the knowledge of good and evil you shall not eat, for in the day that you eat from it you shall surely die."

Because the manifestations of the Spirit have been with us for so long, we tend to lose the concept that these are the very experiences that people fought so hard for in their faith. They are experiences that had been lost to the Church. You don't have to go back very far in history to find a time when most churches no longer believed in the baptism of the Holy Spirit and the gifts of the Spirit. It is important for us to remember the faith that obtained what we have today, because there are still more things that God has set before His people. He is bringing us to a tremendous banquet, and He has set a table before us (Isaiah 25:6). You do not want to come to that table and just pick at a few things and walk away still hungry. Even worse, you do not want to walk away satisfied. However, that is what we tend to do. Even though everything we are walking in now was born out of tremendous sacrifice and intercession to see what is in the Bible restored, we can easily lose that very cry that brought us to this place. Today we need to pursue the Lord on another level.

Personally, I want to make sure there is nothing in my heart that is satisfied with the way things are. We tend to be satisfied with what we have, and in that satisfaction, we let go of what the real potential is in God. Many doctrines have been formed by people seeing what the Scriptures say, but then mixing that with their interpretation of what is possible based on what they see around them. If something does not seem possible, we tend to negate what the Scriptures say and thereby make those things unattainable. That is literally what happened with regard to the gifts of the Spirit. Because it had been so long since anyone had moved in the gifts, scholars and others just assumed, "These gifts do not exist. We obviously don't have them, so let's create doctrines that say they don't exist in our generation. Then we will feel much better." It doesn't feel good to believe that something is available when we do not seem to have it. For me, I want

---

Isaiah 25:6   And the LORD of hosts will prepare a lavish banquet for all peoples on this mountain; a banquet of aged wine, choice pieces with marrow, and refined, aged wine.

to live in the assurance that there is so much available and possible in God. If we do not have something yet, that does not mean we cannot have it. Let God be true and every man a liar (Romans 3:4). The truth exists in God. If I have not appropriated something, that is not God's problem. Because I do not have it does not mean it is not available. Because I do not see it does not mean it does not exist. If it is in the Word of God, then it is available. The resurrection of Jesus Christ makes it available. The problem is that our doctrines put our resurrection way off into the future, so we don't concern ourselves with what we should have today by virtue of Christ's resurrection (John 11:23-26). In reality, we should be extremely concerned about what we do not have that has been made available to us.

In Mark the 9th chapter is a great Scripture about what happened after the transfiguration of Jesus on the mountain. When Jesus came down from the mountain, He saw a crowd surrounding the disciples:

> And He asked them, "What are you discussing with them?" And one of the crowd answered Him, "Teacher, I brought You my son, possessed with a spirit which makes him mute; and whenever it seizes him, it dashes him to the ground and he foams at the mouth, and grinds his teeth, and stiffens out. And I told Your disciples to cast it out, and they could not do it." And He answered them and said, "O unbelieving generation, how long shall I be with you? How long shall I put up with you? Bring him to Me!"

Romans 3:4 May it never be! Rather, let God be found true, though every man be found a liar, as it is written, "That Thou mightest be justified in Thy words, and mightest prevail when Thou art judged."

John 11:23-26 Jesus said to her, "Your brother shall rise again." 24 Martha said to Him, "I know that he will rise again in the resurrection on the last day." 25 Jesus said to her, "I am the resurrection and the life; he who believes in Me shall live even if he dies, 26 and everyone who lives and believes in Me shall never die. Do you believe this?"

And they brought the boy to Him. And when he saw Him, immediately the spirit threw him into a convulsion, and falling to the ground, he began rolling about and foaming at the mouth. And He asked his father, "How long has this been happening to him?" And he said, "From childhood. And it has often thrown him both into the fire and into the water to destroy him. But if You can do anything, take pity on us and help us!" [This is what we are interested in.] And Jesus said to him, "'If You can!' All things are possible to him who believes." Immediately the boy's father cried out and began saying, "I do believe; help my unbelief." (Mark 9:16-24)

Jesus accused the disciples of being an unbelieving generation, but we have a generation today in which people do not even believe in demon possession. I am sure that our level of faith would not have been any better than theirs. The young man fell down, foaming at the mouth, and was rolling on the ground. We would probably be yelling, "Oh my God!" But Jesus simply ignored it, turned to the father and said, "How long has he been this way?" The young man had been that way from childhood. His father had lived with this condition for all of his son's life. He believed in Jesus; he had brought his son to Him to be healed. But he also had unbelief based on what he had seen during the lifetime of his son. He said, "I do believe; help my unbelief." This story is a tremendous example for us, because this is where we all live.

We have a general faith. We believe in healing, but the real challenge comes when **we** need a healing. The difference between believing in healing and receiving a healing is believing that God will do it for you. First of all, you have to believe that He loves you and wants to heal you. Secondly, you have to deal with the conditioning from your long association with your need that has formed unbelief. Can God heal? Will He heal? Absolutely! In fact, there is a long list of things that God can do. But when we read through that list, we think of all the things that God has not done for us. This father said it perfectly: "Lord, I believe; help my unbelief."

I want to get over my unbelief because unbelief, like those doctrines we mentioned earlier, is rooted in what we have never seen or experienced before. When you study the history of the outpouring of the Holy Spirit, as it was restored to the Church, you find that it took a long time. Our founder, John Stevens, used to tell stories about the early days of the Pentecostal movement. When he was a young man, he watched people come to receive the baptism of the Holy Spirit, and at times it would take hours, days, or months before people received it. Why did it take so long? Because they had to overcome their unbelief that resulted from the fact that people had not received it up until then. They were seeking the Holy Spirit, so you cannot say that they did not believe that God could fill them. They did believe. But there was an unbelief that they had to overcome because the experience had never been theirs before. We are still in a time of restoration; it did not stop with the renewed outpouring of the Holy Spirit. There were many things that the early Church walked in that we are yet to experience. But we are stopped by a wall of unbelief that is based on the fact that none of us have ever experienced those things.

In this account of Jesus healing the young man who was possessed by a spirit, it is interesting that the Lord never put down the father. When the father said, "I believe; help my unbelief," Jesus did not say, "If you only have half-faith then I am not going to do this for you. You can't believe and also have unbelief." Jesus knew well that this was part of the condition of mankind, something that we all face. However, we must recognize that we in this fellowship have had a faith to be constantly moving the line of experience forward into the Kingdom. The question that we face is, "Are we too settled and happy with what we have? Are we passive because it takes too much energy to obtain the promises?" The people who first broke through into the baptism of the Holy Spirit had to put a great deal of time, energy, and intercession into it. Today, we lay hands on people and right away they receive the Holy Spirit and start speaking in tongues. Soon they are moving in prophecy, psalms, and gifts of the Spirit. It happens by impartation almost instantly because we have overcome the unbelief that says those things cannot happen.

Receiving the Holy Spirit is not a problem today; the problem is all the things that we do not yet have. We need to be a people who move beyond the present line of unbelief. We should be ones, like the men and women of faith in the past, who are driven to see the world change by virtue of what is possible in God. Are we doing that? Are we walking in our heritage? We cannot say, "Our forefathers did it. Look at all the things that John Stevens attained! You can hardly count all the things that he changed." But what have we changed in the last year? That is what I care about. What are we going to change in the next two weeks? Do we even care about change anymore? Are we still here to do that? We should not be able to keep ourselves back from change, because it is our spiritual heredity. It should be so innate to who and what we are that we cannot stop from pressing into God until there is breakthrough after breakthrough, until everything in the Word of God has been fulfilled.

The apostle Paul had that quality in his spirit. His cry was, "That I may know Him, and the power of His resurrection and the fellowship of His sufferings, being conformed to His death; in order that I may attain to the resurrection from the dead" (Philippians 3:10-11). Today doctrine and theology take everything about the resurrection and put it off into heaven, or after death. But Paul was not talking about the resurrection because he wanted to die. He recognized that there is the ability to know Christ. And when you come to know

Him, He is the way, the truth, and the life (John 14:6). He is the resurrection (John 11:25). In Christ, Paul saw the power of resurrection that he could experience in this life. Paul emphasized Jesus' death on the cross because he was focused on His resurrection. He wanted to be conformed to His death that he might attain to the resurrection from the dead, because the power of God is in the resurrection. The power is not in the cross devoid of the resurrection. The cross provides our forgiveness from sin; it brings our deliverance. We are thankful for that, but we should not forget that it is the resurrection that brings life. It is the resurrection that brings the power to the Church. Paul contended for that. He wanted to know Christ and the power of His resurrection. That power was evident at the resurrection of Jesus, as we read in Matthew 27:50-53:

> And Jesus cried out again with a loud voice, and yielded up His spirit. And behold, the veil of the temple was torn in two from top to bottom, and the earth shook; and the rocks were split, and the tombs were opened; and many bodies of the saints who had fallen asleep were raised; and coming out of the tombs after His resurrection they entered the holy city and appeared to many.

Did you notice the time change in this Scripture? It jumped from the moment Jesus died on the cross to events after His resurrection. Here is the point: when Jesus was resurrected, everything that we are believing for happened right then. Many who were dead were raised at that moment. There is nothing that we are waiting for; Jesus did it all. We have all this doctrine and teaching that tells us we have to wait. But Jesus did not wait. He resurrected many saints at the time of His resurrection. They came out of the tombs in resurrected bodies by virtue of His resurrection. Where did they go? Remember,

---

John 14:6 Jesus said to him, "I am the way, and the truth, and the life; no one comes to the Father, but through Me."

when Jesus ascended, He ascended in a cloud (Acts 1:9). The Book of Hebrews tells us about the great cloud of witnesses, referring to those who had died before the coming of Christ (Hebrews 12:1). These were people of faith, like Abraham and David, who had waited centuries for the resurrection. When Jesus was crucified, He went to be with them. And when He was resurrected, the power of the resurrection was so strong that it resurrected all of them as well (Ephesians 4:8-10).

Everything that is to be available by virtue of the resurrection is available **now** by virtue of Christ's resurrection. We don't want to be those who say, "I can't have this." Who are we to decide what we can or cannot have in Christ? Who are we to place limits on the power of the resurrection of Jesus Christ? Yet we do limit it because we have never seen, personally, the life that comes from His resurrection. Jesus said, "I am the door; if anyone enters through Me, he shall be saved, and shall go in and out, and find pasture. The thief comes only to steal, and kill" (John 10:9-10). If you ever wanted to know what satan is doing at any given time, here you have it out of the mouth of Jesus. The thief, who is satan, is always stealing and killing. What is he stealing? He is stealing your faith in what is available to you in the resurrection of Jesus Christ. By doing that, he subsequently kills you, because you either have the life that is available through the resurrection, or you die because you are

---

Acts 1:9   And after He had said these things, He was lifted up while they were looking on, and a cloud received Him out of their sight.

Hebrews 12:1   Therefore, since we have so great a cloud of witnesses surrounding us, let us also lay aside every encumbrance, and the sin which so easily entangles us, and let us run with endurance the race that is set before us.

Ephesians 4:8-10   Therefore it says, "When He ascended on high, He led captive a host of captives, and He gave gifts to men." 9 (Now this expression, "He ascended," what does it mean except that He also had descended into the lower parts of the earth? 10 He who descended is Himself also He who ascended far above all the heavens, that He might fill all things.)

devoid of that life. Jesus said, "I came that they might have life, and might have it abundantly" (John 10:10).

You can say, "I have life! I got up this morning; I brushed my teeth, combed my hair, and ate my breakfast. I am alive." Not according to Jesus. "Jesus therefore said to them, 'Truly, truly, I say to you, unless you eat the flesh of the Son of Man and drink His blood, you have no life in yourselves'" (John 6:53). Humans are not really alive, not in the way this Scripture talks about. We may use the same word— "life"—but it has an entirely different meaning. We do not have life in ourselves. We are absolutely dependent on external things for our life. If you don't believe that, stop breathing for a minute and then tell me if you have life in yourself. If you were to stop drinking water, it would not be too many days before you died. That death would simply reflect the true state of your being. What we call "life" is totally dependent on something outside of us to sustain it. Jesus said, "That is not the life I am talking about." He made it very clear that, in this state, we have no life in ourselves. Life in yourself means you exist as an independent being, needing nothing. The life of God is resident within Himself. He does not breathe, He does not drink water, and yet He remains alive. He cannot be separated from that life.

Jesus said about Himself, "Truly, truly, I say to you, an hour is coming and now is, when the dead shall hear the voice of the Son of God; and those who hear shall live. For just as the Father has life in Himself, even so He gave to the Son also to have life in Himself" (John 5:25-26). As we read in Matthew 27:52-53, the dead heard the voice of the Son of God and lived. That happened. They received the same life that God has, because He imparted it to Jesus. I do not believe that Jesus was born with that kind of life, but there was a time when God imparted it to Him. He had to be human first. If He had been born with life in Himself, then He would not have been human in the same way that we are human. The fact that we have no life in ourselves is what differentiates us from God. God is life. So it is extremely significant that the Father gave Jesus life until He had it within Himself. Jesus said, "I am the way, and the truth, and the life" (John 14:6). He also said, "No one takes My life from Me; I lay it down" (John 10:17-18). Jesus had to lay His life down because you cannot take away that kind of life. In contrast, someone could take away your life, or my life, in the blink of an eye. Why? Because it is not the same kind of divine life that Jesus spoke of.

When we talk about resurrection life, we are talking about something completely different than what we have now. This is what Paul meant when he said, "I am pressing in to know Him, and the power of His resurrection, being conformed to His death." In other words, he was putting off this so-called life because he was reaching into Christ's life. When Jesus said, "I came that you might have life, and have it more abundantly," He was not talking about the life we have right now. He was talking about imparting His life to us. Jesus is the light of the world, the light of life (John 8:12). His life is the power that breaks death, and it was turned loose at His resurrection. We cannot say, "That was just for Jesus." If that resurrection was just for Jesus, what were all those other people doing coming out of their graves? Many people take the promises in the Bible and say, "These are not for us. They were for a different dispensation, or will be for us in the future." I attended a Bible school that was steeped in unbelief. To them, almost everything in the Scriptures was not available. And I thought, "That cannot be!" Jesus came to make everything in the Word available to us. He came to give us life.

John 10:17-18 "For this reason the Father loves Me, because I lay down My life that I may take it again. [18] No one has taken it away from Me, but I lay it down on My own initiative. I have authority to lay it down, and I have authority to take it up again. This commandment I received from My Father."

John 8:12 Again therefore Jesus spoke to them, saying, "I am the light of the world; he who follows Me shall not walk in the darkness, but shall have the light of life."

Let's look at another Scripture to determine if the Bible tells us that the life of God is available to us in the "here and now" or only in the "sweet by and by."

> For the mind set on the flesh is death, but the mind set on the Spirit is life and peace, because the mind set on the flesh is hostile toward God; for it does not subject itself to the law of God, for it is not even able to do so; and those who are in the flesh cannot please God. However, you are not in the flesh but in the Spirit, if indeed the Spirit of God dwells in you. But if anyone does not have the Spirit of Christ, he does not belong to Him. And if Christ is in you, though the body is dead because of sin, yet the spirit is alive because of righteousness. But if the Spirit of Him who raised Jesus from the dead dwells in you, He who raised Christ Jesus from the dead will also give life to your mortal bodies through His Spirit who indwells you. (Romans 8:6-11)

"But if anyone does not have the Spirit of Christ, he does not belong to Him." In other words, if you are not saved you do not have the Spirit of Christ dwelling in you; you do not even belong to God. But if you have accepted Christ, then the Spirit of Christ dwells in you. From the moment of salvation, Christ is in you. What does Christ do? He reconciles us to God (2 Corinthians 5:18-19). How does He do that? He makes your spirit come alive, out of death into life, reconciling you to the Father. Through salvation, your spirit is regenerated unto God. But what happens to the physical body? The body is still in the same state it was in before the salvation experience. The physical body, as Jesus pointed out, has no life in

---

2 Corinthians 5:18-19 Now all these things are from God, who reconciled us to Himself through Christ, and gave us the ministry of reconciliation, [19] namely, that God was in Christ reconciling the world to Himself, not counting their trespasses against them, and He has committed to us the word of reconciliation.

it. "If Christ is in you, though the body is dead because of sin, yet the spirit is alive because of righteousness" (Romans 8:10). The state of your physical body does not change when Jesus Christ comes into your heart at the moment of salvation, but your spirit comes alive because of Christ's righteousness alone. Your spirit becomes connected to the Father, and then you can receive the Holy Spirit, which gives you access to all the Trinity and its functions. And yet, even with all of that, the salvation experience leaves the physical body in a state without the life of God. He has not given it to you yet. Remember how Jesus received that life. The Father gave it to Him. "But if the Spirit of Him who raised Jesus from the dead dwells in you, He who raised Christ Jesus from the dead will also give life to your mortal bodies through His Spirit who indwells you" (Romans 8:11). Who raised Jesus from the dead? God the Father raised Him from the dead. This is the kind of life that Jesus was talking about when He said, "I came that they might have life, and might have it abundantly" (John 10:10). How does that work? Christ reconciles us to the Father because the Father is the giver of life.

Let's look at Romans 8:11 again: "He who raised Christ Jesus from the dead will also give life to your mortal bodies through His Spirit who indwells you." Does this verse say that you have to be dead and go to heaven for the Father to give life to your mortal body? I don't read that in this verse. In the resurrection of Jesus, the saints were given access to resurrection life; but there is only one way to have that kind of life, and that is through the Father. We are believing for the Father to indwell us. The Father, who raised Jesus from the dead, has the ability to make alive our mortal bodies through the process of resurrection. Do you believe that? Yes, we believe it, but we have unbelief about actually experiencing it. Therefore, we should contend for it. Our prayer should be, "Father, come and take up Your abode within us; impart Your life to us as You dwell in the hearts of Your saints."

In John chapter 8, Jesus said, "If anyone keeps My word he shall never see death." When the Jews heard this, they accused Him of being demon possessed (John 8:51-52). They did not have the ability to grasp it because they had never seen it before. Their response to Jesus was, "No! Abraham died; all the prophets died; you can't talk about this kind of life because we have never seen it. Therefore You are demon possessed." Just like these Jews, we have never seen it either. It has never happened in our experience, but resurrection life is what we live for. We live to have the Lord help us overcome our unbelief. Just because we have not seen it does not mean it has never happened. Elijah was taken up to heaven without experiencing death (2 Kings 2:11). But we did not witness that, so we pray, "Lord, we believe; help our unbelief!" We determine not to live in this place of unbelief anymore. Like Paul, we strive to lay hold of the power of Christ's resurrection. I do not know all that is embodied in that, but I know some of it. However, I believe that there is more available to us through the resurrection of Jesus Christ than we have laid hold of. And it is available right here and right now.

This truth is contained in the sacrament of water baptism. Water baptism was derived from Old Testament traditions of purification. It is interesting how it has come through to the new covenant. Baptism has great significance to us. In the Book of Romans, Paul explains what baptism is all about:

> What shall we say then? Are we to continue in sin that grace might increase? May it never be! How shall we who died to sin still live in it? Or do you not know that all of us who

---

John 8:51-52 "Truly, truly, I say to you, if anyone keeps My word he shall never see death." [52] The Jews said to Him, "Now we know that You have a demon. Abraham died, and the prophets also; and You say, 'If anyone keeps My word, he shall never taste of death.'"

2 Kings 2:11 Then it came about as they were going along and talking, that behold, there appeared a chariot of fire and horses of fire which separated the two of them. And Elijah went up by a whirlwind to heaven.

have been baptized into Christ Jesus have been baptized into His death? Therefore we have been buried with Him through baptism into death, in order that as Christ was raised from the dead through the glory of the Father, so we too might walk in newness of life. For if we have become united with Him in the likeness of His death, certainly we shall be also in the likeness of His resurrection, knowing this, that our old self was [notice the tense] crucified with Him, that our body of sin might be done away with, that we should no longer be slaves to sin; for he who has died is freed from sin. Now if we have died with Christ, we believe that we shall also live with Him, knowing that Christ, having been raised from the dead, is never to die again; death no longer is master over Him. For the death that He died, He died to sin, once for all; but the life that He lives, He lives to God. Even so consider yourselves to be dead to sin, but alive to God in Christ Jesus. Therefore do not let sin reign in your mortal body that you should obey its lusts, and do not go on presenting the members of your body to sin as instruments of unrighteousness; but present yourselves to God as those alive from the dead, and your members as instruments of righteousness to God. For sin shall not be master over you, for you are not under the law, but under grace. (Romans 6:1-14)

Paul began by saying, "Are we to continue in sin that grace might increase? May it never be! How shall we who died to sin still live in it?" One of the precursors to the Pentecostal movement was the revelation of sanctification by faith. Have you ever seen anyone who was really sanctified and sinless? No, but Paul is saying that we should have it. This is an aspect of the resurrection life that is imparted by the Father. Because we have not seen it does not mean we are not to have it. And we definitely will not have it if we do not pursue it. "Or do you not know that all of us who have been baptized into Christ Jesus have been baptized into His death? Therefore we have been buried with Him through baptism" (Romans 6:3-4). Do you really understand what Paul is saying here? He said that we **were** buried (past tense) with Jesus through baptism. Imagine being literally buried with Jesus at the time of His burial. Do you know what would have happened to you? You would have been among those who came up out of their tombs and walked through the streets of Jerusalem. Wow! Wouldn't you like to have a baptism service with faith for that kind of experience today?

"We have been buried with Him through baptism into death, in order that as Christ was raised from the dead through the glory of the Father, so we too might walk in newness of life" (Romans 6:4). Why were we buried in baptism into death? So that we will be raised, as Christ was, to walk in the newness of life that only the Father can give.

> For if we have become united with Him in the likeness of His death, certainly [assuredly] we shall be also in the likeness of His resurrection, knowing this, that our old self was crucified with Him, that our body of sin might be done away with, that we should no longer be slaves to sin. (Romans 6:5-6)

I am so sick and tired of being a slave to sin. What is the result of that every day of my life? "The wages of sin is death" (Romans 6:23). The reason we are getting older every day and eventually dying is because we are still living in that old body of sin and death, which we should have thrown off when we were first baptized. You were saved, you were baptized in water, and you were baptized in the Holy Spirit. So removing the body of sin should have been something we experienced at the beginning of becoming a

---

Romans 6:23 For the wages of sin is death, but the free gift of God is eternal life in Christ Jesus our Lord.

Christian. And yet, because Christianity has been around for so long without that experience, we have made it impossible. It is easy to live in sin because when I look around me everyone is sinning. So why shouldn't I sin? That is what is influencing us. We morph the Scriptures into a doctrine born out of how conditioned we are by what we have seen. Every Christian I know still commits some form of sin. But that does not mean that we have to live in sin. That does not mean that there is no real deliverance from the old self.

This passage in Romans chapter 6 contains tremendously dynamic statements that are expressed in the "here and now." Does this Scripture say that we get baptized in order to live after we die? No, that is not what it says. It says that we go into the experience of baptism and we are raised in newness of life. I know we have never seen it, but it is going to happen. At some point, someone will say, "Lord, I believe; help my unbelief," and they will go into the water of baptism, literally be buried with Christ, and be raised up in the likeness of His life. That is why baptism was given.

All of these experiences are for us, and we repent of our passivity in pursuing them. We repent of allowing ourselves to be so conditioned by what we see, or do not see, around us that we say, "This lack of fulfillment is the Christian experience." Thank God for the men and women of faith down through history who stood up and said, "This cannot be right! There is more to possess." As pioneers in the Kingdom of God, they laid hold of it. Paul talked about laying hold of that for which he was laid hold of (Philippians 3:12). Let us begin to lay hold of those things for which God has laid hold of us.

Father, we believe; help our unbelief. Break off of us the conditionings and the unbelief of the age around us. Break off of us the unbelief

---

Philippians 3:12 Not that I have already obtained it, or have already become perfect, but I press on in order that I may lay hold of that for which also I was laid hold of by Christ Jesus.

of our own hearts that cannot believe the Scriptures because of what our eyes see and our ears hear. When Jesus came, He did not judge by what His eyes saw and what His ears heard. He judged by what God said (Isaiah 11:3). Let us follow in those footsteps. Lord, let Your Word have preeminence in our hearts, in our lives, and especially in our minds, until we walk by faith in all that You have made available to us. Father, help us to pursue, with tenacity, the power of the resurrection of our Lord Jesus Christ.

Isaiah 11:3 And He will delight in the fear of the Lord, and He will not judge by what His eyes see, nor make a decision by what His ears hear.

CHAPTER 14

Faith That Is a Gift

There is an impartation that comes from the young prophets out of their drive for the Lord and their drive to speak His Word and create by that Word. They have taken the Word that was imparted to them and have developed a determination and intensity toward the Lord. They are, as the Scripture says, violent to take the Kingdom by force; you can feel that from their spirits (Matthew 11:12). But the Lord is adding something more. He is adding faith, which is a gift of the Spirit. "For to one is given the word of wisdom through the Spirit, and to another the word of knowledge according to the same Spirit; to another faith by the same Spirit, and to another gifts of healing by the one Spirit" (1 Corinthians 12:8-9). The first thing they have to understand is that what they are receiving is a gift. True faith is a gift of the Holy Spirit to His people. No matter what measure of faith any of us have had up to this point, starting now, we need to have the faith that is a gift from God.

Matthew 11:12 "And from the days of John the Baptist until now the kingdom of heaven suffers violence, and violent men take it by force."

A gift is not something you work for; it is not something you pay for; it is not something you deserve. It is simply given. If you are going to have faith as a believer, as a prophet or prophetess, it is not something that you develop or work up within yourself. From its very beginning within you, this faith is something that comes as a gift from God. In other words, it will never be your faith; it will always be His faith. Your faith will fail, and your intensity will fail too. The gift of faith can make your intensity permanent, something that will never disappear. But you have to remember that you are receiving a gift. Let that be burned into your heart and your mind. Faith is capable of accomplishing great things, but while you are accomplishing those great things, you must never forget that they are not from you; they are His gift of faith.

Another aspect of the gift of faith is found in Hebrews chapter 6: "Therefore leaving the elementary teaching about the Christ, let us press on to maturity, not laying again a foundation of repentance from dead works and of faith toward God" (Hebrews 6:1). Maturity is what the school of prophets is all about. That is why we have a school of prophets and not just church; we are seeking to press into maturity in Christ. In writing about maturity, Paul laid out some of the elementary things that are foundational to a walk with God. One of these is repentance from dead works. What are dead works? They are the works that we try to accomplish by our own energy, by our own faith. Therefore, one of the first things that we do when we begin to press into maturity is to leave behind those works that we try to accomplish on our own. Another one of these foundational things is faith toward God. Not only is faith a gift from God, not a thing we can do of ourselves, but there is also only one way to exercise faith. Faith is always exercised **toward** God. It is never faith **for** things. It is not faith for miracles, or for healings, or for prophecy, or for works. You can only exercise the gift of faith toward God. Faith says, "Father, I believe in You. I believe that You can, and will, accomplish Your will." Faith without works is dead, but the works are not our works; they are His works (James 2:26; Ephesians 2:10). His works are accomplished by His faith that is given to us, which we express back to Him as the Creator of everything. Faith locks you into a deep relationship with the Father. He gives you the gift, and you exercise that gift back toward Him. This deep relationship between you and the Father is the true prophetic relationship that matures you.

Now let's read part of Paul's exposition about faith in Romans the 4th chapter. You should study the entire chapter to get an understanding of what faith really is. Paul's way of writing may seem a little difficult to understand at first, but let's read two verses that will help it all come together for you:

> For this reason it is by faith, that it might be in accordance with grace, in order that the promise may be certain to all the descendants, not only to those who are of the Law, but also to those who are of the faith of Abraham, who is the father of us all, (as it is written, "A FATHER OF MANY NATIONS HAVE I MADE YOU") in the sight of Him whom he believed, even God, who gives life to the dead and calls into being that which does not exist. (Romans 4:16-17)

Our faith is in accordance with grace. What is grace? It is a free gift; we do not do anything to earn it. By its very definition, grace is something we do not deserve. We also do not deserve faith. God gives it to us by His grace "in order that the promise may be certain to all the descendants, not only those who are of the Law, but also to those who are of the faith of Abraham, who is the father of us all." Abraham is the father of faith and we, as Gentiles, are brought into

---

James 2:26 For just as the body without the spirit is dead, so also faith without works is dead.

Ephesians 2:10 For we are His workmanship, created in Christ Jesus for good works, which God prepared beforehand, that we should walk in them.

the promises by the faith of Abraham. He believed for something in God that, through Christ, included us. By faith Abraham became a father of many nations "in the sight of Him whom he believed, even God, who gives life to the dead and calls into being that which does not exist" (Romans 4:17). This is fundamental to the school of prophets. The idea of prophecy is that we participate with the Father, through His Word, in calling into being that which does not exist. We manifest in this earth things that do not exist today. The school of prophets is always framing the age to come. According to the Book of Hebrews, the worlds that we see, that we know, were created out of that which did not exist (Hebrews 11:3). The ages were framed by the Word of God, as men and women of faith spoke that Word. That is what Abraham did. He brought forth many nations, and as Gentiles, we are among those nations. He brought us into a oneness with the promise that was for him and the nation of Israel. He brought us into that by faith, because he believed that he would be the father of many nations. By faith, he created us into a nation that did not previously exist.

This faith that is able to bring into being that which does not exist is so strong that it gives life to the dead. Faith is greater than death. Throughout history, we have seen people with faith raise the dead; we know that it has happened. How does it happen? It happens by faith toward God, because He is not affected by death. We are. But because God is free from death, He can bring life even when there is death. That is the faith Abraham had. The reason that Abraham could put his son Isaac on the altar and prepare to kill him was because Isaac was the child of promise. And the promise, if it is from God, is greater than death. When God said, "Put Isaac on the altar and sacrifice him to Me," Abraham had faith, not because he could

---

Hebrews 11:3 By faith we understand that the worlds were prepared by the word of God, so that what is seen was not made out of things which are visible.

raise the dead but because he knew that God could (Genesis 22:9-10; Hebrews 11:17-19). He knew that the promise could live, even if to him the promise seemed dead. Therefore, what he did, he did with faith toward God. He knew God had the ability to bring life out of death, to bring a new nation out of nothing.

God is beginning to develop you on an individual basis through the gift of faith, and by challenging that faith. He is getting ready to do something—and when He begins to give you this gift of faith, it comes with a warning. As you receive this faith, you have to remember that it is His faith. You did not work for it. Even though you may have it, it is still not yours. He gave it to you, and you must exercise it toward Him. People too often feel that it is their faith, and think, "Now I can exercise my faith and ask whatever I want and it will be done" (John 15:7). They get the idea that they are the ones who are doing it: "God gave me faith; now I can work miracles. I can pray and it happens; I get what I want." That is not likely, not if you are a part of a prophetic community looking to establish the Kingdom of God in the earth. You have to exercise that faith back toward Him, saying, "What You said, what You will, is going to happen. Even if You have to create it out of nothing, even if You have to bring it back from the dead, You are able to do it." That is what Abraham did, and we are getting ready to walk as he walked.

Genesis 22:9-10 Then they came to the place of which God had told him; and Abraham built the altar there, and arranged the wood, and bound his son Isaac, and laid him on the altar on top of the wood. [10] And Abraham stretched out his hand, and took the knife to slay his son.

Hebrews 11:17-19 By faith Abraham, when he was tested, offered up Isaac; and he who had received the promises was offering up his only begotten son; [18] it was he to whom it was said, "In Isaac your descendants shall be called." [19] He considered that God is able to raise men even from the dead; from which he also received him back as a type.

John 15:7 "If you abide in Me, and My words abide in you, ask whatever you wish, and it shall be done for you."

The intensity of the school of prophets will continue, and it will grow because that intensity will be toward God. It will be born out of knowing who He is. God will put you in situations to test you, to ask you, "Are you exercising your faith toward Me and My ability, or are you exercising something of yourself from what you believe and the way you think it should be?" There may be promises, but we are not the ones who fulfill those promises. God's promise to Abraham and Sarah was that they would have a child, but that promise was not fulfilled until it was impossible. There was not a child of promise until Abraham and Sarah were no longer able to have children. There will never be any fulfillment of God's promises until we know in our hearts, in our heads, and in our spirits that only He can do it. It is when we exercise faith toward God that we open the door for the impossible to happen. The sooner we learn that lesson, the sooner we can see faith work.

Abraham received the promise that he would have a child and be the father of many nations during the years in which he and Sarah were able to have children. Abraham was an amazing person. He was very wealthy. He was a tremendous warrior; he went out and destroyed the nations and kings that took his nephew Lot captive (Genesis 14:14-17). He was a force to be reckoned with. He was also a man of boldness. When God spoke to him to move from Ur of the Chaldees, he left everything. He left his father, his mother, and his country and went out to a place he had never seen or

---

Genesis 14:14-17 And when Abram heard that his relative had been taken captive, he led out his trained men, born in his house, three hundred and eighteen, and went in pursuit as far as Dan. [15] And he divided his forces against them by night, he and his servants, and defeated them, and pursued them as far as Hobah, which is north of Damascus. [16] And he brought back all the goods, and also brought back his relative Lot with his possessions, and also the women, and the people. [17] Then after his return from the defeat of Chedorlaomer and the kings who were with him, the king of Sodom went out to meet him at the valley of Shaveh (that is, the King's Valley).

known (Genesis 12:1-4; Hebrews 11:8). This was a man who was bold to believe and willing to do what God directed. You can imagine him in his youth, in his virility, saying to Sarah, "Let's go fulfill the promise of God. I know we can do this." You know that feeling. You have promises. You have Words over your life, and you have probably tried to fulfill them. But as long as those Words are still possible for you to fulfill with your own faith and energy, they will not happen.

I do not think that God necessarily wanted to wait for Abraham and Sarah to grow old, but He could not allow the promise to be fulfilled by them alone. The promise had to be fulfilled by Him. Do you remember what happened when Sarah heard the angel say, "You will have a child at this time next year"? She laughed, because in her heart she knew that it was impossible (Genesis 18:10-12). Like Sarah, when we come to the point where we are no longer saying, "Yes, I have the promise!" and we start laughing because the promise seems impossible, then we know that we are close to its fulfillment. The promises will not happen because of us; they will happen when they are impossible for us. However, I do not think

---

Genesis 12:1-4 Now the LORD said to Abram, "Go forth from your country, and from your relatives and from your father's house, to the land which I will show you; ² and I will make you a great nation, and I will bless you, and make your name great; and so you shall be a blessing; ³ and I will bless those who bless you, and the one who curses you I will curse. And in you all the families of the earth shall be blessed." ⁴ So Abram went forth as the LORD had spoken to him; and Lot went with him. Now Abram was seventy-five years old when he departed from Haran.

Hebrews 11:8 By faith Abraham, when he was called, obeyed by going out to a place which he was to receive for an inheritance; and he went out, not knowing where he was going.

Genesis 18:10-12 And he said, "I will surely return to you at this time next year; and behold, Sarah your wife shall have a son." And Sarah was listening at the tent door, which was behind him. ¹¹ Now Abraham and Sarah were old, advanced in age; Sarah was past childbearing. ¹² And Sarah laughed to herself, saying, "After I have become old, shall I have pleasure, my lord being old also?"

that we have to wait for fulfillment until we are a hundred years old and every other possibility is dried up. There is something that God is trying to accomplish in a relationship with us. Fulfillment can happen in our youth if there is a true revelation that everything that God has spoken is already impossible. I do not care how young you are, how strong you are, how virile or how capable you are; it is still impossible. We do not have enough energy, or enough ability, to bring the living back from the dead. These are things that are outside of our capacity. Yet that is what we can manifest by faith toward God.

All the men and women of faith described in Hebrews chapter 11 brought forth that which did not exist in the earth. That is what we are to do as a prophetic community. We are to bring forth the Kingdom of God, to change nations, to see every knee bow and every tongue confess that Jesus Christ is Lord (Philippians 2:10-11). That will not be done by our energy. God will have to do it, but we will trigger it as we express our faith toward Him. There are many impossible things that need to be accomplished. There are ages to be framed out of that which does not exist. We have the promises. God said He will do it. Christ said He will return and bring forth His Kingdom. God said that He will create a people. We can look around like Sarah and laugh, or say like Mary, "How can these things be?" (Luke 1:34) They can be because God can do them. When we know in our own hearts that He will accomplish what He said by our gift of faith exercised toward Him, then things which "eye has

---

Philippians 2:10-11 That at the name of Jesus EVERY KNEE SHOULD BOW, of those who are in heaven, and on earth, and under the earth, [11] and that every tongue should confess that Jesus Christ is Lord, to the glory of God the Father.

Luke 1:34 And Mary said to the angel, "How can this be, since I am a virgin?"

not seen and ear has not heard" will begin to manifest before us (1 Corinthians 2:9).

Smith Wigglesworth, the evangelist and faith healer, had a very simple saying: "Only believe." That is all he knew. Throughout his ministry, many tremendous healings and miracles took place; yet he was constantly challenged, like Abraham, about his own physical body. He would heal the sick, raise the dead, and cast out demons. Everyone he laid hands on would recover, but he would go home and be in such pain that he would literally roll on the floor all night as he was passing kidney stones.[14] He believed in healing because he knew that it was not him, the man with the kidney stones, who was healing people. He knew how to exercise faith toward God. What was impossible for him to accomplish for himself and his family, he was able to do for thousands of other people. When you look at the life of Smith Wigglesworth, or someone like Abraham, you understand how this process of maturing and becoming a school of prophets is God working in us to be those who exercise a gift of faith back toward God. In the school of prophets, there will never be any confusion about who is doing it, and why it is happening. It is a gift of faith exercised toward God, who is capable of accomplishing everything that He has promised us. He will give us that which He has spoken. He is capable of doing it, and He will do it. His Word promises it and He will complete it.

Do you believe that you can out-minister Abraham? Do not wait until you are a hundred years old to learn this lesson of how to exercise the gift of faith that you have received. Believe that you can cut the time short and, in your youth, move into a pure exercise of

---

1 Corinthians 2:9 But just as it is written, "THINGS WHICH EYE HAS NOT SEEN AND EAR HAS NOT HEARD, AND WHICH HAVE NOT ENTERED THE HEART OF MAN, ALL THAT GOD HAS PREPARED FOR THOSE WHO LOVE HIM."

[14.] Roberts Liardon, "Smith Wigglesworth—'Apostle of Faith,'" in *God's Generals: Why They Succeeded and Why Some Failed* (Tulsa, OK: Albury Publishing, 1996), 221-222.

faith toward God. Exercise your faith that God will fulfill all He has said He will do. Appropriate this special gift of the Spirit, the gift of faith. When you receive the gift, turn and bless others with it. Pass it on. Keep going until everyone has it. Lord, we draw Your faith, a gift of faith, in the name of the Lord.

CHAPTER 15

The Witness
and the Works

I want to get you moving in miracles. I experienced being miraculously healed from a terminal illness. After I was healed, I really anticipated a breakthrough for our fellowship into many more miracles and signs. I felt a shift for us as a people, and I fully expected to see us moving in more of the works of the Lord. Isn't that what the Scriptures tell us? "For we are His workmanship, created in Christ Jesus for good works, which God prepared beforehand, that we should walk in them" (Ephesians 2:10). God has prepared us for these works! What I saw in the Lord was that something is changing from the way we have walked in the past into a greater moving of the Spirit, not only having to do with healings, but with many aspects of our walk with God. Let's begin by reading the Lord's commission to the disciples in Mark chapter 16:

> And He said to them, "Go into all the world and preach the gospel to all creation. He who has believed and has been baptized shall be saved; but he who has disbelieved shall be condemned. And these signs will accompany those who have believed: in My name they will cast out

demons, they will speak with new tongues; they will pick up serpents, and if they drink any deadly poison, it shall not hurt them; they will lay hands on the sick, and they will recover." (Mark 16:15-18)

Jesus said, "These signs will accompany those who believe." This means that everyone who believes—everyone who is saved—will experience these signs. This is an elementary Scripture about believing in the Lord Jesus Christ as our Savior. It is very matter-of-fact that for those who go through this process of believing and being saved, these signs will follow them. It does not say that these signs will accompany some who believe. It does not say that these signs will accompany most who believe. These signs will accompany everyone who believes.

I have faith that we will move into this because these signs will accompany everyone who believes, and it is time to move in them. These works are a necessity, especially with the things that are coming upon the earth in these end times. One manifestation of the end time will be the lying signs and wonders. We know that when the enemy comes he will come with false works, false wonders, and false healings (2 Thessalonians 2:9-10). Do not let that scare you, because you will always know the difference. The difference is that whenever Jesus does something, it is filled with His love. However, satan is incapable of love. When he does a miracle it will be like the sound of fingernails scraping on a blackboard; it will be very disturbing because it will be devoid of love.

It is extremely important for us to move in these works because God is raising us up to be part of the mighty people that Joel spoke

---

2 Thessalonians 2:9-10   That is, the one whose coming is in accord with the activity of Satan, with all power and signs and false wonders, [10] and with all the deception of wickedness for those who perish, because they did not receive the love of the truth so as to be saved.

of (Joel 2:2). I believe that I am here to help raise up that mighty people, but there cannot be a mighty people to walk in the end time if they are incapable of working the works of God. That is why I have a drive in the Lord to see us moving in more miracles and healings. I want to impart an understanding of the works of God and the working of miracles—how they work, what is actually at work, and what blocks the works from being manifested.

After I was healed, I looked to the Lord and said, "God, I don't get it! I expected to see a breakthrough of healings happening through this people, and I am not seeing it." We have people who are in the hospital, as well as others who have real physical, emotional, or spiritual needs. That should not be. Why isn't it working for us? I don't think it is something we need to be condemned about, but it is something we need to look at. There could be different blocks for different people, so I want to cover several points in this message and break something loose for you. As I cover each point, search your heart for things that are personally holding you back, and believe for a deliverance to work the works of Him who sent you (John 9:4).

1. First, Cast Out the Demons

There is a great need for healing, for getting rid of afflictions, but the first thing that we have to do is take authority over the demons that are involved. As we read in Mark 16:17, "In My name they will cast out demons"; that's where we start. The first of the works of God is the casting out of demons and the devil. As the Scriptures state, "For this purpose the Son of God was manifested, that he might destroy

---

Joel 2:2 A day of darkness and gloom, a day of clouds and thick darkness. As the dawn is spread over the mountains, so there is a great and mighty people; there has never been anything like it, nor will there be again after it to the years of many generations.

John 9:4 "We must work the works of Him who sent Me, as long as it is day; night is coming, when no man can work."

the works of the devil" (1 John 3:8, KJV). It is the first sign that will accompany a true believer and it must be exercised before you will see other signs following as you work the works of God. The Lord recently gave me a Word to lay hands on a woman who was legally blind, and He showed me the spirits that were coiled around the optic nerve blocking her ability to see. If there is a need to minister recovery or health, you cannot do it with the demons there. You must first cast out the demons. That is why Jesus stated that as the first step when He commissioned the disciples. You have to get the devil out of the way because he is there to block the works of God. So when I blessed this woman, I said, "Lord Jesus, You showed it, and now by Your authority we, the Body of Christ, cast them out. You demons of blindness, we bring judgment on you, we take authority, and we cast you out. You have no place here; you have no hold on her or any aspect of her life, and we end your influence now. Begone, in Jesus' name." We see in the Scriptures examples of the Lord healing simply by casting out the demons, and not praying specifically for physical healing (Luke 11:14; Matthew 17:18). That's where you start. You start by taking authority over the devil.

2. "But I've Never Seen a Miracle"

The Lord showed me that another problem for many people is that you may have been walking with God for a long time but have never seen a healing or a miracle take place. When you don't see it, you feel as though that is why you cannot move in it. But consider that the disciples saw many miracles, yet when the Lord was coming down off the Mount of Transfiguration, they were unable

---

Luke 11:14 And He was casting out a demon, and it was dumb; and it came about that when the demon had gone out, the dumb man spoke; and the multitudes marveled.

Matthew 17:18 And Jesus rebuked him, and the demon came out of him, and the boy was cured at once.

to cast the demon out of the young man because of their unbelief (Mark 9:17-19).

We have to realize that when things do not happen, there is nothing wrong with the Word of God. Get that into your mind. There is never anything wrong with God's Word or His promises. It is like working with computers. When you do something that causes a computer to malfunction, you are never convinced that it was something you did but it is usually operator error. When the works that God promised do not happen, we have to recognize that the problem is operator error. So Jesus said to the disciples, "It is because of the littleness of your faith," and He became very frustrated with them about that (Matthew 17:17, 19-20). Again, these disciples had seen Jesus perform so many miracles. And I know a lot of people have struggled with this in their minds: "I've just never seen God move like that." Don't let that become a block in your mind. This feeling, "It is hard for me to believe for healing because I have never seen it," is never the truth. The disciples saw healings over and over again, and in fact, they had actually moved in healings themselves. Remember, Jesus had commissioned them and sent them out, so they had moved in these things (Luke 9:1-2). Yet they were still

---

Mark 9:17-19   And one of the crowd answered Him, "Teacher, I brought You my son, possessed with a spirit which makes him mute; [18] and whenever it seizes him, it dashes him to the ground and he foams at the mouth, and grinds his teeth, and stiffens out. And I told Your disciples to cast it out, and they could not do it." [19] And He answered them and said, "O unbelieving generation, how long shall I be with you? How long shall I put up with you? Bring him to Me!"

Matthew 17:17   And Jesus answered and said, "O unbelieving and perverted generation, how long shall I be with you? How long shall I put up with you? Bring him here to Me."

Matthew 17:19-20   Then the disciples came to Jesus privately and said, "Why could we not cast it out?" [20] And He said to them, "Because of the littleness of your faith; for truly I say to you, if you have faith as a mustard seed, you shall say to this mountain, 'Move from here to there,' and it shall move; and nothing shall be impossible to you."

Luke 9:1-2   And He called the twelve together, and gave them power and authority over all the demons, and to heal diseases. [2] And He sent them out to proclaim the kingdom of God, and to perform healing.

blocked by unbelief. You have to recognize that unbelief can be in your heart like a living, breathing entity at any time. It does not matter what you saw or moved in yesterday; that does not prevent you from letting unbelief creep into your heart.

3. Step Out in Trust

A great deal of this unbelief is based on self. It is based on embarrassment, not wanting to put yourself out there, not really trusting the Lord. "If I step out on the water, will the Lord really hold me up (Matthew 14:28-31)? If I really go for this, is the Lord going to come through?" You have a fear of what people will think about you or how you will look if you try something and it doesn't work. Here is the response to that: Who cares? The worst that could happen is that you will look like a fool. It does not matter how you appear to others. You moved in faith, and that is what matters. If the Lord shows you to do something, then do it. When Jesus was led by the Father to go to the cross, He appeared to those watching to be a false prophet, a failure, and a fool (Mark 15:29-30).

To work the works of God, you must learn to do what the Lord shows you and not be concerned about those observing. That was the first thing that Mary tried to teach people about working with Jesus: "Whatever He says to you, do it" (John 2:5). This is what I am trying to teach you as well: how to work with Jesus, because it is all about His presence. It will not happen just because you show up. It

---

Matthew 14:28-31   And Peter answered Him and said, "Lord, if it is You, command me to come to You on the water." [29] And He said, "Come!" And Peter got out of the boat, and walked on the water and came toward Jesus. [30] But seeing the wind, he became afraid, and beginning to sink, he cried out, saying, "Lord, save me!" [31] And immediately Jesus stretched out His hand and took hold of him, and said to him, "O you of little faith, why did you doubt?"

Mark 15:29-30   And those passing by were hurling abuse at Him, wagging their heads, and saying, "Ha! You who are going to destroy the temple and rebuild it in three days, [30] save Yourself, and come down from the cross!"

will happen because He shows up. Of course, He shows up because you show up with faith; then He does the works. That is the faith that Smith Wigglesworth had. He said of the gift of healing, "I just move, and I expect God to be there by the time I get there."[15] But he knew that it was not just him showing up; it was the presence of God that did it. He knew that nothing would happen unless God was there. Healing happens because you show up with that same faith, and then God shows up and He does the works. It is always by virtue of His presence.

What is your faith in? Your faith is not, "I can perform a miracle." Your faith is in God. That is exactly what the Scriptures tell us. Our faith is that the Lord will show up. When He shows up, nothing is impossible (Matthew 19:26). We lay hands on the sick and they **will** recover, because He is the One who is there (Mark 16:18). Therefore, get out of your mind how you will look or feel, or what might happen.

The main thing you have to learn is the voice of the Lord. The Holy Spirit speaks to you, and then you do it. As you practice that, your relationship with the Lord will grow deeper and deeper. However, if you do not do what He is showing or telling you, you tend to quiet that voice and quench the Holy Spirit (1 Thessalonians 5:19). It is easy to turn it off and say, "That's just a voice in my head. I don't really think that was the Lord." Why? Because He was asking you to do something that would be really embarrassing to you if it did not work; that's why. No, that is not the right response. When the Lord speaks to you, do it.

Matthew 19:26 And looking upon them Jesus said to them, "With men this is impossible, but with God all things are possible."

1 Thessalonians 5:19 Do not quench the Spirit.

15. John Robert Stevens, "God's Response to Our Worship," in *Meditations for Worshipers* (North Hollywood: The Living Word, 1975), 33.

4. I Believe; Help My Unbelief – A New Level of Faith

We are dealing with long-standing issues with regard to unbelief. But don't let that bother you. You could say, "I've heard all this before." First of all, you have not heard it like this before. We are on a new level. We have turned a corner. Something has happened. You must believe what I am telling you, because the Lord healed me in an amazing way, and your faith did it. You prayed my healing into existence. However, we continually face spiritual warfare, which is simply satan trying to rob us of what God did just a short time ago. We know the story of Elijah. One moment he is calling fire down from heaven, and the next he is in the desert lying under a tree wishing he was dead (1 Kings 18:37-38; 19:4). You read that and think, "How could that happen?" You should know how that happens, because it happens to you. That is the reality of spiritual warfare. It robs you of the sense of blessing that God just used you and moved through you to accomplish His work. But more than that, it tries to take away from you the reality of what just happened so that when you face the next situation you feel as if you are starting from scratch. We take authority over satan's attempts to rob you of who you are, what you are, and what you have accomplished, until you feel as if you are living year after year without seeing the moving of God as your reality.

---

1 Kings 18:37-38 "Answer me, O LORD, answer me, that this people may know that Thou, O LORD, art God, and that Thou hast turned their heart back again." [38] Then the fire of the LORD fell, and consumed the burnt offering and the wood and the stones and the dust, and licked up the water that was in the trench.

1 Kings 19:4 But he himself went a day's journey into the wilderness, and came and sat down under a juniper tree; and he requested for himself that he might die, and said, "It is enough; now, O LORD, take my life, for I am not better than my fathers."

In Mark chapter 9, a mute boy had suffered seizures since his childhood (Mark 9:20-21). We do not know how old this boy was. For all we know, he could have been in his twenties. With the condition that he had, he could not live on his own, so his father was still caring for him. Think about the father because the father was the one who initiated the healing. After years and years of watching the boy suffer, he brought his child to Jesus to be healed. Imagine how many times a day that young man was having seizures. People with epilepsy can have seizures ten, even twenty, times a day. Imagine that happening ten times a day for a period of ten years, and you get a picture of what this father had gone through. Still, he had so much faith in Jesus that he took this young man to see Him. It must have been a very difficult journey while his son was having seizures the entire way. In fact, the seizures probably increased the closer they got to Jesus because satan knew what was going to happen. Jesus said to the father, "All things are possible to him who believes." He replied, "I believe, Lord; help my unbelief" (Mark 9:23-24).

This applies to us. We have so much faith as a people, but there is just a little shroud of unbelief that comes over us. You believe in miracles. You know that the Lord can do it, but now it's time to see one. It's time to move in miracles. But in your heart, you realize that there is a little question or a little measure of unbelief. This is really important for you to get out of this message: unbelief is horrible! And you really need to repent of unbelief. I want you to go after unbelief in a way that you have never gone after it before. I want you to see that it is as vile as the Lord said it was when He was angry at

---

Mark 9:20-21 And they brought the boy to Him. And when he saw Him, immediately the spirit threw him into a convulsion, and falling to the ground, he began rolling about and foaming at the mouth. [21] And He asked his father, "How long has this been happening to him?" And he said, "From childhood."

Mark 9:23-24 And Jesus said to him, " 'If You can!' All things are possible to him who believes." [24] Immediately the boy's father cried out and began saying, "I do believe; help my unbelief."

the disciples because of their unbelief (Mark 9:19). Unbelief is a slap in God's face because it denies everything that He is and everything He has done. However, there is no condemnation to those who are in Christ Jesus, so we are not going to be condemned about it (Romans 8:1). But this one thing is certain: we are going to root out unbelief in a way that we have never done before.

Many of the greatest healings that we read about in the Bible were of people who had diseases and problems for a very long time. Still, no matter what they had been through, they believed in Jesus and His ability in God to heal them. The reason was that they had the promise of it in the Scriptures, and they were looking for that promise to take place.

Remember the man at the pool of Bethesda? He had endured the same sickness for thirty-eight years, and yet somehow he found a way to get to the pool every day and wait for a miracle to happen. As a result, he was there when Jesus came and he was healed (John 5:5-9). There is also the story of the woman with the issue of blood. She had been bleeding for twelve years and was weak from the loss of blood, yet she forced her way through a crowd of people that was pressing around Jesus. She moved through that crowd just to touch His garment and be healed (Matthew 9:20-22). I want you to

---

Romans 8:1 There is therefore now no condemnation for those who are in Christ Jesus.

John 5:5-9 And a certain man was there, who had been thirty-eight years in his sickness. [6] When Jesus saw him lying there, and knew that he had already been a long time in that condition, He said to him, "Do you wish to get well?" [7] The sick man answered Him, "Sir, I have no man to put me into the pool when the water is stirred up, but while I am coming, another steps down before me." [8] Jesus said to him, "Arise, take up your pallet, and walk." [9] And immediately the man became well, and took up his pallet and began to walk.

Matthew 9:20-22 And behold, a woman who had been suffering from a hemorrhage for twelve years, came up behind Him and touched the fringe of His cloak; [21] for she was saying to herself, "If I only touch His garment, I shall get well." [22] But Jesus turning and seeing her said, "Daughter, take courage; your faith has made you well." And at once the woman was made well.

remember that it was after twelve years that she was healed. Some of you need healings and a touch from the Lord but you say, "This has been going on for so long that I feel like the woman with the issue of blood. I have been this way for so long that I have gotten used to it. I have even made peace with God over it and it has become my way of life." No, today is the day that you touch God in a different way! You can press through into His presence just like that woman did.

After I experienced my healing, I asked the Lord, "Why aren't people moving in miraculous works and healings?" One of the things the Lord spoke to me is that He is working in us a new level of faith. Remember the story of Lazarus? The Lord loved Lazarus, who was one of His real friends, along with his whole family. Jesus heard that Lazarus was sick, so what did He do? He could have gone there immediately and healed Lazarus, but He did not do that. He waited until Lazarus died (John 11:3-6). When Jesus finally arrived at their home, Martha said to Him, "Lord, if You had been here earlier You could have healed Lazarus, but now he is dead." Jesus said to her, "Your brother will rise again" (John 11:21-24). What Martha was really saying is, "You just went beyond my level of faith. I know I have faith; I have seen healings. I have gotten rid of my unbelief surrounding healing. But raising dead people? I'm not quite there yet." What was Jesus doing? He was literally bringing those who were following Him up to another level of faith beyond what they had. There are levels of faith. We already have a level of faith that is amazing, so I do not want you to take this in a negative way because

John 11:3-6 The sisters therefore sent to Him, saying, "Lord, behold, he whom You love is sick." [4] But when Jesus heard it, He said, "This sickness is not unto death, but for the glory of God, that the Son of God may be glorified by it." [5] Now Jesus loved Martha, and her sister, and Lazarus. [6] When therefore He heard that he was sick, He stayed then two days longer in the place where He was.

John 11:21-24 Martha therefore said to Jesus, "Lord, if You had been here, my brother would not have died. [22] Even now I know that whatever You ask of God, God will give You." [23] Jesus said to her, "Your brother shall rise again." [24] Martha said to Him, "I know that he will rise again in the resurrection on the last day."

it is all positive confirmation. The Lord is simply bringing you up to the next level of faith that you are to move in. You are to be the mighty people who are to move in the end time. You are going to lay hands on people, cast out the devils, and heal the sick. You must understand what the Lord is doing in you.

5. Are You Witnessing?

One of the things we have to realize is that the works of God happen for a reason. They are given as signs to the unbelieving (John 10:37-38). The working of miracles, signs, and wonders is part of your testimony. It is part of you being a witness. The apostles were called witnesses, and they moved in signs and wonders (Acts 1:8; 2:43). You cannot separate the two. The signs come for a witness to those who do not believe; they do not come for the believer. That is why you have to be careful as you sit in church with the same people and relationships. These signs were really not given to be exercised in church; they were given to be exercised by the *ekklesia* for those to whom they were witnessing. And to be honest, some of you have not seen or moved in these signs because you do not witness to people.

I believe that is a fault that we have as a fellowship. Some of it can be traced back to conditionings from our past. We were living in a different era, and God was doing something then to change the

---

John 10:37-38 "If I do not do the works of My Father, do not believe Me; [38] but if I do them, though you do not believe Me, believe the works, that you may know and understand that the Father is in Me, and I in the Father."

Acts 1:8 "But you shall receive power when the Holy Spirit has come upon you; and you shall be My witnesses both in Jerusalem, and in all Judea and Samaria, and even to the remotest part of the earth."

Acts 2:43 And everyone kept feeling a sense of awe; and many wonders and signs were taking place through the apostles.

Christian landscape. That has happened, is happening, and will continue to happen. But it's important to recognize that what was said and done during that time does not necessarily apply to today. As a fellowship of people, we tend to feel that there is an old order aspect to the way people witness that we do not want to be involved with. So don't be involved with an old order way of witnessing. Instead, go out and heal people. That is the biblical testimony—laying hands on the sick and seeing them recover. That is how the apostles witnessed to people about Jesus; they talked about Him either before or after they healed. Believe me, when you heal the sick, you have their attention. When you raise the dead, you have people's attention. I love the prayer that Jesus made when He raised Lazarus from the dead. He said, "Father, I don't really need to pray to You about this, but I'm praying for those who are standing around, so that they will know I raised the dead through You" (John 11:41-42).

The original intent of the miracles was to be the testimony of Jesus, and the testimony of Jesus is the spirit of prophecy (Revelation 19:10). That is why we should prophesy, because it testifies of Jesus. But part of prophecy is walking up and prophesying to someone, giving them a revelation. Tell them what is going on in their lives, then pray for them. The spirit of prophecy is the revelation over people's lives. It is the testimony of Jesus, the witness of Jesus. If you do not witness to unbelievers about Jesus, you will not move in very much of the miraculous. You would be blown away by what would happen through you if you started talking to people about the Lord.

John 11:41-42   And so they removed the stone. And Jesus raised His eyes, and said, "Father, I thank Thee that Thou heardest Me. [42] And I knew that Thou hearest Me always; but because of the people standing around I said it, that they may believe that Thou didst send Me."

Revelation 19:10   And I fell at his feet to worship him. And he said to me, "Do not do that; I am a fellow servant of yours and your brethren who hold the testimony of Jesus; worship God. For the testimony of Jesus is the spirit of prophecy."

6. Have You Lost Your First Love?

Another issue you may be dealing with is that you may have lost your first love. If you have, the Bible is very clear in telling you what to do: go back and do the things that you did when you had your first love (Revelation 2:4-5). Even on a natural level, if you are having problems with your marriage relationship, go back and do the things you did when you were first in love. Your first love generated certain actions and ways of relating. You can easily test where you are at in your relationship. Just ask yourself if you are still doing, on a daily basis, those things that you did when you were first in love. People fall in love and get married, have children, get jobs to support the family, and struggle with finances and other problems. Then at some point they look around and say, "What happened to our relationship?" It may not necessarily be bad; it is just not what it was. It is not that first love. So you can understand what the Lord means when He says, "You have lost your first love for Me." But He tells us the way to change. Go back and do the things that you did when you were crazy, head-over-heels in love with Him. Take down the walls that you have built to Him because of your perception about how it has been going in your life, and see what changes.

To talk to people about the Lord, you have to be excited about something. I am excited about the Lord healing me! I can talk to anyone about that, and I do: "Do you know what just happened to me? The Lord just healed me!" I can bring it up in any conversation. The very definition of first love is that something happened between you and the Lord, and you are excited about it. The natural response is to go tell someone what just happened for you. When you fall in love with someone, you go tell your friends, "You have to meet this

---

Revelation 2:4-5 "But I have this against you, that you have left your first love. [5] Remember therefore from where you have fallen, and repent and do the deeds you did at first; or else I am coming to you, and will remove your lampstand out of its place—unless you repent."

new person in my life that I am so excited about. I'm in love!" Love is exciting, and that is just human love. Imagine what divine love is really like. Get that first love back so that you feel this drive to go talk to people. We all know what it's like when someone comes to your door and witnesses to you out of a sense of obligation. You are aware that they would rather be doing anything else besides knocking on your door. I do not want to be made to tell people about the Lord. I want to be excited to tell people about the Lord. I want to be bubbling over with the excitement of knowing Him.

People need salvation in this day, so I pray that the Lord does something for you that restores the excitement of that first love and it becomes your drive. Then be led by the Spirit. Do it with real wisdom and follow the leading of the Lord. If you are excited and connected with the Lord, He will show you the ones to talk to. Something will happen for them. Their lives will change because it is the Lord who is doing it and not you. When you are excited and relating to the Lord, then things are going to happen.

When we talk about being a mighty people, we are talking about God sending Christ into the earth again. You become the manifestation of Christ. We are His Body, the fullness of Him who fills all in all (Ephesians 1:22-23). Jesus was sent into the world as an expression of love. "For God so loved the world, that He gave His only begotten Son" (John 3:16). Everything about the sons of God coming forth, about a mighty people moving in the end time, is about a tidal wave of God's love in people that will minister to the world. Yes, we will stand up in church and prophesy, and things will change, but that is not what it's all about. That is one aspect; witnessing to the world is another aspect. Jesus said, "Go into all the world and preach the

---

Ephesians 1:22-23 And He put all things in subjection under His feet, and gave Him as head over all things to the church, [23] which is His body, the fulness of Him who fills all in all.

gospel" (Mark 16:15). Tell people about Jesus, but don't do it if you are not excited. Witness because you are excited to share your first love.

The Lord has given us several practical steps. Let's review them. To work the works of God, remember to first cast out the devil. If you feel, "I can't move in healing because I've never seen it," know that is a lie and throw it off. If you are scared of looking like a fool—who cares! Put your faith in God, not in yourself. If your problem is unbelief, repent of your unbelief. If you are not witnessing because of a reaction to an old order expression, move in this new expression. Or if you have lost your first love, return to your first love. Be excited! Then just move! If we are believers these signs will follow us, but we have to move in faith.

7. We Are His Witnesses

We have to move in healings and miracles because we are to be the manifestation of Christ in the earth, and healing was Jesus' calling card. Let's read about this in a conversation that Jesus had with the disciples of John the Baptist:

> Now when John in prison heard of the works of Christ, he sent word by his disciples, and said to Him, "Are You the Expected One, or shall we look for someone else?" And Jesus answered and said to them, "Go and report to John what you hear and see: the BLIND RECEIVE SIGHT and the lame walk, the lepers are cleansed and the deaf hear, and the dead are raised up, and the POOR HAVE THE GOSPEL PREACHED TO THEM. And blessed is he who keeps from stumbling over Me." (Matthew 11:2-6)

I like the term "the works of Christ" rather than healings or miracles. They are His works. They are what He does because of who He is. John the Baptist said, "I want to make sure this is the Messiah that we're dealing with," so he sent his disciples to ask Jesus, "Who are You really?" Jesus gave them His calling card: "Go back and tell John that the blind see, the deaf hear, and all these signs are happening." All of these works were the things God gave Jesus to show who He was. When Jesus spoke this, He was quoting Isaiah chapter 35 back to John. He answered him with Scripture. He knew that John would get it because Isaiah 35 is a messianic prophecy about the One who was to come. It was a logical response. John sent his disciples to ask Jesus, "Are You the Messiah?" And Jesus replied, "Go quote Isaiah 35 to John and tell him that it is speaking of Me."

> Then the eyes of the blind will be opened,
> And the ears of the deaf will be unstopped.
> Then the lame will leap like a deer,
> And the tongue of the dumb will shout for joy.
> For waters will break forth in the wilderness
> And streams in the Arabah. (Isaiah 35:5-6)

So what are you doing when you follow the Lord's command: "And these signs will accompany those who have believed" (Mark 16:17)? You are handing people Jesus' calling card and saying, "Do you want to know who I am? These signs are the calling card of Christ." Honestly, without the works of God we are nobody, but Jesus has given us His calling card. Jesus had only one thing to say when asked to prove who He was. He went back to the prophecies about the Messiah and said, "That is Me. This is what you are witnessing. Aren't you watching the blind see? Don't you see the deaf hear, the lame walk, and the Gospel being preached to the poor? Those are the prophecies. I am here as the fulfillment of those Scriptures." Read the messianic prophecies in the Bible. Time and time again they declare that these signs and works will occur when the Messiah appears. Read Isaiah 29:18-19: "And on that day the deaf shall hear words of a book, and out of their gloom and darkness the eyes of the blind shall see. The afflicted also shall increase their gladness in the Lord." There is also Isaiah 42:6-7: "And I will appoint you as a covenant to the people, as a light to the nations, to open blind eyes, to bring out prisoners from the dungeon, and those who dwell in darkness from the prison." Look at Psalm 146:7-8: "Who executes justice for the oppressed; who gives food to the hungry. The Lord sets the prisoners free. The Lord opens the eyes of the blind." Everywhere you read about the Messiah, you find the same works spoken about.

That is why it was so important that Jesus did these things when He came. That is why He said, "Don't stumble over Me. Just look at the works. The very works that I do testify about Me" (John 5:36). They started to stone Him and He said, "For which of the works are You stoning me?" (John 10:31-32). When they handed Jesus the scroll of Isaiah in the synagogue, what did He do? He opened it and read, "The Lord has anointed me to preach the gospel to the poor, to proclaim release to the captives and recovery of sight to the blind" (Luke 4:17-18). These things are repeated over and over in the Bible about Jesus, and He kept saying it over and over about Himself. He kept showing it to people. And now Jesus is saying to those who believe, "I'm sending you with My calling card. I'm sending you with the only thing I had to hand to people when I was on earth." The world needs the calling card of Jesus, and you need to be able to

---

John 5:36 "But the witness which I have is greater than that of John; for the works which the Father has given Me to accomplish, the very works that I do, bear witness of Me, that the Father has sent Me."

John 10:31-32 The Jews took up stones again to stone Him. ³² Jesus answered them, "I showed you many good works from the Father; for which of them are you stoning Me?"

Luke 4:17-18 And the book of the prophet Isaiah was handed to Him. And He opened the book, and found the place where it was written, ¹⁸ "The Spirit of the Lord is upon Me, because He anointed Me to preach the gospel to the poor. He has sent Me to proclaim release to the captives, and recovery of sight to the blind, to set free those who are downtrodden."

hand them that card. Show the works of God and say, "These works that you see are the fulfillment of the prophecies of the Messiah."

There are many who need that messianic confirmation. The Jewish people need that. The Arab people need a messianic confirmation. You can say, "I didn't need signs to believe." That is good. "Blessed are they who did not see, and yet believed" (John 20:29). You did not see but you believed, and the Lord blessed you in that. But there will be many who will need to see, because the seeing of these works will show them the glory of God. When Jesus healed a man who had been blind from birth, the disciples asked, "Lord, who sinned, this man or his parents? We know that if he is blind, someone must have sinned." And the Lord answered, "Neither, but this is that the glory of the Lord may be manifested" (John 9:1-3). There were others who were sick and Jesus said the same thing: "This sickness is so that the glory of the Lord will be revealed" (John 11:4). That is the way you are going to think. You are here for the glory of the Lord to be manifested. Did God actually bring sick and demon-possessed people around solely for Jesus to deliver? How would He do the works of God if there was no one to work on? That is why Jesus did not condemn them. He was not afraid to have sinners around Him, because He was able to forgive their sins and make the lame walk and give sight to the blind. Those people had been waiting, often for a very long time, not because they were sinners, but because God was going to manifest His glory in them through Christ.

When I was sick, I kept repeating Psalm 118:17: "I shall not die, but live, and tell of the works of the LORD." I pray that the Lord

---

John 9:1-3   And as He passed by, He saw a man blind from birth. ² And His disciples asked Him, saying, "Rabbi, who sinned, this man or his parents, that he should be born blind?" ³ Jesus answered, "It was neither that this man sinned, nor his parents; but it was in order that the works of God might be displayed in him."

be glorified in everything that He did in me. Every time there is a healing, it manifests the glory of the Lord. The truth is that He created us to be the expression of His glory. His glory will be seen in us through eternity (Ephesians 3:21). In the Kingdom, we will be like possessions in the Lord's house that He is very proud of. We will be there for God to say, "See what I did in these?" We will forever speak of the glories of the Lord. He will be glorified in what He has done in us.

You may not need a healing, but as you behold His glory you will be transformed from glory to glory into His image (2 Corinthians 3:18). Talk about a miracle! That is what we want. We want to be out healing the sick and raising the dead. Bring people in for the miracles and they will stay for sonship. They will stay for the transformation of their lives because there is a lot more after the miracles. After Jesus healed the two blind men they followed Him (Matthew 20:30-34). They became disciples. That is what I am saying. People will come in for the miracles, but then they will become a disciple out of it. Remember when the Lord healed the ten lepers? Only one came back to worship the Lord. Jesus said, "What happened to the other

---

Ephesians 3:21 To Him be the glory in the church and in Christ Jesus to all generations forever and ever. Amen.

2 Corinthians 3:18 But we all, with unveiled face beholding as in a mirror the glory of the Lord, are being transformed into the same image from glory to glory, just as from the Lord, the Spirit.

Matthew 20:30-34 And behold, two blind men sitting by the road, hearing that Jesus was passing by, cried out, saying, "Lord, have mercy on us, Son of David!" [31] And the multitude sternly told them to be quiet; but they cried out all the more, saying, "Lord, have mercy on us, Son of David!" [32] And Jesus stopped and called them, and said, "What do you want Me to do for you?" [33] They said to Him, "Lord, we want our eyes to be opened." [34] And moved with compassion, Jesus touched their eyes; and immediately they regained their sight and followed Him.

nine?" (Luke 17:11-18). They went back to living their lives. That is not what the Lord is looking for. He is looking for us to come and give our lives to Him after we have been healed. There is a great prayer for healing from blindness in Psalm 119:18. "Open my eyes, that I may behold wonderful things from Thy law." The Lord heals the blind so that they can behold His Word.

As you read in these Scriptures, there were often healings that took time. What is the time doing? It is entrenching your faith. Instead of going back into unbelief, you hold the miracle. These works need to explode on the earth! Something needs to explode in you where the works of God are concerned. All of this probing into your heart and spirit is for you to answer the question: why isn't it happening?

There was one healing the Lord performed where He took a blind man out of the city to heal him (Mark 8:23). Remember that story? Jesus had to walk him out of the city to get him out of the atmosphere of unbelief that He was in. Can you walk out of the city? Can you walk out of everything that has been a weight of unbelief on you? Whatever it is, work it out between you and the Lord, because doing these works is why He came. This is what He does. This is who He is. At some point there will be so many healings that we will lose

---

Luke 17:11-18 And it came about while He was on the way to Jerusalem, that He was passing between Samaria and Galilee. ¹² And as He entered a certain village, ten leprous men who stood at a distance met Him; ¹³ and they raised their voices, saying, "Jesus, Master, have mercy on us!" ¹⁴ And when He saw them, He said to them, "Go and show yourselves to the priests." And it came about that as they were going, they were cleansed. ¹⁵ Now one of them, when he saw that he had been healed, turned back, glorifying God with a loud voice, ¹⁶ and he fell on his face at His feet, giving thanks to Him. And he was a Samaritan. ¹⁷ And Jesus answered and said, "Were there not ten cleansed? But the nine— where are they? ¹⁸ Was no one found who turned back to give glory to God, except this foreigner?"

Mark 8:23 And taking the blind man by the hand, He brought him out of the village; and after spitting on his eyes, and laying His hands upon him, He asked him, "Do you see anything?"

count, but first something has to take place in your heart with the Lord that takes the lid off. Do something that walks you out of your atmosphere of unbelief, then never turn back. Once Jesus had healed the blind man, "He sent him to his home, saying, 'Do not even enter the village'" (Mark 8:26). He had to leave the atmosphere of unbelief to be healed, and he had to stay out of it to keep that healing. Find a way to stay out of your old atmosphere of unbelief.

I believe that the young people are getting this and they should move in it freely. Instead of just going to the elders, have the kids bless you. Believe in the healing and stay with it. God bless your faith. You are going to have faith. This is your opportunity to minister to people. There are probably many people you already know who really need a healing and a touch. Believe me when I tell you that we are going to have that explosion of works that the Lord showed me after I was healed. You are the ones who reached into that healing, not me. Something changed for you and you turned a corner. This message is only a booster to what has already happened. It all came together and it was explosive. So I know that you have this, and I am not going to let go of the fact that you have it. Now is the time for you to move in the glorious works of God!

CHAPTER 16

Intimate,
Creative Prayer

John Stevens had an intense drive to pray into existence the
will of God on the earth, to manifest into the visible realm what
is now invisible, and to call into being that which does not exist
(Hebrews 11:3; Romans 4:17). Through our intercession and travail,
we give birth to things that never existed in the earth before. This is a
major aspect of who John was and what he imparted to us. We are to
be those who bring the Kingdom of God, which is in heaven, to this
earth. One of the greatest burdens I feel for the younger generations
coming forth is that they have this drive in their spirits. God wants to
create a people of intercession and prayer. He wants this generation
to be those who know how to engage in prayer in a tremendous way.
However, when we talk about prayer, we immediately introduce our
own concepts of what prayer is and how we are to pray. I want to
start by throwing those concepts out the window. I want to give the

---

Hebrews 11:3 By faith we understand that the worlds were prepared by the word of God,
so that what is seen was not made out of things which are visible.

Romans 4:17 (As it is written, "A FATHER OF MANY NATIONS HAVE I MADE YOU") in the
sight of Him whom he believed, even God, who gives life to the dead and calls into being
that which does not exist.

Holy Spirit a clean slate to work with, because there is something more regarding prayer that God wants us to get ahold of right now.

If you study the previous outpourings of the Spirit, going back into the 1800s and the early 1900s, you will find that whatever God did in moving on the earth was always initiated by groups of people who prayed. The Moravians kept intercession going twenty-four hours a day for 100 years. It was this lifestyle of prayer that led to the experiences in God that happened for many years to follow. We know that we need God to move in this generation, but that is dependent on this generation being able to interact with God in a way that creates that moving. One of the first Scriptures that comes to mind concerning this issue, and gives us a place to begin talking about prayer and intercession, is in 2 Chronicles chapter 7. God said,

> "If I shut up the heavens so that there is no rain, or if I command the locust to devour the land, or if I send pestilence among My people, and My people who are called by My name humble themselves and pray, and seek My face and turn from their wicked ways, then I will hear from heaven, will forgive their sin, and will heal their land." (2 Chronicles 7:13-14)

The fact is, we usually talk about creating a new prayer life because something is missing in our current prayer life. This is what God was talking about to those people in Israel. They went so far in ceasing their prayer, their hunger, and their seeking after God, that things began to go wrong in the world around them. Do you believe that God controls your circumstances? God is Spirit, but He has to get your attention on the natural level, so He often arranges your circumstances to do just that. God wants to get our attention, and right now He is trying to get the attention of the whole world. I believe that we are in the end times and that events are moving along a certain course. As we come to the end of the age, we see God moving more and more through the situations that are happening in the world. Why? Because He is screaming to get our attention. He told Israel, "I will get your attention through these circumstances. Once I have your attention, if you will turn, humble yourself, pray, and seek My face, your circumstances can change." We have to have that sense, and our young people have to have that sense. Things can change through prayer and seeking God's face. That is what He wants from us. God wants things to change.

We do not believe the same way as many Christians do concerning end-time events. Part of the difference in our eschatology is this belief that things can change through prayer. Just because something is written in the Book of Revelation does not mean it has to happen. I believe that many problems happen because no one is doing anything to prevent them from happening. The truth is that if we pray, the mercy of God can intervene. I dislike the emphasis on a "rapture," the belief that God will take the Christians out of the tribulation, because it makes people almost delight in the horrible things that are happening in the world. Believers should say, "No, these events do **not** have to happen." We should have the faith of our father Abraham and contend with God and say, "Wilt Thou indeed sweep away the righteous with the wicked?" (Genesis 18:23). Let's see something different happen. Let's see a great outpouring of God's Spirit. After all that God went through to send Jesus Christ, His only Son, to suffer on the cross and bring about our salvation, I do not see why a single person has to go to hell. Why don't we pray instead for a wave of salvation to sweep over the earth and literally open people's hearts to the Lord? I am fine with satan ending up in hell, but I think that only he and his angels should be tormented there; he should be extremely lonely. Let's not give him anyone else to play with.

We need to move into a prayer life that can begin to change things, and one of the greatest ways we can do that is to learn from the prayer that Christ taught. We call it the Lord's Prayer, but it would be better identified as the disciples' prayer because He was teaching His disciples to pray. This prayer is not the Lord praying; it is Him teaching us and bringing us into His prayer. One of the reasons that the Lord's Prayer does not really work for people is because it is honestly not that meaningful to them. And we do not tend to live in something that is not meaningful to us; we drift away from it. I am looking for an impartation of a completely new feeling about prayer, and an entirely different way to engage in it.

"But you, when you pray, go into your inner room, and when you have shut your door, pray to your Father who is in secret, and your Father who sees in secret will repay you" (Matthew 6:6). Jesus said, "When you pray, go into your inner room." Go into that inner place within you. Go into the secret place, the deep place of your spirit, the deepest depths of who and what you are. Go into the place you probably rarely go, into that most intimate core of who you are. Then, when you enter that place, shut the door. Do not let anything else in. How do we do that? According to the Scriptures, Christ is the door; He has a way of closing us in with the Father (John 10:7). He came to reconcile us to the Father, and He is the One who can hold us in that place of His presence (Romans 5:10). He did not reconcile us just so we can say, "Now I can relate with the Father. I have access. When it suits me, I can tune into Him." No, He came to hold us, to enfold us in that place with the Father. So go into your inner room, shut the door, and pray to your Father who is in secret.

We know that God is Spirit. Most of the time He is invisible in a physical sense. That does not mean He cannot, or does not, manifest in the physical realm. He does, but for the most part He is invisible

---

John 10:7 Jesus therefore said to them again, "Truly, truly, I say to you, I am the door of the sheep."

Romans 5:10 For if while we were enemies, we were reconciled to God through the death of His Son, much more, having been reconciled, we shall be saved by His life.

to us. Yet we can be with Him in that secret, invisible place because Christ said, "Where I am, there may you be also" (John 14:3). We have a spirit, and Christ wants us to be with Him in the spirit. He wants us to come into a relationship with the Father who sees in secret. In this deep inner place within you, the Father sees you. He knows you in the depth of that place, and "your Father who sees in secret will repay you" (Matthew 6:6). The word "repay" is a valid translation of the Greek here, but another word that can be used is "restore." The Father will restore you. From that inner place with Him, He will restore us. Restore us to what? He will restore us back to Himself, back to the Garden of Eden, back to what we were created for. We were created for a relationship with the Father. That is what Eden was all about—a relationship with the Lord. God involved Adam with Himself in the creation. Adam named all of the animals; he was part of it (Genesis 2:19). We also read that the sons of God rejoiced when the earth was created (Job 38:4-7). God included you with Him at the time of creation.

God will restore you, but He will also give to you. It is not necessarily repayment, but it is giving to you that which you are asking for. Jesus explains this process. Before He teaches the Lord's Prayer, He sets the atmosphere. He dims the lights for us. He creates an atmosphere of intimacy. Get this into your mind: prayer is intimacy with God. According to the definition we have, we tend to think of prayer as something that we do from down here on earth to try to reach God

---

John 14:3 "And if I go and prepare a place for you, I will come again, and receive you to Myself; that where I am, there you may be also."

Genesis 2:19 And out of the ground the LORD God formed every beast of the field and every bird of the sky, and brought them to the man to see what he would call them; and whatever the man called a living creature, that was its name.

Job 38:4-7 "Where were you when I laid the foundation of the earth? Tell Me, if you have understanding, [5] who set its measurements, since you know? Or who stretched the line on it? [6] On what were its bases sunk? Or who laid its cornerstone, [7] when the morning stars sang together, and all the sons of God shouted for joy?"

up in heaven. Just the word "prayer" mentally evokes distance and separation. It evokes the idea that there is something we have to do because of the distance that we have from Him. Yet what Christ is trying to create for us is the exact opposite of that. He is trying to create a sense of intimacy. We are to go into our secret place, close the door behind us, and not let anyone else in, because we are about to engage in something very private and very intimate.

Intimacy is an essential part of a relationship. By its very definition, intimacy is something that you do with another person that no one else witnesses or is involved in. You do not do intimate things in front of an audience, at least you shouldn't. What satan is doing today in the area of lust and sex is bringing it out into the open and completely taking all of the intimacy out of it. Everything satan does works through a lie. He is a liar and the father of lies (John 8:44). So he makes sex a lie, and he tries to raise our children on a lie. But what satan is projecting is not what sex really is. It is all about intimacy. What happens when a husband and wife are intimate, when they go into their secret place and close the door behind them? They create something that prior to that intimate moment had never existed before. They create a child. All of a sudden, brought into the physical realm, is the beginning of something that did not exist before that time. Out of one moment of intimacy, something that no one has seen, something that could not be imagined, is conceived physically. This is what God is trying to teach us on a spiritual level. God is all about making the invisible visible (Hebrews 11:3).

That is what Christ teaches us in the Lord's Prayer. "Pray, then, in this way: 'Our Father who art in heaven, hallowed be Thy name. Thy kingdom come. Thy will be done, on earth as it is in

---

John 8:44 "You are of your father the devil, and you want to do the desires of your father. He was a murderer from the beginning, and does not stand in the truth, because there is no truth in him. Whenever he speaks a lie, he speaks from his own nature; for he is a liar, and the father of lies."

heaven'" (Matthew 6:9-10). We pray to our Father, "Thy Kingdom come. Thy will be done." God has a Kingdom, but right now that Kingdom is invisible. God has a will, but often His will is invisible to us. But if we allow ourselves to be locked in with Him, and engage in this intimate moment with Him, we will find a way to bring into existence that which now is invisible. I never find a limit to how intense I can be in my spirit with the Lord's Prayer. "Thy Kingdom come! Thy will be done!" The Greek verbs used in the prayer are in the imperative mood. You are not praying, "Oh, please let Thy Kingdom come." You are declaring, "Thy Kingdom come!" You are engaging in a creative process with the Father, and you literally make it happen. That is the best expression of prayer that there is. When we are with Him in oneness of spirit, and in that intimate moment, we literally manifest the Kingdom of God into this earth.

Does the Kingdom of God exist? Of course it does. It exists in heaven. God's Kingdom is already there; He is already the King. The problem with prayer, as we exercise it now, is that we are constantly praying for the Kingdom to come. What we miss when we pray that way is that the Kingdom already is. Christ **is** the King of kings and Lord of lords (Revelation 19:16). "The earth is the LORD's, and the fulness thereof" (Psalm 24:1, KJV). We are not waiting for something to happen. Get out of the waiting mode. When we are under that old religious teaching about going to heaven and getting a harp, we just grit our teeth through life, waiting to die so we can go there. It's as if the Church is teaching us to love dying. We spend our lives thinking, "I can't wait to get to heaven." What we should say is, "I can't wait to get heaven here," because this is where God is establishing His Kingdom. It is about Christ's return, not about your departure. We need the intimacy of the relationship between us and the Father that manifests what is right now invisible to a

---

Revelation 19:16 And on His robe and on His thigh He has a name written, "KING OF KINGS, AND LORD OF LORDS."

large extent. Don't you find yourself wanting to get closer with Him and to engage in this process with the Lord? We need the same spirit on us that was on our father Abraham, "who is the father of us all, (as it is written, 'A father of many nations have I made you') in the sight of Him whom he believed, even God, who gives life to the dead and calls into being that which does not exist" (Romans 4:16-17).

As believers in Christ, we have been grafted into Abraham as our father. Therefore, we have been grafted into the promises of God's chosen people (Romans 11:17). The Word highlights Abraham and emphasizes that he is our father because he engaged in a relationship with God that brought into being that which did not exist. That is why Abraham was able to sacrifice Isaac, because he knew that God was able to raise Isaac from the dead. Abraham knew that if God let him sacrifice Isaac, then God would have to resurrect Isaac, because Isaac was the son of the promise (Genesis 21:12). Let me tell you, if you are the one doing the sacrificing, you had better be convinced of that. And Abraham was convinced that God is the One who raises the dead and calls into being that which is invisible, that which at this moment does not exist.

God's Kingdom does not exist visually on the earth. Also, in many ways, God's will does not exist visually on the earth; it is not manifested. Do you believe that God has a will in every situation? Do you believe that He has a will for every minute of your life? Do you believe that He has a will for your family, for this body of people, for this planet, and for things that are far beyond our capacity to know?

Romans 11:17   But if some of the branches were broken off, and you, being a wild olive, were grafted in among them and became partaker with them of the rich root of the olive tree.

Genesis 21:12   But God said to Abraham, "Do not be distressed because of the lad and your maid; whatever Sarah tells you, listen to her, for through Isaac your descendants shall be named."

I believe that He does. I believe that God has a will, and He wants us to be a part of bringing His will into visual, physical manifestation, just as it now exists in His Kingdom in heaven. In heaven, satan was cast out because there was no longer a place found for him. Christ ascended to the right hand of the Father, and satan and his angels, the principalities and powers, were cast out (Revelation 12:7-9). We should know that well because we live with them now. We know where they went. They got halfway to hell; they came to earth. But we are going to see them go the rest of the way, and it will be a short trip; it does not have to take a long time. God's Kingdom was created in heaven, and now He is saying to bring it here. "But it's invisible!" That's okay. Call it into being. That is what God does. He calls into being what does not exist. He declares with a shout, "Come into being!" We have the ability, in our intimacy with Him, to bring to birth what right now cannot be seen. Doesn't that sound different than having all nights of prayer where we are shouting at God to answer our prayers? There is nothing wrong with starting there; it is just not where God wants us to end up.

"Now faith is the substance of things hoped for, the evidence of things not seen" (Hebrews 11:1, KJV). When we talk about faith, we are talking about manifesting that which is hoped for but not seen. That means prayer is the greatest expression of faith that there is. According to the Scriptures, faith without works is dead, but the true works of faith begin in prayer (James 2:26). We can work very hard and try to do many good Christian works, but the only thing that will manifest the invisible is prayer. Do you want

---

Revelation 12:7-9 And there was war in heaven, Michael and his angels waging war with the dragon. And the dragon and his angels waged war, [8] and they were not strong enough, and there was no longer a place found for them in heaven. [9] And the great dragon was thrown down, the serpent of old who is called the devil and Satan, who deceives the whole world; he was thrown down to the earth, and his angels were thrown down with him.

James 2:26 For just as the body without the spirit is dead, so also faith without works is dead.

to feed the hungry? Good. Pray the food into existence; then find where it manifests and bring it to the hungry. In the conception of a child, a husband and wife bring into existence that which is unseen. That is something that is very possible to do! It just requires the relationship and the intimacy that allows it to manifest. We tend to get into doing works without beginning with, and staying into, that intimate relationship with the Father. That is where prayer brings into existence what is unseen.

The more you get into prayer, and the more intimate your relationship with the Father becomes, the bolder you are to ask. A while ago, I was complaining about something that did not seem to be working and the answer I got from the Lord was, "Did you ask?" You have not, because you ask not (James 4:2). We can start to feel, "I don't know if God is going to do this for me anyway, so why should I ask? I'll just sit here and desire it. Then I'll secretly get mad at God because I never got it." But God is saying, "Why don't you ask Me? Why don't you come into the relationship with Me that has the capacity to produce what you want and bring it into manifestation?" One thing that all of us should be doing is persistently asking (Luke 11:9-10). You should be asking far more than you are asking now. You should be asking for things far greater than anything you have ever thought to ask Him for. You are shy and reserved with God. That is proof that the relationship is missing the intimacy. To get intimate you have to take your clothes off, and you cannot do that if you are shy. Our shyness before God simply shows us that we are really not intimate enough with Him so that we honestly feel comfortable in His presence. We have to get over that sense

---

James 4:2 You lust and do not have; so you commit murder. And you are envious and cannot obtain; so you fight and quarrel. You do not have because you do not ask.

Luke 11:9-10 "And I say to you, ask, and it shall be given to you; seek, and you shall find; knock, and it shall be opened to you. [10] For everyone who asks, receives; and he who seeks, finds; and to him who knocks, it shall be opened."

of shyness. We should be able to come boldly before the throne of grace because of the blood of Jesus Christ (Hebrews 4:16; 10:19).

There is nothing to hide. We can go into that innermost place to pray because there is nothing in there that we are hiding. You may be trying to hide things from other people, and you are probably trying to hide things from yourself, but if you are going to be in this relationship with God, you have to go into that innermost place to pray. You have to be willing to find that place of intimacy with Him where there is no embarrassment, where you can stand before Him like Joshua the high priest in your filthy garments, and have God take all of those garments off of you (Zechariah 3:3-4). That seems like the stuff of nightmares, doesn't it? Have you ever had dreams where you are running around naked and you could not find your clothes? Imagine what it was like for Joshua the high priest standing in heaven with all those people around him. When you read about heaven, you read about myriads of angels and other beings, and here they were taking off all of Joshua's clothes while he was standing before the Lord (Revelation 5:11). You cannot be embarrassed. If we believe the blood of Jesus Christ covers us, there is nothing to be ashamed of.

That is why forgiveness is so important. Experiencing God's forgiveness for us is essential, because if that is not real to us, and

---

Hebrews 4:16 Let us therefore draw near with confidence to the throne of grace, that we may receive mercy and may find grace to help in time of need.

Hebrews 10:19 Since therefore, brethren, we have confidence to enter the holy place by the blood of Jesus.

Zechariah 3:3-4 Now Joshua was clothed with filthy garments and standing before the angel. ⁴ And he spoke and said to those who were standing before him saying, "Remove the filthy garments from him." Again he said to him, "See, I have taken your iniquity away from you and will clothe you with festal robes."

Revelation 5:11 And I looked, and I heard the voice of many angels around the throne and the living creatures and the elders; and the number of them was myriads of myriads, and thousands of thousands.

we do not feel totally free from all that has held us in bondage, we will never come into an intimate relationship with Him. We will always be embarrassed, always shying away and hiding something. We will say, "I want to get into prayer, but I'm not going into that secret place! Let me go out to the backyard and pray." The apostle John wrote, "And now, little children, abide in Him, so that when He appears, we may have confidence and not shrink away from Him in shame at His coming" (1 John 2:28). Maybe a better translation of the Greek is, "Don't be embarrassed out of His presence." We must get rid of all shame, all sin, and everything that prevents us from staying in God's presence. I want us to be able to stand before Him. I want us to be able to come into His presence and have that sense of intimacy with Him. I believe that God is doing this for you even as you read this. He is taking down your walls. He is stripping away that which would embarrass you out of His presence.

This will take us to a new level in our prayer life. We read in 1 Thessalonians 5:16-18, "Rejoice always; pray without ceasing; in everything give thanks; for this is God's will for you in Christ Jesus." There are several verses like this in the Bible that we think are impossible because they are way too impractical. For example, "stop sinning" (1 Corinthians 15:34). We think, "That's just impractical. Who can walk in that Scripture? God was having a bad day when He said that. He didn't really mean it." No, the Word means what it says, and it tells us to pray without ceasing. How do we do that? "For if I pray in a tongue, my spirit prays, but my mind is unfruitful. What is the outcome then? I shall pray with the spirit and I shall pray with the mind also; I shall sing with the spirit" (1 Corinthians 14:14-15). That is what we do in worship. We call it "singing in the spirit." We sing in tongues together unto the Lord. What words are we singing? I have no idea, but I know He loves it, because He

---

1 Corinthians 15:34 Become sober-minded as you ought, and stop sinning; for some have no knowledge of God. I speak this to your shame.

is looking for those who will worship Him in spirit and in truth (John 4:23). Our prayer should be the same way. When God gave us the Holy Spirit, He gave us the ability to pray without ceasing. That is not a Scripture that we can throw out because we think it is impossible to walk in. It is more possible to walk in than you think. One of the reasons praying in the spirit without ceasing is so important is that it constantly retains the intimacy with the Lord. When you have had an intimate moment with someone, you just carry that glow with you all day long. It is something that stays with you. And I believe there is an ability to pray without ceasing; it is something that we should exercise.

When I have the opportunity to go into that secret place and be intimate with the Lord, I like to speak to God in English because that is the language He gave me. It is the language in which I am able to be the most intimate with Him. When I really have an intimate time with the Lord, I do not express myself in tongues. When I talk to Him, I do not call Him God; I call Him Father. "Father, I love you. I want to be one with You. I want my spirit to immerse itself into Your Spirit. I want You, Father, to take up Your abode in me. I want to dwell in You, and I want You to dwell in me." When you are having those intimate moments with the Lord, I encourage you to speak in a language you understand, where you can really express your intimacy, your thanks, your love, your wonder at who and what He is. However, you still have the rest of the day that you are supposed to be praying. How do you do that? How do you pray without ceasing? Is it actually possible? Yes it is. You can pray in tongues all the time. Have you ever wondered, "Why should I speak in tongues? What's the use of it?" We have yet to tap into the power of speaking in tongues. The Scriptures tell us to build ourselves up

---

John 4:23 "But an hour is coming, and now is, when the true worshipers shall worship the Father in spirit and truth; for such people the Father seeks to be His worshipers."

in our most holy faith, praying in the Holy Spirit (Jude 20). "My schedule is very busy. It is hard enough to just find time to read the Word or pray, much less talk in tongues all day long." You can do more than one thing at once, can't you? You do multiple things all the time. You are multitasking continually. Why is it that you cannot be praying in tongues all the time?

You don't have to speak in tongues out loud. You can talk to yourself in tongues. You can do that sitting at your desk at work. If people are around looking at you, then don't move your lips, but you can still be speaking in tongues. I don't think the Scriptures are teasing us when they talk about praying without ceasing. Pray all the time. One thing it does, it keeps your spirit at the forefront of your being; you will find yourself leading with your spirit. When you walk into a room, you will find that your spirit is analyzing what is going on in that room. We talk about being a witness of the Lord in our testimony to people. One way that happens is by praying constantly in the spirit. As you do that, you will know something about someone, or be aware of something about to happen, because your spirit begins to be dominant. However, most of you, in the way you live your day, basically put your spirit in a closet. You close the door on the secret place, and you shut up the Holy Spirit and your own spirit inside of you; then you try to go about living your day. But there is no reason why we cannot live our day in the spirit as spiritual people, praying without ceasing, always exercising our spirits in the Holy Spirit. You don't have to be a religious weirdo to do it. You don't have to walk around mumbling in tongues and drawing attention to yourself. We don't have to act strange to exercise the gifts of the Holy Spirit, but we should know what we are doing. If I am in an atmosphere where I can move my lips and speak softly in tongues, then I do that. If it

---

Jude 20 But you, beloved, building yourselves up on your most holy faith; praying in the Holy Spirit.

is inappropriate, I stop moving my lips, but in my head I am still speaking in the Holy Spirit.

Do you want to be a spiritual person? Just begin to constantly speak in tongues. This is something that you can exercise. It will bring you into being spiritual more quickly than anything else. Set yourself to do this at work. Do this during your normal day, and as you do it you will find how quickly you will forget and stop. That means your spirit just turned off; your focus just shifted off of the Lord. Don't worry about it. Simply pick it back up and begin again. Pretty soon you will find yourself having a fixed focus on the Lord. "Thou wilt keep him in perfect peace, whose mind is stayed on thee" (Isaiah 26:3, KJV). Is that possible, or is that just another one of those verses that we reject? "I can't do that one!" No, it is possible. The apostle Paul did this:

> For this reason also, since the day we heard of it, we have not ceased to pray for you and to ask that you may be filled with the knowledge of His will in all spiritual wisdom and understanding, so that you may walk in a manner worthy of the Lord, to please Him in all respects, bearing fruit in every good work and increasing in the knowledge of God; strengthened with all power. (Colossians 1:9-11)

Paul told the Colossians that he had not ceased to pray for them. Do you believe he was telling the truth, or was he just saying that so they would feel like he really cared for them? No, it was an apostolic prerogative that he never cease praying for them to see these things happen for them. Look at what Paul was constantly imparting to the churches. It was very creative. He was literally creating in them the ability to have more and more intimacy with God; he was bringing into existence that which did not exist before.

I want this to change your life. I want it to change the way you think about prayer, what it is and how to engage in it. I want you to take the time to find that intimate, inner, secret place with the Lord. Then I want you to continually exercise that and understand what you are doing. We often talk about prophetic proclamation because that conveys more of the sense that we are calling into being that which does not exist; we are bringing something to birth. That is what we really have to get into. That is what this generation of young people have to do. They have to bring to birth that which is in God's heart for His Kingdom, and for the earth. We will not do that outside of this intimacy in a relationship with the Father. Christ died to give us this opportunity. Formerly, we were separated from the Father (Ephesians 2:12). Now, we not only have the ability to be His people and for Him to be our God, but we also have the ability to have an intimate relationship with Him. Let's not lose that. Do you believe this can happen for you? Do you believe you can do this? I do. I know this is what you want, because when you have this intimate relationship with the Father, it fills the void you feel in your heart, even as a believer.

Now when someone says, "Let's pray," does it have a different meaning? A good way for us to start moving in this kind of prayer is to really humble ourselves before the Father and confess that we have not prayed as we ought to pray. We have the Holy Spirit in us, but we have not exercised the intercession of the Holy Spirit as we should have. Therefore, we come to the Father and say, "We are sorry for taking lightly the opportunity that we have to pray. More than that, we repent that we have not even recognized the power You have given us to move in through prayer. We have a determination in our hearts to change. We thank You, Father, for Your grace and for Your forgiveness. Cleanse us from all unrighteousness; put in our hearts the drive, the determination, and the love for prayer. Father, we ask that You teach us the intimate relationship with You that will bring

---

Ephesians 2:12 Remember that you were at that time separate from Christ, excluded from the commonwealth of Israel, and strangers to the covenants of promise, having no hope and without God in the world.

to birth, out of the invisible, Your Kingdom in the earth. We hunger to know You and to be with You on this level. It is not what we will receive by way of answers; it is what we will have in a relationship with You. That is what our life is all about. Thank You for this Word, Father. Let it live in our hearts like a little leaven that will change our lives totally, in Jesus' name."

CHAPTER 17

Let Him Love You

Everything that is happening in the world today magnifies the absolute need for the sons of God to come forth and be manifested in the earth at this time (Romans 8:19-21). The Scriptures are very clear about it; this is something that must take place. It is something we have been pressing into for a long time. We are not those who are looking around at the world and crying out for a "rapture" to take us out of it. We are looking for God to make us the solution for the world. The sons of God coming forth is not a luxury; there needs to be more authority to impact what is going on in the earth. How will the sons of God come forth? Through the process of maturity in the believers, "until we all attain…to the measure of the stature which belongs to the fulness of Christ" (Ephesians 4:13). We all know, from watching people grow up on a natural level, that maturity is a process. When you look at photos that parents take of the many stages in their child's development, you can easily recognize the process of maturity that is taking place. So when we talk about sonship, we are

---

Romans 8:19-21   For the anxious longing of the creation waits eagerly for the revealing of the sons of God. [20] For the creation was subjected to futility, not of its own will, but because of Him who subjected it, in hope [21] that the creation itself also will be set free from its slavery to corruption into the freedom of the glory of the children of God.

talking about the completion of this maturing process that is taking place in the life of the believer. What then is the reason that we do not have more of a manifestation of mature sons? Our inability to receive God's love is what is holding us back from becoming sons of God who have come into complete maturity.

This is a major issue for us in The Living Word Fellowship. Everything that we have in our drive to become mature sons of God came from our father in the faith, John Robert Stevens. That is part of our spiritual DNA, our makeup, as a people. However, included in this tremendous impartation that we received from John is something that is actually a limitation for us, and that was John's inability to experience God's love for himself. He would say, "I feel God's love when I minister to people, but I don't feel it for myself personally. I know God's love only because I see how much love He has for everyone else." Whether this was the spiritual battle against John or something in his own spirit, it caused him to feel cut off from the Lord, even when He appeared to him personally. When the Lord appears to you, you should be absolutely blown away by His love, even if He is correcting you. Yet John was left, and I think we are left, with this inability to really know the love of God and feel it when it comes through to us personally. Do you realize how much of a lie from satan that is?

Right now for us as a body, this is what blocks our ability to receive more from the Lord. We can ask of Him all we want, but if we do not really feel that He loves us and wants to give us whatever we need or ask for, then our asking is in vain. We are still putting up a wall to Him. Even if you see a promise from God, how do you appropriate it if you do not feel that it is for you, or that God will do it for you? Unless you are truly overwhelmed by how much God loves you, you will never open up to receive what He wants to give you. Recently, I went through a very serious illness and was miraculously healed. It is very real to me why the gift of healing does not work more than it does. God heals you because He loves you. If you cannot receive His love, you cannot be healed. When Jesus healed people, He said, "Be it done to you according to your faith," but remember that faith works through love (Matthew 9:29; Galatians 5:6). We really get hung up about faith: "I need more faith. I tried this, but it didn't work. I believed for that, but I didn't have enough faith." We beat ourselves up all the time over how much faith we don't have. We have plenty of faith. We only need faith the size of a mustard seed (Matthew 17:20). If you have received salvation, then you have faith, because to receive salvation you must believe in Jesus Christ and what He did for you on the cross. We have faith, but faith works through love, and what we are missing is the love.

I really want us to open our hearts on a new level to the love of God that is behind everything that He does and everything that He is. God is love (1 John 4:8). He works through love. Jesus Christ came because God so loved the world that He sent us His Son (John 3:16). Everything from God is based on His love, but it is very difficult for us as humans to really open up to let anyone love us that intensely. As long as I have been in the ministry, I have never counseled anyone who does not have some problem with themselves. It manifests in many different ways. It may be that you do not like your physical body, "I've got too much fat here," or your personality, "I am just not a fun person. People don't like me." Those perceptions block your

---

Matthew 9:29 Then He touched their eyes, saying, "Be it done to you according to your faith."

Galatians 5:6 For in Christ Jesus neither circumcision nor uncircumcision means anything, but faith working through love.

Matthew 17:20 And He said to them, "Because of the littleness of your faith; for truly I say to you, if you have faith as a mustard seed, you shall say to this mountain, 'Move from here to there,' and it shall move; and nothing shall be impossible to you."

1 John 4:8 The one who does not love does not know God, for God is love.

John 3:16 "For God so loved the world, that He gave His only begotten Son, that whoever believes in Him should not perish, but have eternal life."

openness to God's love, because anything you see as being wrong with yourself you ultimately blame on God since He created you that way. He is the One who formed you from your mother's womb; He brought you forth out of nothing. So whatever you are having a problem with about yourself is born out of you having a problem opening up to God's love.

If you want to get rid of your problems, open up to His love. If we could just receive a fraction of how much God loves us, we would never have a problem with ourselves again. There is no one who does not need something from God; we are all praying for something for ourselves. I was certainly crying out to God for a healing, because it was life or death. But God does not just heal you; He wants you to let Him love you. Healing is not an action that God performs. He **is** health. Jesus taught us to pray, "Thy Kingdom come on earth as it is in heaven" (Matthew 6:10). In heaven there is no disease. There are none of these problems that we have here on earth. What is heaven? Heaven is an atmosphere that is made up of an unresisted receptivity to God's love. What is the Kingdom of God? The Kingdom of God is God's love being an unresisted reality in the earth. I guarantee you that the answer to whatever you need is in opening your heart to let God love you.

People think of God as being some big, scary figure who brings about judgments, but the truth is, He is not that way. In Ezekiel 6:9 we read about how God's people resisted His love and hurt Him. He said, "I loved you; I did all of these things for you, but you rejected Me. You hurt Me." That brings it down to something we can relate

---

Matthew 6:10 "Thy kingdom come. Thy will be done, on earth as it is in heaven."

Ezekiel 6:9 "Then those of you who escape will remember Me among the nations to which they will be carried captive, how I have been hurt by their adulterous hearts which turned away from Me, and by their eyes, which played the harlot after their idols; and they will loathe themselves in their own sight for the evils which they have committed, for all their abominations."

to. Does God get mad? Yes, He gets mad, but look behind His anger. If you really look behind the anger of someone who is lashing out, you will usually find a hurt of some kind. The response to hurt often appears as anger, so we should not be misled by that when it comes to God. We should not misunderstand who God is and how He is moving. He is not really mad; He is hurt. He has provided so much for us, but when we refuse to receive it we hurt Him. Isn't that what happens on a human level? What do you normally do when someone hurts you? When you do things for people and they don't receive it, you think, "I did all of this for them and they don't really care." It is very hurtful. God loves us beyond words, beyond our ability to comprehend it. We need to take down every wall, take down every resistance, and open up to His love. We have to realize that whatever is not being fulfilled in all of the promises He has given, is directly related to how open we are to receive His love. According to the Scriptures, His love is being beamed at us. His love is the power that reached down into the grave and resurrected Jesus Christ from the dead (Ephesians 1:19-20). It was His love that broke the bonds of death. To God, death is nothing. If we can receive His love, there is nothing that can stop what He wants to do for us and what we are believing to see happen.

There is something very deep in us that resists opening up to God's love, and we really need to grapple with that. Start giving your heart over to the Lord in a new way. Open up and honestly analyze the resistance that you have. You might think, "People don't love me." Maybe they do love you and you are just not open to it. "No, I'm sure they don't love me. And I know God doesn't love me. He just wants to discipline me." No, God wants to bless you. If He disciplines you, it is to get you to open up to His love so He can bless you. According

---

Ephesians 1:19-20   And what is the surpassing greatness of His power toward us who believe. These are in accordance with the working of the strength of His might [20] which He brought about in Christ, when He raised Him from the dead, and seated Him at His right hand in the heavenly places.

to the Book of Hebrews, the end result of His discipline is that we receive His nature (Hebrews 12:10). God does not discipline us to hurt us. He disciplines us to get us to open up to all that He wants to give us, which ultimately is His divine nature. However, we don't see it that way. Discipline is hard; it hurts. We tend to not want to be around people who discipline us. "All discipline for the moment seems not to be joyful, but sorrowful" (Hebrews 12:11). At the moment when discipline is coming, it is not fun. But that is not the point; you have to see the purpose of the discipline. In God's heart, it is to get you to open up to His love. Our attitude about discipline is, "God doesn't love me! I prayed for this and He didn't do it." But the Word says, "God causes all things to work together for good to those who love God" (Romans 8:28). Your response is, "I have quoted that Scripture all my life and the good things don't seem to happen for me." Maybe the problem is that you do not really love God the way you think you do. It is very easy for us to give Him a love that is not what He is looking for. We say we love God, and in our hearts we are convinced that we love Him. We come and worship, which is an expression of our love to God, but He wants our love to come into another level. In John chapter 21, we read about how Jesus challenged Peter on this very point.

> So when they had finished breakfast, Jesus said to Simon Peter, "Simon, son of John, do you love Me more than these?" He said to Him, "Yes, Lord; You know that I love You." He said to him, "Tend My lambs." He said to him again a second time, "Simon, son of John, do you love Me?" He said to Him, "Yes, Lord; You know that I love You." He said to him, "Shepherd My sheep." He said to him the third time, "Simon, son of John, do you love Me?" Peter was grieved because He said to him the third time,

---

Hebrews 12:10   For they disciplined us for a short time as seemed best to them, but He disciplines us for our good, that we may share His holiness.

"Do you love Me?" And he said to Him, "Lord, You know all things; You know that I love You." Jesus said to him, "Tend My sheep." (John 21:15-17)

This was the third time that Jesus appeared in a glorified state to the disciples after the resurrection (John 21:12-14). He prepared breakfast for them, and when they finished, Jesus said to Simon Peter, "Simon, son of John, do you love Me?" The root in the Greek for the word "love" that Jesus used here is *agape*. Peter replied, "Yes, Lord; You know that I love You." The word for "love" that Peter used comes from the Greek word *phileo*. The definition of *phileo* is "love," but it is more like affection, as in kissing someone on the cheek when you meet them. So we get the idea that *phileo* is not the same love as the divine love expressed by the word *agape*.

Jesus was trying to get something across to Peter when He asked him, "Do you love Me?" Christ loves us with the love of the Father, and He was asking Peter, "Do you love Me with the love that I am giving to you? Do you love Me with a divine love?" Peter's response was, "You know that I love You with a human affection, with feelings of association and wanting to be around You." He was confessing that he did not have the same kind of love. To this Jesus replied, "Tend My lambs." Then Jesus said to him a second time, "Simon, son of John, do you love Me?" Here again we see the word *agape*. "Do you love Me with this deeper love, this greater love?" Peter replied, "Yes, Lord; You know that I love You," and again He used the word *phileo*, meaning, "You know that I have a human affection for You." So Jesus said to him, "Shepherd My sheep." Then Jesus asked a third time, "Simon, son of John, do you love Me?" This time the Lord used the word *phileo*. He came down to Peter's level: "Peter,

---

John 21:12-14 Jesus said to them, "Come and have breakfast." None of the disciples ventured to question Him, "Who are You?" knowing that it was the Lord. [13] Jesus came and took the bread, and gave them, and the fish likewise. [14] This is now the third time that Jesus was manifested to the disciples, after He was raised from the dead.

do you have a human affection for Me?" At this Peter was grieved, not because Jesus asked him three times if he loved Him; Peter was grieved because he finally understood what Jesus was saying. When Jesus used the word *phileo,* He was saying, "Peter, is that all you have for Me, *phileo* love? You only love Me on a human level? You have some good human affection for Me?" Peter finally understood the difference between what Jesus was saying and what his response had been.

Obviously we love God. We know that we love Him, and that He loves us, but there is a vast difference between His love and ours. We substitute our human love and emotions for what He is trying to impart to us in His divine love. Love is the root of everything that we have in our relationship with the Lord. "We love, because He first loved us" (1 John 4:19). When He loves us with all the love that He has for us, He wants us to open up to receive that. But we can't handle it. God loves us with His divine love, but that is too much for us. It is intimidating because it means that we have to get rid of all the feelings we have about ourselves and about everyone around us.

When we say that we have walls, what does that mean? First and foremost, walls are feelings that we have toward ourselves, but they are also feelings that we have toward others. So when God's powerful divine love begins to touch us, these feelings come up, and unless we can bring them down, they become a wall of resistance that limits what we can receive from Him. As a result, what we receive from God is commensurate with what we have experienced in human love. We can tolerate human love because it is not so great that it pounds down our walls. Most relationship problems that we have are because we block the level of love that would really bring change in our lives and make us whole. That is what is meant by two becoming one flesh (Genesis 2:24). When you really open up

---

Genesis 2:24 For this cause a man shall leave his father and his mother, and shall cleave to his wife; and they shall become one flesh.

to someone who is totally in love with you, not just on a human level but with a spark of divine love, it will change your life. It will deliver you from the things that bind you and hold you in captivity. But again, our walls protect us from having to change. Our walls protect us from having the discomfort of being loved beyond what we can handle. We know that we do not deserve that kind of love, and because of these complex feelings within us we just cannot receive it.

Jesus said that everything depends on the great commandment that you love the Lord your God with all your heart, all your mind, and all your strength (Matthew 22:37-38). You love Him with everything you have within you. You can take the Law, the Prophets, the rest of the Scriptures, everything about religion, and boil it all down to one thing: loving God. However, that cannot be a *phileo* love, where we just have this human love, friendship, and kindness for Him. We already have that; we love Him because He first loved us. Therefore, we must come into a divine love; that is the love He is looking to receive back from us. He does not want our *phileo* love. He wants His divine love mirrored back to Him with the same strength with which He is beaming it toward us. When we have that, then we will fulfill everything that God is looking for. We must love Him with all of our hearts, but it is with the love that we receive first from Him. We have to open up to this reality.

The second great commandment is that you love (*agape*) your neighbor as yourself (Matthew 22:39). However, if I tell you that I love you, I am lying if I do not have divine love, because if I cannot receive that love myself, then I cannot give it to you. The truth is, I do not feel about myself the way God feels about me, with that

---

Matthew 22:37-38 And He said to him, "'You shall love the Lord your God with all your heart, and with all your soul, and with all your mind.' [38] This is the great and foremost commandment."

Matthew 22:39 "The second is like it, 'You shall love your neighbor as yourself.'"

divine impartation of love. Therefore, I may think that I really love you, but if I am honest with myself, I cannot love you more than I love myself. So in reality, I must not have that much love for you. We go through life confusing these two kinds of love. Divine love is the foundation of everything, but we continually replace it with our human love because we feel more comfortable there. We can work with it; it is something we know how to do. I can love you with a human love. People all over the world love each other with human love. That is why the divorce rates are so high, because human love fails. But God's love never fails. His love is forever, even when we hurt Him and offend Him.

God is looking for us to open up. This may sound a little strange, but you need to have a salvation experience. Your response is probably, "I've already been saved!" Good, now go deeper with it. Receive the love that is behind your salvation experience. "For God so loved the world, that He gave His only begotten Son" (John 3:16). Jesus came to the world to show God's love for all of mankind, for all of creation. He loved the Father and He knew that the Father loved Him. He was the reflection of the Father's love in the earth, and He went to the cross as an expression of God's love for each of us personally. I know that we have received salvation, but that does not mean we have opened up to the fullness of His love. For the most part, we have only opened up to the concept of His love. We keep it on a doctrinal shelf: "I know God loves me." Yes, but I need to **let** Him love me. I don't need to mentally accept that He loves me; I need to know and receive in my heart the love that God has for me (1 John 4:16). We read in Ephesians chapter 3,

> So that Christ may dwell in your hearts through faith; and that you, being rooted and grounded in love, may be able to comprehend with all the saints what is the breadth

---

1 John 4:16 And we have come to know and have believed the love which God has for us. God is love, and the one who abides in love abides in God, and God abides in him.

and length and height and depth, and to know the love of Christ which surpasses knowledge. (Ephesians 3:17-19)

It doesn't matter whether we are talking about the love of Christ or the love of God, because Christ is the expression of the love of the Father. When Philip requested of Jesus, "Show us the Father," He said, "If you have seen Me, you have seen the Father" (John 14:8-9). Why? Because Jesus was the love of God expressed to the world. That was His ministry. And we are to know the love of Christ which surpasses knowledge. There is no way to grasp that with our minds. All we can do is open our hearts to receive it.

I know this seems impossible. There were many times during my illness when I prayed, "Lord, I know I'm dead, because there is no way I can open up to Your love on the level that I need to. I don't need to receive a healing; I need to receive Your love. If I receive Your love, the healing will be there." Everything is provided if we can receive His love. When we have this love, there is nothing that we are missing. It seems impossible, but with God nothing is impossible (Matthew 19:26). God can help you with this. You have to take this word and start crying out to God, because He will not do it if you do not want it more than your breath. You have to want to know the love of God more than anything else you have ever wanted in your entire life. You cannot have any ulterior motives. You cannot want to receive the love of God so that you can get something out of it. "You ask and do not receive, because you ask with wrong motives, so that you may spend it on your pleasures" (James 4:3). Do not ask with wrong motives; receive all that He has for you in His love.

John 14:8-9 Philip said to Him, "Lord, show us the Father, and it is enough for us." ⁹ Jesus said to him, "Have I been so long with you, and yet you have not come to know Me, Philip? He who has seen Me has seen the Father; how do you say, 'Show us the Father'?"

Matthew 19:26 And looking upon them Jesus said to them, "With men this is impossible, but with God all things are possible."

This is a key to the sons of God coming forth, because the sons of God have no greater ministry than imparting the love of God to the world. We are to follow up with what Christ has already done. Christ came into the earth to express the love of the Father to all the world, and to each of us individually. He was not here for anything else. He had to go to the cross to make it work, but His death on the cross was the love of God being expressed to you individually. So why do we need the sons of God? What are they coming forth on the earth to do? Is it to prophesy judgment? Jesus said, "I did not come to judge the world. I came to bring salvation. I came to express the love of the Father" (John 3:17). The ministry of the sons of God coming forth on the earth is to follow in the footsteps of Christ, to be the expression of the love of the Father to the world. However, we cannot do that if we cannot receive the Father's love ourselves.

Do you see how blocked we are? Have you ever wondered, "For as many years as we have believed, prayed, and looked for the sons of God to come forth, what is stopping it?" Our inability or refusal to receive the love of God is what is stopping it, because the love of God is the ministry of the sons of God to the earth. We will minister that love to our neighbors and to the whole world; but if we cannot receive it, we cannot give it. That is why we are stuck. We have to go back and seek God with all of our hearts for His love. First, understand that you do not have to love God in order to seek Him. Hunger is not based on love. Hunger is something that we can determine to have. "In the day that you seek Me with all of your heart, I will be found of you" (Jeremiah 29:13). Determine to seek the Lord with all of your heart! We

---

John 3:17 "For God did not send the Son into the world to judge the world, but that the world should be saved through Him."

Jeremiah 29:13 "And you will seek Me and find Me, when you search for Me with all your heart."

are going to seek Him and find this love of God. Don't start feeling miserable about yourself and say, "I don't have this love of God! I know I'm falling short." Don't think like that! Realize that there is an answer. Nothing is stopping you from seeking God. You can seek Him with all your heart, and He will be found by you.

There is only one way: you have to seek God. I love the Lord's Prayer. It begins by telling you to go into your secret place with the Father. It requires your initiative to be where He is. You pray, "Our Father, who art in heaven" (Matthew 6:6-9). You have to go where He is, in heaven. Your pursuit of Him has to start there. And in the process of seeking Him with all your heart, you will find the ability to open up to His love. We can have it. The love of God is possible. We can open up to the pure force of His love. The cry of Moses was, "Lord, reveal Thy glory." He had been on the mountaintop, he had received God's Word, but his cry was, "Let me see You! Let me behold Your glory." What happened? The Lord answered his prayer. As much as Moses was able to handle, God let him see His glory (Exodus 33:18-23). God will do the same for us. If Moses could cry, "Show me Thy glory," we can cry, "Show us Your love." Let us really see and come to know the love of God that was behind our salvation.

Matthew 6:6-9 "But you, when you pray, go into your inner room, and when you have shut your door, pray to your Father who is in secret, and your Father who sees in secret will repay you. 7 And when you are praying, do not use meaningless repetition, as the Gentiles do, for they suppose that they will be heard for their many words. 8 Therefore do not be like them; for your Father knows what you need, before you ask Him. 9 Pray, then, in this way: 'Our Father who art in heaven, hallowed be Thy name.'"

Exodus 33:18-23 Then Moses said, "I pray Thee, show me Thy glory!" 19 And He said, "I Myself will make all My goodness pass before you, and will proclaim the name of the LORD before you; and I will be gracious to whom I will be gracious, and will show compassion on whom I will show compassion." 20 But He said, "You cannot see My face, for no man can see Me and live!" 21 Then the LORD said, "Behold, there is a place by Me, and you shall stand there on the rock; 22 and it will come about, while My glory is passing by, that I will put you in the cleft of the rock and cover you with My hand until I have passed by. 23 Then I will take My hand away and you shall see My back, but My face shall not be seen."

We have found a way to receive salvation and yet separate it from being open to the amazing power of the love of God. That is why the power is missing from us. When we open up to the love of God, everything will work because it is all God. God is One. When you get God, you get everything. It is not like going through a shopping basket and saying, "Look, I got the gift of prophecy. Oh, I also got this gift of tongues." When we really receive God, we get all that He is, and He is love. All the other things flow out from that. Where there is prophecy, it will pass away. Where there are tongues, they will cease. Where there are gifts of the Spirit, they will be done away. What is left when all of these things go away? Love. Love never goes away; love never fails. When everything else is finished, we will always have the love of God. Our knowledge is partial, but we will know even as we are fully known. We will truly come to know ourselves in the love of God because we will see ourselves in that mirror (1 Corinthians 13:8-12). You need to get rid of the mirror that you are using, and use His love as the new mirror to see yourself.

The sons of God have to come forth in the earth; there has to be the fulfillment of that Word. We do not need them tomorrow; we need them to manifest today. The only way that will happen is if we break through to know and receive the love of God, so that we have something to minister. Whatever we have now may be great, but it is not what God is looking to give to the world. There is only one thing to minister to the world. It is the same thing that Christ ministered to us: the love of the Father. He came because of the love of the Father. Salvation is God's love ministered to us, and we have

---

1 Corinthians 13:8-12 Love never fails; but if there are gifts of prophecy, they will be done away; if there are tongues, they will cease; if there is knowledge, it will be done away. [9] For we know in part, and we prophesy in part; [10] but when the perfect comes, the partial will be done away. [11] When I was a child, I used to speak as a child, think as a child, reason as a child; when I became a man, I did away with childish things. [12] For now we see in a mirror dimly, but then face to face; now I know in part, but then I shall know fully just as I also have been fully known.

received it. We have received the Holy Spirit. We have received His love in part. But now we are throwing out the *phileo* love and we are going after the divine love that God has. We can have all of it. Seek God for it. Do not let Him rest (Isaiah 62:6-7). Show Him the drive that you have to know His love in its fullness.

Father, let Your Spirit create in us what You are speaking. Break us free from that which resists or hinders the manifestation of Your love in our lives. Lord, we declare that every block, every wall, every resistance, every hindrance that we have had, comes down. We take them down willingly. We ask for Your love to blow us away. We ask that our hearts, our minds, and our spirits be open to the fullness of the divine love that was behind You sending Christ to the earth. We ask that the power of the love expressed in Christ's death on the cross remove every area of resistance and ignorance from us. Lord, we declare that everything changes and, by Your love, the sons of God will manifest in the earth.

Isaiah 62:6-7 On your walls, O Jerusalem, I have appointed watchmen; all day and all night they will never keep silent. You who remind the LORD, take no rest for yourselves; [7] and give Him no rest until He establishes and makes Jerusalem a praise in the earth.

CHAPTER 18

Worship That Brings His Presence

We are in an exciting time of transition because we are moving into the realm of spirit in a way that we never have before. There is a door open for us in our worship, and we should be pressing into it. I am believing for an impartation of the Lord's Spirit that lifts us into this Word that He is speaking to our hearts. The Lord spoke to me that worship will replace the intercession that we have had in the past. Now don't misunderstand that; God is not doing away with intercession. When God brings something new and greater, you add it to what you already have. We were thrown into the depths of prayer, intercession, and crying out to God for John Stevens in the years prior to his passing. We have seen many all nights of prayer; intercession is something that is very real to us. In showing us something greater, the Lord is not taking away from intercession and what it is to us. We have had, and will continue to have, a great deal of intercession; but He is saying that worship will replace how we have used intercession in the past. Over the last many years of our walk with God, we have used intercession to achieve what we were seeking for in God, but getting to where God is taking us now will be accomplished through worship. This means a new level of worship beyond what we have known. What we have now is good, but God wants to replace the good with the best. What we have now may be sixtyfold, but God wants to take us to a hundredfold fruitfulness in what we do (Matthew 13:8).

The worship that we have is a gift. That should tell us something right there, because God blesses the ones who increase their gift. Read the parable of the talents in Matthew chapter 25. A man gave talents to his servants and went away on a journey. When he came back he asked each one, "What did you do with the talent I gave you?" Those who increased their talents were blessed and put in a place of authority. So what do we do with this gift of worship that we have been given? We certainly cannot hold on to the same level of worship that we had when the gift was given to us. Otherwise, when the Lord returns we will come to Him and say, "You know the talent that You gave us? Here it is; I kept it for You." What happened to those who did that in the parable? The Lord banished them to the outer darkness. He was not at all happy with those who did not grow their gift.

We want to grow this gift of worship, but first we need to understand how much it really is a gift from God. Our worship is something that was born in the outpourings of the Holy Spirit and the moves of God that began in the early 1900s. The outpouring at Azusa Street in Los Angeles began in April of 1906, and continued through to about 1915. Actually, we cannot put what happened in a convenient historical box, because so many outpourings of the Spirit happened before, during, and after that time period. However, the Azusa Street revival was a focal point; almost everyone has heard about it. We know that there were many manifestations of miracles, signs, and wonders. Many things happened, including worship in the spirit, during those early outpourings.

Matthew 13:8 "And others fell on the good soil, and yielded a crop, some a hundredfold, some sixty, and some thirty."

Moving on from Azusa Street, one of the next junctures is the outpouring known as the "Latter Rain." The people who initiated the Latter Rain movement were concerned about losing the spiritual impetus in the Pentecostal churches, because things were starting to dry up and die out. The outpouring started when a group of people met at Sharon Bible College in Saskatchewan, Canada, in October 1947. Again, the dates are not necessarily hard and fast, because things began before that and went on for some time. Nevertheless, in the first half of the twentieth century, God was really moving and there were tremendous outpourings. Many miracles occurred, and there was a revival of speaking in tongues and the gifts of the Holy Spirit. One of the things that happened, which to my knowledge had not happened before to the same extent, was the style of worship that we have. If you have visited other churches, you know that the style of worship that we have is different than what most people have. Some churches are beginning to move into the worship in the spirit, singing in tongues, and there is a tremendous anointing on that. But this worship in the spirit is still something very unique to us, at least as far as what I have seen in North and South America.

I want those in our fellowship, especially the younger ones who have grown up in it, to have a sense that our worship is unique. It is something that God has graced us with that was born in those early outpourings. Some people have tried to move into it, but it is still not quite the same thing. The style of worship for many groups is really more of a praise worship, in which there is a lot of independence. If you go to some Charismatic churches, you will find people lying in the aisles, slain in the Spirit, and they will lie there for hours. You will also find people who are yelling and others who are laughing. It is not that we are against being slain in the Spirit, or that we don't believe in laughing. I know that God can be in those manifestations, but we do not express them in our congregational worship. Why? Because oneness is in the DNA of this worship. Many of these outpourings, especially the Azusa Street and Latter Rain outpourings, were born out of a real sense of oneness in those who ignited them. The Azusa Street revival was led by William Seymour, an African-American, and it was one of the breakthroughs in race relations in this country. When God poured out His Spirit, the races came together. Consequently, when the worship came, it had that element of oneness because oneness is also a gift from God. Oneness is something that Jesus prayed for, and we see it as a very real expression in our worship (John 17:21).

In our worship services, we do not have some being baptized in the Holy Spirit, some running around the church, and others falling over or walking across the chairs. These kinds of expressions have been around for many years. In the early days of Pentecostalism, there were many different manifestations. I am not saying that the Spirit was not in those expressions, but one thing unique to us is the deep sense of oneness in our worship. When we come together to worship, we are looking for a Body experience rather than individual experiences. If we wanted individual experiences, then we would see some of these other manifestations, which are very real and can meet people and change their lives. But there are other ways to receive personal experiences, rather than in a congregational worship service. If you need a personal experience, then go to the ministries after the service and have them bless you. Better yet, wait on the Lord before you show up at a service so that you arrive already filled. Then, when we come together, what we have in our worship is a collective experience. We are looking for God to pour Himself out on the Body, not just on individual members. When you look at previous outpourings, this is very much what happened. They were not expressions of just one or two individuals getting something from God. When God began to move, everyone received

---

John 17:21 "That they may all be one; even as Thou, Father, art in Me, and I in Thee, that they also may be in Us; that the world may believe that Thou didst send Me."

the experience. This is what I want to see: everyone receiving it together. Why is that so important? Because at some point, there will not be enough individual ministries to meet the needs; but if there are those who, like a little leaven, start an outpouring, then thousands of people could have a meeting with God. Rather than trying to evangelize the world by witnessing to one person at a time, what about thousands of people meeting God all at once? This is what the spirit of oneness in our worship can bring.

This worship in the spirit broke through because the spirit of oneness was involved. As much as those outpourings seemed to happen a long time ago, the real importance of this worship is for today. It is for what God is doing now in His Kingdom. This worship will bring into reality our ability to experience, and to live in, two realms at once. We have to face the fact that the Kingdom of God is in heaven. In the Scriptures it is called the "kingdom of heaven" (Matthew 4:17). We know that the Father is in heaven and Jesus is seated at His right hand (Ephesians 1:20). Jesus taught His disciples to pray, "Our Father who art in heaven" (Matthew 6:9). The first thing that Jesus wants you to grasp is the fact that God is in heaven, in His Kingdom. The point is for you to know where you need to be also, not to separate you from God. It is to show you what you should be doing, where you should be going, and where your focus should be. You should not say, "God is in heaven and I am down here. We are very far apart and I can only have a long-distance relationship with Him." On the contrary, before telling us to pray to the Father, Jesus

---

Matthew 4:17 From that time Jesus began to preach and say, "Repent, for the kingdom of heaven is at hand."

Ephesians 1:20 Which He brought about in Christ, when He raised Him from the dead, and seated Him at His right hand in the heavenly places.

Matthew 6:9 "Pray, then, in this way: 'Our Father who art in heaven, hallowed be Thy name.'"

said, "First go into your inner room" (Matthew 6:6). That expresses the fact that you are to take the initiative to go into His presence. We do not wait for God to come down here for us to pray, and we do not wait for Him to come down here for us to worship. We take the initiative to go to where He is.

If we are those charged with bringing the Kingdom of God to the earth, then we need to be those who dwell in the heavens with Him. Jesus said, "Where I am, there you may be also" (John 14:3). We are too passive about living in the flesh on the natural plane. We feel that there is no way for us to really dwell where He dwells, but we have a real answer in the Lord's Prayer: "Thy kingdom come… on earth as it is in heaven" (Matthew 6:10). We know that we are to bring heaven to the earth, but how do we do that if we ourselves are not part of that heavenly Kingdom? If we do not know what heaven is, how do we know what to bring to earth? We have to know it. We have to be familiar with it. Therefore, the Lord is bringing us to the reality of living in the spirit, of being a spiritual people.

The initial experience of salvation is your spirit coming alive to God. Your spirit was dead to God, but now has been made alive to Him (Ephesians 2:4-5). That opens the door for us to begin to relate in the realm of spirit. We must have that ability, because God Himself is Spirit (John 4:24). In this hour, God will not relate to you in a fleshly body. Christ may have a resurrected body, but it is a heavenly body. It is not a body from this world, as we know it. When we talk about pressing into resurrection life, we are talking about having a

---

Matthew 6:6 "But you, when you pray, go into your inner room, and when you have shut your door, pray to your Father who is in secret, and your Father who sees in secret will repay you."

Ephesians 2:4-5 But God, being rich in mercy, because of His great love with which He loved us, [5] even when we were dead in our transgressions, made us alive together with Christ (by grace you have been saved).

John 4:24 "God is spirit, and those who worship Him must worship in spirit and truth."

similar experience as Christ, where we put on our heavenly body (1 Corinthians 15:40-44; 53-54). It is there in the heavens; it has already been made for us (2 Corinthians 5:1-4). The tailor may be making a few alterations, but it is basically ready for us to put on. That is something we have to see and understand, and we have to be determined to put it on, as the Scripture says, "Put on the Lord Jesus Christ" (Romans 13:14). There has to be an initiative on our part to live in the spirit and to be a spiritual people. That has been talked about from the beginning of our fellowship, and through our worship, there is an actual way for us to move into the realm of spirit. The worship allows us to move into the heavenly places.

This worship in the spirit is not like our concept of prayer. Our concept isn't to pray in heaven where He is; we tend to pray from down here on earth, and God who is in heaven hears us (2 Chronicles 6:21). All of our works are done on a natural level,

---

1 Corinthians 15:40-44 There are also heavenly bodies and earthly bodies, but the glory of the heavenly is one, and the glory of the earthly is another. [41] There is one glory of the sun, and another glory of the moon, and another glory of the stars; for star differs from star in glory. [42] So also is the resurrection of the dead. It is sown a perishable body, it is raised an imperishable body; [43] it is sown in dishonor, it is raised in glory; it is sown in weakness, it is raised in power; [44] it is sown a natural body, it is raised a spiritual body. If there is a natural body, there is also a spiritual body.

1 Corinthians 15:53-54 For this perishable must put on the imperishable, and this mortal must put on immortality. [54] But when this perishable will have put on the imperishable, and this mortal will have put on immortality, then will come about the saying that is written, "Death is swallowed up in victory."

2 Corinthians 5:1-4 For we know that if the earthly tent which is our house is torn down, we have a building from God, a house not made with hands, eternal in the heavens. [2] For indeed in this house we groan, longing to be clothed with our dwelling from heaven; [3] inasmuch as we, having put it on, shall not be found naked. [4] For indeed while we are in this tent, we groan, being burdened, because we do not want to be unclothed, but to be clothed, in order that what is mortal may be swallowed up by life.

2 Chronicles 6:21 "And listen to the supplications of Thy servant and of Thy people Israel, when they pray toward this place; hear Thou from Thy dwelling place, from heaven; hear Thou and forgive."

using our physical bodies to accomplish things; but worship takes us into the realm of spirit. We have all wondered, "How do we become a spiritual people?" The key is worship because true worship only works from a place of spirit. That is why it is so important that we worship the way we do. We call it "singing in the spirit." When we sing in tongues, we are literally singing in the spirit, because tongues are a heavenly language. Paul wrote, "For if I pray in a tongue, my spirit prays, but my mind is unfruitful. What is the outcome then? I shall pray with the spirit and I shall pray with the mind also; I shall sing with the spirit and I shall sing with the mind also" (1 Corinthians 14:14-15). This exercise of your spirit, which through Christ has been made alive to God, is preparation for you to move into a spiritual relationship with the Lord. It can seem difficult to relate to God, because He is Spirit and we are not solely given to living in the spirit. However, you have a spirit and your spirit is alive; therefore you have the same makeup as God. When the Lord created man in the beginning, He said, "Let Us make man in Our image" (Genesis 1:26), and so the very image of God resides in your spirit.

We read in the Book of John, "But an hour is coming, and now is, when the true worshipers shall worship the Father in spirit and truth; for such people the Father seeks to be His worshipers. God is Spirit, and those who worship Him must worship in spirit and truth" (John 4:23-24). We **must** worship in spirit and in truth. There is only one way to worship God, and that is with our spirit. We need to be functioning in our spirit. I know that our spirit is alive, but we still have not learned our spirit the way we need to. We have not lived in the spirit the way we need to. We have not emphasized being spiritual. We have not made it the expression that supersedes our carnal mind and our fleshly body. We are in a learning experience.

Genesis 1:26 Then God said, "Let Us make man in Our image, according to Our likeness; and let them rule over the fish of the sea and over the birds of the sky and over the cattle and over all the earth, and over every creeping thing that creeps on the earth."

That is not a problem to God, but we have to learn how to move into the realm of spirit. You ask, "How do I do that?" Your spirit has the ability to do it because it **is** spirit. "But I don't understand." If you do not feel anything, see anything, or hear anything—if nothing of it is real to you—just do it by faith.

You can go after salvation in the same way. If you think, "I don't know if God is real or not," then test Him. Find out if He is real. Go after Him and say, "Lord, if You really are real, if You really are alive, then I want You to meet me. I want You to be real to me. I want You to give me salvation. I want to serve you." You can start from a place of complete unbelief and lay hold of God. It is just a matter of your determination. It is a matter of how badly you want it (Jeremiah 29:13). When it comes to worship, you may feel, "I'm not spiritual!" That's okay; your spirit can come alive and stand before God. Just determine to do it. Even if you are not sure if He is there, pray, "God, I don't know that You love me; I don't know that You will do anything for me, but I determine to worship You." That is the beauty of worship. It is something you do for Him. Prayer and intercession is all about what you want Him to do for you. Worship is not. Worship is about what you are giving to the Lord. Regardless of whether you know Him, understand Him, or have ever felt Him, you can give your worship to Him. And the way we are to worship is in our spirit. Our spirit is able to go into His presence and worship Him. That is where worship must be done. It is not to be done outside of His presence.

It comes down to something very simple. With all the things that we read about in the Bible, and all the confusion that we deal with in life, we truly can know what God is looking for. Have you ever wondered, "What does God do all day?" He looks for a people to be His worshipers. The Father seeks those who will worship Him

---

Jeremiah 29:13 "And you will seek Me and find Me, when you search for Me with all your heart."

in spirit and in truth. That means that all I have to do is seek to worship Him in spirit and in truth. Even if I don't think I can find Him, I can trust that He will find me. At some point, what I am seeking and what the Father is seeking will come together. We read in Philippians, "For we are the true circumcision, who worship in the Spirit of God and glory in Christ Jesus and put no confidence in the flesh" (Philippians 3:3). We worship in the Spirit of God. This is not a new doctrine; this is exactly what has always been in the Word. This is where the Lord has always been and where He is coming from. This is why Christ made our spirits alive. For if our spirits come alive, then we have the ability to become His worshipers. And if we become His worshipers, then God will find us and connect with us.

We read in the Scriptures about singing psalms, hymns, and spiritual songs (Colossians 3:16; Ephesians 5:19). When we worship in the spirit, we are singing spiritual songs to the Lord. We do not understand what we are saying, because we are speaking a heavenly language. Don't worry; God understands it. He is the One that gave us the language; we are speaking the tongue of His realm. That is why we do not use tongues to talk to others in church. The way we use tongues in church is to worship and sing spiritual songs. We sing in the spirit, with our spirits, and bring offerings to the Lord. We sing psalms, hymns, and spiritual songs with thankfulness in our hearts to God (Ephesians 5:20). There has to be the element of spirit in our worship, because God is making us a spiritual people. What that actually means is that He is enabling us to live where He

---

Colossians 3:16 Let the word of Christ richly dwell within you, with all wisdom teaching and admonishing one another with psalms and hymns and spiritual songs, singing with thankfulness in your hearts to God.

Ephesians 5:19 Speaking to one another in psalms and hymns and spiritual songs, singing and making melody with your heart to the Lord.

Ephesians 5:20 Always giving thanks for all things in the name of our Lord Jesus Christ to God, even the Father.

lives, and to function in a real way with Him in the spirit. That starts with worship because worship is a spiritual activity.

How do we know that worship is really something we do in the spirit? Let's look at Psalm 5:7: "But as for me, by Thine abundant lovingkindness I will enter Thy house, at Thy holy temple I will bow in reverence for Thee." The Hebrew word for "lovingkindness" is *hesed*, which is a very deep word in the Hebrew language for steadfast, unfailing love. "By Your abundant lovingkindness I will enter Your house." Where is God's house? "Our Father who art in heaven" (Matthew 6:9). His house is in heaven, and we are seated with Him in heavenly places (Ephesians 2:6). "At Your holy temple I will bow in reverence for You." The word "at" would be better translated from the Hebrew as "in." We should read it: "I will enter Your house; in Your holy temple I will bow in reverence for You." The very idea of worship is that there is only one place to worship God, and that is in His house. We bring our worship to Him. Worship down here is not worship in the spirit. If we are worshiping from down here, then we are worshiping in the flesh from a physical plane. But if we worship in the spirit, we are worshiping in His house.

According to the Hebrew Scriptures, people did not worship at home; they worshiped in the Temple (Deuteronomy 12:5). That is why it was so important for the Israelites to go to Jerusalem during all of the biblical feasts. They had to worship in God's house. They could have services in the synagogues; they could read the Scriptures; they could get together and pray all they wanted to; but if they were going to worship the Lord, they worshiped in the Temple. That was

---

Ephesians 2:6 And raised us up with Him, and seated us with Him in the heavenly places, in Christ Jesus.

Deuteronomy 12:5 "But you shall seek the Lord at the place which the Lord your God shall choose from all your tribes, to establish His name there for His dwelling, and there you shall come."

where worship was done; there was no worship outside of being in His house. Psalm 100 describes this temple worship:

> Shout joyfully to the Lord, all the earth.
> Serve the Lord with gladness;
> Come before Him with joyful singing.
> Know that the Lord Himself is God;
> It is He who has made us, and not we ourselves;
> We are His people and the sheep of His pasture.
> Enter His gates with thanksgiving,
> And His courts with praise.
> Give thanks to Him; bless His name.
> For the Lord is good;
> His lovingkindness is everlasting,
> And His faithfulness to all generations. (Psalm 100:1-5)

In this beautiful psalm about worship, we read, "Come before Him with joyful singing." Where do we sing? Before Him. Just as the children of Israel did, we must also worship in His temple. The Israelites had to travel up to the Temple, because it was located on a high hill in Jerusalem. The Psalms of Ascent speak about going **up** to the house of the Lord (Psalm 122:1-4). In order to worship, they had to leave their houses and travel upward. We also have to move up into another level in order to enter God's house, His temple, and worship Him. Our Father is in heaven, and we should be there with Him to bring our worship and lay it before Him. If we are going to be thankful, if we are going to sing praises, if we are going to worship Him, we must come into His presence. God has set it up that way. He wants us in His presence.

Psalm 122:1-4   I was glad when they said to me, "Let us go to the house of the Lord." [2] Our feet are standing within your gates, O Jerusalem, [3] Jerusalem, that is built as a city that is compact together; [4] to which the tribes go up, even the tribes of the Lord—an ordinance for Israel—to give thanks to the name of the Lord.

When we enter into His presence and worship Him, then something very significant happens. We learn what that is in Jeremiah chapter 33, a beautiful chapter about restoration:

> " 'The voice of joy and the voice of gladness, the voice of the bridegroom and the voice of the bride, the voice of those who say,
>> "Give thanks to the LORD of hosts,
>> For the LORD is good,
>> For His lovingkindness is everlasting";
> and of those who bring a thank offering into the house of the LORD. For I will restore the fortunes of the land as they were at first,' says the LORD." (Jeremiah 33:11)

For those who bring the offering of worship into the house of the Lord, God restores the land as it was at first. After we worship Him, He restores the land. Our worship does more than bring releases or healings; it brings restoration to the earth. God has spoken to us about restoration for many years. We have had Words about the revealing of the sons of God. What do the sons do? They bring God's presence into the earth. They bring the blessing and the anointing, and they release creation from futility (Romans 8:19-21). Do you want to know how we can bring about the fulfillment of the Lord's Prayer: "Thy kingdom come. Thy will be done, on earth" (Matthew 6:10)? As we go up to worship God in His presence, He comes down to earth. What is the result of those who give thanks to the Lord of hosts? The outcome is that God comes down to earth.

It is only in this level of worship that we will see the two realms being blended together. If we really come into the worship that the Lord is looking for, we will be seated with Christ in heaven;

Romans 8:19-21 For the anxious longing of the creation waits eagerly for the revealing of the sons of God. [20] For the creation was subjected to futility, not of its own will, but because of Him who subjected it, in hope [21] that the creation itself also will be set free from its slavery to corruption into the freedom of the glory of the children of God.

we will know that realm and we will dwell there. Our worship will also initiate a response from God: He will come down to earth and begin to dwell and move here. If we begin to move in heaven, won't the physical realm be left out? No, God will bless the physical realm. When the Father indwells us, He will give life to our mortal bodies (Romans 8:11). Why? God wants to restore this planet, because at some point His Kingdom will engulf the entire earth (Daniel 7:27). Stop waiting for the Kingdom. The Kingdom is already here. Christ is already King of kings and Lord of lords (Revelation 19:16). The earth is already "the LORD's, and the fulness thereof" (Psalm 24:1, KJV). However, there is something in our minds that keeps going back to an old religious way of thinking in which everything is put off in the future or in heaven. Forget about longing to die and go to heaven. There is no need to die if we can get His presence here.

The 22nd Psalm says, "Yet Thou art holy, O Thou who art enthroned upon the praises of Israel" (Psalm 22:3). The root word for "enthroned" here is the Hebrew word *yashav*. More than "enthroned," it means "to dwell, live, or stay." So, when we worship in God's presence, He comes here to stay. God lives and dwells in our worship. Have you ever wondered how we will get into the fulfillment of Romans 8:11, God dwelling in us? His abode, His dwelling place, will be in those who worship Him in spirit and in truth. He is not just enthroned; He comes to live in us. The word "enthroned" still conveys the idea of God being up in heaven somewhere. But the

---

Romans 8:11 But if the Spirit of Him who raised Jesus from the dead dwells in you, He who raised Christ Jesus from the dead will also give life to your mortal bodies through His Spirit who indwells you.

Daniel 7:27 "Then the sovereignty, the dominion, and the greatness of all the kingdoms under the whole heaven will be given to the people of the saints of the Highest One; His kingdom will be an everlasting kingdom, and all the dominions will serve and obey Him."

Revelation 19:16 And on His robe and on His thigh He has a name written, "KING OF KINGS, AND LORD OF LORDS."

outcome of us becoming spiritual worshipers is that He comes and dwells with us here on the earth.

Come before God's throne with worship, with praise, with thanksgiving, and with all of your heart expressing back to Him the love that He has ministered to you. You have to do it personally. There is no delivery service in the Kingdom. You cannot send your worship through someone else. You must deliver it to God personally. You must lay it at His feet; you must come into His house; you must enter His temple. It is time for us to do that. When we do, He will dwell with us as He dwelt in the praises of Israel. God dwells in the worship of His people. If we move into His presence in our worship, He will move into us.

2 Chronicles chapter 5 describes the dedication of Solomon's Temple. We always emphasize the fact that God's presence filled the Temple, but when the priests first went in and began the service of dedication, the Lord was not in the Temple. At their initiative they went in, and after they had put the ark of the covenant in the holy place, we read,

> And when the priests came forth from the holy place (for all the priests who were present had sanctified themselves, without regard to divisions), and all the Levitical singers, Asaph, Heman, Jeduthun, and their sons and kinsmen, clothed in fine linen, with cymbals, harps, and lyres, standing east of the altar, and with them one hundred and twenty priests blowing trumpets in unison when the trumpeters and the singers were to make themselves heard with one voice to praise and to glorify the Lord, and when they lifted up their voice accompanied by trumpets and cymbals and instruments of music, and when they praised the Lord saying, "He indeed is good for His lovingkindness [*hesed*] is everlasting," then the house, the house of the Lord, was filled with a cloud, so

that the priests could not stand to minister because of the cloud, for the glory of the LORD filled the house of God. (2 Chronicles 5:11-14)

That is a picture of what God wants to do now. Those priests knew what it was to worship in the spirit. They worshiped at God's throne in heaven, in His temple in the heavenlies, and His response was to come down, indwell them, and fill that house with His presence. That is the response we are looking for today. We are looking to bring God's Kingdom to the earth. That is what Jesus taught us to pray: "Thy kingdom come. Thy will be done, on earth as it is in heaven" (Matthew 6:10). That will not happen just through our prayer and prophetic proclamation, but also through our worship. One of the greatest and most effective ways to bring the Kingdom of heaven to this earth is to begin to worship at His house, in His temple. Then He will come and fill all the earth. He will have a reason to be here, because the worshipers that He has been seeking are here. The exciting thing is that we really already have this worship. It is a gift that was given by the grace of God in the spiritual outpourings of the past. We are going to grow this gift of worship into the manifestation of His presence. The worship we have now is wonderful, but it can increase. We can take faith to grow this gift of worship that we have. We can anticipate a greater worship. We can contend for it with all of our hearts. Let's cry out to God for it. When we come together, let's expect another level of worship. Remember, the style of worship that we have was not conceived; it was poured out. So why can't a new level of worship be poured out upon us by His grace? Why can't our oneness once again be the catalyst for God to pour out on us an entirely new level of worship?

By our faith, in this generation, we are going to grow this gift of worship into exactly what God was looking for when He poured it out in the beginning. God is looking for a people who will grow and multiply the gifts that He has given them. And that is what we will do. Lord, we are going to be a people of spirit. We long to dwell with You in the heavenly places (Ephesians 2:4-6). No longer will our worship be something that is at arm's distance, separate from You, but we will worship before Your throne. We don't want our worship detached from who You are and where You are. We want to know You and the power of Your resurrection (Philippians 3:10). We want to move into the heavenlies. We are going to enter into the realm of spirit by faith and come before You to give our offerings of praise, thanksgiving, and worship. We thank You for all that You are. We thank You for Your unbelievable lovingkindness toward us. We bless You and proclaim, "HOLY, HOLY, HOLY, IS THE LORD GOD, THE ALMIGHTY" (Revelation 4:8). By the determination of our spirits, and the access that we have through the blood of Jesus Christ, we come boldly before the throne of grace determined to be Your worshipers and to obtain all of the promises that you have provided for us in Your Word. By this worship, not one Word that You have spoken will fall to the ground, but we Your people will possess them all.

Philippians 3:10 That I may know Him, and the power of His resurrection and the fellowship of His sufferings, being conformed to His death.